Symptom-Focused
Dynamic Psychotherapy

Symptom-Focused Dynamic Psychotherapy

Mary E. Connors

THE ANALYTIC PRESS

2006   Mahwah, New Jersey   London

Published by
The Analytic Press, Inc., Publishers
    Editorial Offices:
    10 Industrial Avenue
    Mahwah, NJ 07430

    www.analyticpress.com

Designed and typeset by CompuDesign, Charlottesville, VA

Library of Congress Cataloging-in-Publication Data

Connors, Mary E., 1953–
  Symptom-focused dynamic psychotherapy / Mary E. Connors.
    p. cm.
  Includes bibliographical references and index.
  ISBN 0-88163-444-1
  1. Psychodynamic psychotherapy. I. Title.
  [DNLM: Behavior Therapy. 2. Behavioral Symptoms—therapy.
  WM 425 C752s 2006]
RC489.4.P72C66 2006
616.89'14—dc22

                                     2005054550

Printed in the United States of America

10 9 8 7 6 5 4 3 2 1

FOR MY BROTHER, ROBERT J. CONNORS

1951–2000

CONTENTS

Preface and Acknowledgments

MY EARLY BEHAVIORAL TRAINING EMPHASIZED that psychotherapy was something to "do." I learned a variety of active intervention strategies, implemented them, and assessed the outcome. My psychoanalytic training led me to think that perhaps therapy was more about how to be with someone rather than what to do (which was a relief, as I had little idea what I was supposed to do, and how and when to do it!) Yet I liked the idea of being as effective as possible with the various problems that people brought to treatment, and it seemed that knowing some specific things to do at times might facilitate my ability to help. Gradually I began to develop a psychotherapeutic style that incorporated symptom-focused interventions into a dynamic treatment, and I found that such integration seemed coherent as I employed it with my patients.

However, that is not what I was taught. When I began my graduate program in psychology in 1977, the available theoretical paradigms were very different from current versions. The perspectives with which I became most familiar—psychoanalytic and behavioral—were more distant from people's actual experience than is the case today as well as more at absolute odds with one another. The dominant psychoanalytic paradigm was drive theory, and the behavioral theory that I was taught focused primarily on classical and operant conditioning. I began seeing my first patients when I was a young graduate student, and they displayed some complex difficulties, including sexual fetishes, paranoid delusions, and desperate relationship seeking. I found the theories I knew to be disappointing in furthering my understanding of my patients. Try as I might to apply those theories, I had to conclude that response schedules and oedipal issues were of limited explanatory value with my cases. I sought a psychoanalytically oriented internship, for I believed that a theory based on what might be going on inside a person had more potential to illuminate clinical phenomena than a strictly behavioral approach that declared one's inner workings to be irrelevant. I learned about self psychology, some of which strongly resonated with me; for the first time, here was a theory that made sense to me in terms of my own experience. I continued to immerse myself in psychoanalytic theory and found much that was helpful. But I remained unsatisfied concerning what might constitute the most useful explanations and treatment techniques for the range of problems my patients were presenting.

Fortunately, in the last two decades several major advances have clarified our understanding of development, psychopathology, and treatment. One key factor is the ascendency of what has been termed the relational perspective in psychoanalytic thought, so that relations with others, rather than drives, are a conceptual focus. A second major development is the cognitive revolution in behavior therapy. Internal states have become a legitimate focus of inquiry with a new emphasis on cognitive processes and their relationship to affect. Both within psychoanalytic thinking and in clinical theory in general an increased appreciation of the impact of real events on development and psychopathology is evident, for example, in the current high interest in attachment processes and in trauma. Finally, the polarization that historically resulted in mutual suspicion between psychoanalytic clinicians and researchers has been softening to some degree, so that many analytic therapists welcome findings from empirical studies, and researchers have become more appreciative of the value of in-depth case studies and qualitative work.

These paradigm shifts enable collaborative dialogue that was impossible when behavior theory eschewed the notion of subjectivity and psychoanalytic concepts centered on reductionistic intrapsychic structures and functions. All but the most radical behaviorists now consider mental processes to be a useful arena for exploration and intervention, and psychoanalytic conceptualizations of internal events tend to be less reified and more "experience near," as Kohut put it. Students of today have more options than simply declaring allegiance to one of the two major opposing camps and closing their minds to the possibility that the other might have something to offer. These changes suggest to me that an integrative book might be timely.

My particular blend of data and theory is deeply informed by my own subjectivity; in selecting my favorite ideas, I am necessarily omitting many others that readers may wish to incorporate into their perspectives. I hope that my own distillation of theory, research, and practice might be helpful to those of an integrative bent. I wish to stress, however, that these ideas are evolving, and in no way do I view this work as anything but preliminary and tentative. My Zen Buddhist training suggests that one should avoid clinging to "fixed ideas" that obscure the reality of a vast and continuously changing universe. I fail to embody this profound truth most of the time, but I invite readers to join me in striving for a spirit of respectful inquiry, flexibility, and humility concerning what we know and what we think we know.

This work reflects countless influences, and I am immeasurably grateful for the ideas and support that I have received. I want to thank Dr. Paul Stepansky, Managing Director of the Analytic Press, who was unfailingly helpful and generous to me at a challenging time in the publication of this work. His incisive editorial suggestions enabled me to develop a deeper and more organized perspective on some of the most crucial aspects of symptom-focused dynamic treatment. I would like to thank the members of my long-term consultation group: Steve Stern, Linda Lewis, Janet Leder, Pamela Duhl, John Perri, Darryl Pure, and Maureen Fayen. Our perspectives have been evolving together for many years. I am also grateful to my colleagues in the field of eating disorders: Craig Johnson, Marilyn Stuckey, and Susan Love, with whom I first collaborated in assimilating symptom-focused techniques into psychoanalytically informed psychotherapy. My colleagues, students, and supervisees from the Illinois School of Professional Psychology have been instrumental in the further development of my ideas, and I would especially like to thank Beth Pullen, one of the first readers of this manuscript. I am grateful to Dana Reinhold and Amy Willis for 30 years of sustaining friendship as well as for their confidence in the current project. I would like to thank my patients, whose resilience and creativity are a constant inspiration. I am especially appreciative of their generosity in consenting to be discussed in this book in the hope that it might help others.

Finally, I would like to thank my husband, Roger Thomson. His comments on content and style in every chapter strengthened this work immensely. Many of the ideas in this book arose in the context of our two decades of shared personal and professional lives, and I no longer remember with whom they might have originated. My understanding of such concepts as twinship self-object experiences and secure attachment is deeply informed by our relationship.

CHAPTER ONE

Rationale for a
Symptom-Focused Dynamic Treatment

THE QUESTION OF WHAT CONSTITUTES an appropriate goal of psychotherapeutic treatment has been debated since Freud's time. Freud (1917b) emphasized making the unconscious conscious and enlarging the realm dominated by the ego while constricting that of the id. He stated (1917c) that an analysis was ready to end when the patient no longer suffered from his symptoms, had surmounted his anxieties and inhibitions, and possessed the capacity for enjoyment and for efficiency in functioning. Repressions should be lifted and any gaps in memory filled in. Moreover, these changes ought to be stable and enduring: "Through the overcoming of these resistances the patient's mental life is permanently changed, is raised to a high level of development and remains protected against fresh possibilities of falling ill" (p. 451).

As psychoanalytic thinking evolved in ways less dominated by drive theory, some analytic authors focused on the state of the self and on object relations. For instance, Kohut (1971) emphasized the development of a cohesive self that is capable of achieving its goals and using its talents. Summers (1994, 1999) describes the goal of treatment as enabling the self to function more effectively by changing the ways in which a patient's object relationships are internally structured, and he noted the importance of realizing the self's potential through authentic being and relating. Mitchell (2000) stressed helping the patient find ways of interacting that are genuine and rich, thus expanding a limited relational repertoire characterized by repetition, stasis, and loyalty to the familiar. Stolorow and his colleagues (1987) have described the goal of treatment as the progressive exploration, clarification, and transformation of the patient's subjective world.

In contrast, treatment goals discussed in cognitive behavioral writings tend to be much less lofty, smaller in scope, and more specific. These authors emphasize the correction of problematic behavioral excesses and deficits and cognitive distortions. For cognitive behaviorists, targeting a patient's anxiety disorder symptoms, rather than global change in the self, is the appropriate focus of a helpful treatment. Amelioration or removal of a symptom is viewed as the hallmark of a successful psychotherapy. London (1986), lucidly discussing the conflict between therapies of insight and therapies of action, stated that, whereas insight therapists want to undermine symptoms, action therapists are more interested in directly alleviating them so that patients can feel better: "The technical dispute is thus a function of the importance assigned to symptoms relative to the conditions that sponsor them" (p. 30). He notes that accusations are common on both sides; insight therapists view those more action oriented as superficial and mechanical, while action therapists consider insight treatment ineffectual and pseudoscientific.

The controversy surrounding the proper aims of treatment continues today, with the opinions of managed care reviewers and insurers added to those of mental health professionals. Psychoanalytic clinicians, who already feel beleaguered by diminished cultural and financial support for long-term treatment, may be inclined to dismiss the cognitive behavioral orientation as just another irritating but ultimately irrelevant manifestation of the current wrongheaded zeitgeist. However, at the same time analytic thinkers are not unconcerned about their patients' symptomatic difficulties. It may seem that these divergent perspectives on treatment goals are irreconcilable; I believe, however, that some degree of integration is possible and useful. Throughout this book I develop a model of psychoanalytically informed psychotherapy that includes specific interventions to address particular symptoms. In developing this thesis, I first discuss the distress engendered by symptoms, their formation and function, and then introduce an integrative approach.

People do not tend to seek treatment unless they are suffering. As Freud (1940) noted, "On the patient's side a few rational factors work in our favor, such as the need for recovery which has its motive in his sufferings" (p. 181). The DSM-IV (American Psychiatric Association, 1994) defines mental disorder as a syndrome or pattern that is associated with present distress, such as a painful symptom, or a significant impairment in functioning. Persons may experience intense disturbance when they suffer from Axis I disorders with symptoms that can be debilitating, such as some anxiety disorders and mood disorders. These symptoms might appear alone or in conjunction with characterological difficulties. Some individuals with Axis II disorders may cause more distress to those around them than they experience themselves, but others with personality pathology are disturbed by their repetitive patterns and wish to change. In my experience, many persons are troubled by conditions that do not conform to a specific diagnostic category but, rather, relate to the state of the self or to attachment difficulties that impair relations with others. Such patients may enter treatment complaining that they have "low self-esteem" or that they cannot maintain intimate relationships.

Clinicians who have been trained from behavioral perspectives would view all these problems as appropriate targets of intervention. Psychoanalytic therapists, however, are likely to be far more cautious in their approach to symptoms. The classical psychoanalytic stance toward symptoms has been to conceptualize them as compromise formations resulting from the interplay of reprehended drives, ego defenses, and superego prohibitions (e.g., Freud, 1917a). Traditional theory has thus viewed symptoms as manifestations of underlying conflicts and has proposed that they will resolve only when the dynamic unconscious forces propelling them are brought to awareness in analysis or psychotherapy. Furthermore, the symptom was thought to occupy such an integral position in the psychic economy that attempting to remove a symptom prematurely was believed to result only in the substitution of another symptom. Although numerous current psychoanalytic theorists do not accept many aspects of Freudian metapsychology, few have turned their attention to specific symptomatic disorders.

RATIONALE FOR A SYMPTOM FOCUS

I have proposed that there are several reasons that interventions designed to affect specific symptoms may be indicated (Connors, 2001a). Some symptomatic disorders place patients in actual physical jeopardy. Anorexia nervosa has been estimated to have a mortality rate close to 10% (Sibley and Blinder, 1988). Bulimia nervosa can also be life threatening, with such consequences as cardiac arrest resulting from electrolyte imbalances (Johnson and Connors, 1987). Major depressive disorder often has fatal consequences, with up to 15% of those afflicted committing suicide and many more dying prematurely because of the confluence of depression and other medical conditions (American Psychiatric Association, 1994). Alcohol abuse is involved in at least 100,000 premature deaths annually (McGinnis and Foege, 1993). Drug abuse can be quite dangerous as well, particularly when toxic drugs such as inhalants are used or needle sharing takes place; approximately one-third of AIDS cases in the United States are related to intravenous drug use (Center for Disease Control and Prevention, 1994). Compulsive unsafe sexual activity may have fatal consequences. Violent behavior, including domestic violence and child abuse, constitutes a major public health issue.

The impairment caused by some symptoms may be such that psychotherapy is not a real possibility until the symptoms abate. Here I am referring particularly to symptoms that are so debilitating, frightening, or preoccupying that they interfere greatly with a patient's ability to engage in psychological exploration. A certain measure of physiological well-being, moderate levels of arousal, and a degree of psychological safety and freedom are optimal to promote reflective dialogue between patient and therapist. Obviously patients differ greatly in their capacity for psychological exploration, but conditions outside a certain range will hinder even the most emotionally aware person. If we reflect on our own experience of suffering physical pain, such as from a muscle spasm or a toothache, we may be aware that this severe pain makes it difficult to focus on anything except how much it hurts. Our usual ability to deploy attention to a range of topics and exchange ideas with others is restricted.

I believe that many patients who come to therapy are experiencing the psychological equivalent of a severe pain that dominates their consciousness and precludes conversation about topics other than their suffering. A malnourished anorexic whose cognitive functions are impaired by starvation is in no position to achieve insight into her unconscious motivation. Neither is the alcoholic who is always either inebriated or beginning to experience withdrawal, or the bulimic who is binge eating and purging many times a day. Patients who are feeling terrorized by panic attacks or flashbacks related to traumatic experiences likewise cannot be very present in a therapeutic relationship. Persons with symptoms that affect their arousal levels, such as manic states, anxiety disorders, or severe depressive episodes, may require help in moderating their over- or underarousal before mutual dialogue is possible.

A patient's level of distress about a symptom might also warrant a specific symptom focus. Some symptoms are so ego dystonic, anxiety provoking, or deleterious to self-esteem that their rapid amelioration is desperately sought. Many patients experience great shame concerning their symptoms. Others feel panicked about the potentially disastrous relational consequences of their continuing to engage in substance abuse or compulsive sexual behavior. Many symptomatic conditions affect patients' performance in the workplace, and continued employment may be predicated on improvement in such problems as depression or anxious avoidance that interfere with attendance and task performance.

The classical analytic tradition, with its emphasis on abstinence rather than gratification, renunciation of infantile wishes, and removal of resistances to uncovering unconscious conflicts, may lead clinicians to adopt an unnecessarily harsh stance toward symptom relief (Connors, 2001a). We may believe that nonintervention is appropriate because we think that these symptoms would diminish only over a prolonged period of time as internal conflict resolves, that people in treatment must feel worse before they can feel better, and that in general symptomatic suffering is somehow beneficial and necessary for the therapeutic process or, at any rate, that it is unavoidable. We might also expect that symptom substitution would occur should the original symptom diminish prematurely, rendering intervention fruitless.

My view is that distress resulting from troublesome symptoms is generally not useful, and that many times it can be harmful, promoting rigid and risk-avoidant behavior. I invite clinicians to question their own attitudes about patients' suffering. Should symptoms be alleviated if it means patients will opt for a briefer treatment or fail to explore themselves fully? Is assisting patients with symptoms a "quick fix" that we should eschew, and, if so, is it because of some Nietzcheian ideal that suffering will make our patients stronger? Or, in an era in which psychiatric drugs are advertised on television, are we reacting against the increasing conceptualization of complex human situations as remediable with a prescription for a pill or a technique rather than with self-understanding? As a culture we tend to hold conflicting attitudes toward the relief of suffering; advertisements tout the "fast results" promised by various nostrums, but terminally ill patients are undermedicated because physicians are not taught to prioritize pain management relative to other concerns. Obviously we do not wish to collude with some of the messages promulgated in our consumer culture that the optimal response to distress is its eradication. Yet it might be worthwhile to examine whether we hold views concerning the virtue of suffering that constrain our ability to consider direct techniques of symptom alleviation.

In Buddhist teachings there is a story concerning a follower of the Buddha who expressed his dissatisfaction with his path because the Buddha had not declared his views on such matters as whether or not the world is eternal and what happens after death. The monk determined to abandon his training unless he received answers. The Buddha responded with a tale about a man who had been wounded by a poisoned arrow. Although a surgeon was brought to treat the man, he stated that he would not permit the surgeon to remove the arrow until he knew the name of the man who had wounded him, where the man lived and what his occupation was, what type of bow shot the arrow, what kind of feathers were on the shaft, and so on. "All this would still not be known to the man and meanwhile he would die" (Nanamoli and Bodhi, 1995, p. 535). The Buddha emphasized the need to remove the poisoned arrow of ignorance without wasting precious time on fruitless speculation.

I consider the exploratory process of psychoanalytic psychotherapy to be powerful and transformative, and my use of the Buddha analogy here is not intended to suggest otherwise. But what about that arrow? I suggest that the most empathic and attuned therapist response to a patient in great symptomatic distress is to try to do something about the symptom as quickly as possible, even if it means that understanding is not yet perfect

(Connors, 2001a). Clinicians from different perspectives agree that active crisis intervention is necessary when a patient is suicidal. In such a case, it is obvious that severe consequences could ensue unless the therapist manages the situation and secures the patient's safety—this being the priority in treatment until the crisis has passed. Distressing symptoms are not necessarily life threatening, but they may be so pressing that a patient will not remain in psychotherapy or be able to engage in a therapeutic relationship unless the symptoms are attended to relatively early in the treatment. The immediacy with which a clinician intervenes when a patient is suicidal, regardless of the clinician's views concerning underlying causality, might be appropriate in less extreme situations as well.

Patients with problematic symptoms, particularly those involving substance abuse, eating disorders, or mood disorders, have often been relegated to inpatient treatment. The former availability of inpatient hospitalization meant that some clinicians who felt insufficiently trained in symptom-focused work, or who had theoretical objections to doing it, were able to employ a "split treatment" model, in which patients with disabling symptoms worked on them with an inpatient team. In an era of great concern about health care costs, however, such formerly ubiquitous practices as a four-week hospital stay for alcoholism are exceedingly rare unless a patient has considerable personal means. Because outpatient treatment is far less costly than hospitalization, clinicians will have to manage many situations involving symptomatic disorders without the assistance provided by inpatient care. Hospitalization increasingly is reserved for brief crisis situations such as a medically supervised detoxification from substances or stabilization of an acutely suicidal patient.

SYMPTOM FORMATION AND FUNCTION

A proposal for active intervention with symptomatic behavior raises issues about the origin and function of symptoms. Traditional psychoanalytic theory has focused on the role of internal conflict in the genesis of a symptom and its function in effecting a compromise between adversarial elements of the mind. However, Freud (1937) presciently recognized the complex origin of pathology: "The aetiology of every neurotic disturbance is, after all, a mixed one. . . . As a rule there is a combination of both factors, the constitutional and the accidental" (p. 220). More recent theoretical developments advocate a biopsychosocial approach to understanding symptomatology (e.g., Adams and Sutker, 2001). This multidimensional approach eschews a single-factor theory of pathology and instead suggests that a complete explanation must include such biological variables as genetic vulnerabilities; such psychological factors as attachment security and traumatic history; and the sociocultural milieu, including the impact of gender, race, ethnicity, religion, sexual orientation, and prevailing cultural norms (Connors, 1994). For example, bulimia nervosa has been found to have a considerable genetic component (Bulik, Sullivan, and Kendler, 1998). It has also been linked to particular types of family constellations and to such risk factors as sexual abuse (Connors and Morse, 1993; Connors, 2001b). This symptom is associated with a cultural emphasis on thinness, which is more prominent in certain groups than in others and places Caucasian heterosexual young women of higher socioeconomic status at especially high risk for developing this disorder (Connors, 1996). The expression of a symptom depends on complex interactions of such risk factors as these.

I believe that effective treatment of symptomatic disorders is related to a comprehensive understanding of their etiology. As useful as a biopsychosocial perspective on the development of psychopathology is, however, it does not tell us very much about the role that a particular symptom comes to play in the psyche of an individual. In an earlier work (Connors, 1994), I suggested four particular pathways to symptom formation, although I suspect quite a few more could be enumerated. Common to all is the idea of a vulnerable self in a relational matrix that is or was somehow inadequate. It should be noted, however, that in addition to limitations in the caregiving environment of the child due to such issues as parental psychopathology, intergenerational transmission of trauma, and lack of resources, some children with extreme difficulties due to biological vulnerabilities might present insuperable challenges to the most competent parents.

One pathway to symptom formation represents a reworking of Freud's (1917b) understanding of a symptom as a compromise between conflicting impulses (Connors, 1994). Some patients who have experienced trauma manifest a reduction in functioning to protect the self from overwhelming and unacceptable affects and knowledge. The nature of these affects may be sexual or aggressive, often reflecting what has been done to the person in abusive experiences rather than the wishes for sexual and aggressive expression emphasized by classical theory. Herman (1992) noted that trauma survivors always face a conflict between forgetting and keeping secrets about the trauma, or remembering and telling about it. Symptoms in traumatized patients may represent a compromise between the two. For example, a number of female Cambodian refugees who witnessed atrocities later suffered loss of vision that was found to have no organic basis (Rozee and Van Boemel, 1989). Group treatment was effective in restoring some vision to these trauma survivors who could not bear to see any more horror. Some authors have suggested the term somatoform dissociation (e.g., Nijenhuis and Van der Hart, 1999) for physical complaints subsequent to trauma that may include disorders of movement and sensation. Patients suffering from somatoform dissociation, once considered to be "hysterics," might manifest sensory losses and problems with motor control that they experience as unconnected to the original trauma.

Traumatized patients must find a symptomatic compromise that achieves multiple purposes. First, the self must be protected from knowledge of unbearable events (often perpetrated by family members) and the accompanying rage, pain, sense of betrayal, and hopelessness. Second, ties with caregivers must be preserved to ensure physical and psychological survival. Affects such as rage may be far too dangerous to permit in an abusive interpersonal environment, so that relational bonds are maintained by disavowing and denying large sectors of self-experience, including affects and memories. Finally, a part of the self might retain hope that someday one's story may safely be told and finds a way to hint at it through disguised representations of actual experiences. This compromise could result in such symptoms as amnesia for large portions of one's personal history, self-mutilation, dissociative phenomena, and somatoform disorders.

Another pathway to symptom formation is seen in addictive disorders and some compulsive behaviors. Problems such as alcoholism, substance abuse, bulimia nervosa, and compulsive gambling all involve reliance on an inanimate object or an activity for self-regulation (Connors, 1994). Strong evidence exists that addictive disorders have relatively high genetic heritability (e.g.,

Goodwin, 1984), and individual differences in such areas as physiological tolerance of alcohol have been cited as significant risk factors (e.g., Schuckit, 1989). Other research has shown that addicted behavior tends to be associated with negative emotional states; persons are more likely to abuse substances or engage in addictive activities such as gambling when they are angry, anxious, sad, lonely, and so on (Donegan et al., 1983; Peele, 1985). Such emotional states are also more strongly associated with relapse into addictive behavior after a period of abstinence than is any other factor (Marlatt and Gordon, 1985).

Thus, people who are biologically predisposed to react in particular ways to certain substances and to experience affective difficulty might respond to distressing events by engaging in the addictive behavior, which then will anesthetize or otherwise change the current emotional tone. Eventually the addicted person's primary relationship is with the addictive object or activity, which is often experienced as infinitely more safe and reliable than interpersonal relationships. A patient with binge-eating problems described her relationship with food by stating, "It feels like my best friend—I know it's always there for me." A sense of self-cohesion is restored when the person feels calmed, numbed, or distracted through engaging in the addictive behavior. Although the ability to cope with life in general decreases as involvement in an addiction progresses, it does enable a temporary escape from negative emotional states, which can be so reinforcing that the addictive object will become desperately sought again and again.

A third pathway to symptom formation is seen in anxiety disorders, in which people may experience highly aversive emotional states, but without the more active effort to ward them off that is seen in addictions (Connors, 1994). A key feature of anxiety disorders is a sense of vulnerability (Beck and Emery, 1985); anxious persons continually feel threatened and fear internal or external catastrophe. The feared stimulus may be a particular thought, as in obsessive–compulsive disorder; a bodily sensation, as in panic disorder; or an external object or situation, as in a simple phobia and social phobia (Barlow, 1988). In all these disorders, the person experiences distressing anxiety without a functional solution other than avoidance. Anxiety disorders have some degree of heritability (Torgersen, 1983), and such temperamental differences as behavioral inhibition have been implicated in the development of anxiety (Kagan, 1989). So have certain life experiences; for example, patients with panic disorder described their parents as critical, frightening, controlling, and unsupportive while the patients were growing up (Shear et al., 1993). Anxious patients doubt their capacity to manage themselves in threatening situations and expect that others will be harshly critical and deprecating rather than understanding. Anxious patients generally experience their symptoms as quite aversive but may be loathe to change their avoidant strategies and risk potentially intolerable levels of anxiety.

A fourth type of symptom formation results from what a person may experience as an insoluble dilemma resulting from conflict between her own self-strivings and the requirements of parents (Connors, 1994). When the wishes of needed caregivers conflict with the needs of the evolving self in a profound fashion, the potential for a problematic resolution is great. A person may oscillate between compromising self-development to maintain the relationship, and rebelling in a fashion that preserves the self but at the expense of isolation and alienation. Stolorow and his colleagues (Stolorow et al., 1987; Brandchaft, 1988) suggest that depression will become the dominant affect in a person for whom this is a chronic conflict. The conflict lives on in the adult patient's internal world, and the injunctions of new objects whom the patient perceives as being similarly intolerant of her autonomous strivings may be added to those of parents. Silencing the self (Jack, 1991) has been identified as a particularly important phenomenon in women's depression. Other symptomatic problems associated with the fear that self-initiated activity will entail relational catastrophe might include work inhibitions and behaviors sometimes referred to as self-defeating or self-sabotaging.

It is my experience that symptom substitution is more than a remote possibility in only one of the pathways that I outlined. Occasionally patients who are using addictive behaviors to regulate affect in a fragmentation-prone self will relinquish one addiction only to take up another. However, the most common manifestation of self-regulatory difficulties will be the recalcitrance of the original symptom rather than its disappearance and replacement with another. Moreover, some people will be able to reduce their dependence on a destructive addiction and substitute behaviors that are still rigidly adhered to but that are less harmful, such as daily attendance at self-help groups or compulsive exercise. Wachtel (1977) commented that concerns about symptom substitution may reflect an erroneous conception that behavioral methods such as systematic desensitization "take away" the anxiety; rather, they represent a treatment of the symptom that enables patients to confront previously avoided sources of anxiety.

Numerous other possible routes to symptom development may well exist in addition to the four that I have described. My point is that symptoms result from a multiplicity of biopsychosocial risk factors rather than from a single causative element. Internal conflict is central in the genesis of some symptoms, but others probably result from deficits in such psychological skills as self-regulation of affect. Gedo (1991) commented that we must consider neurocognitive difficulties and ways in which disorganizing experiences interfere with maturational processes in the brain rather than assuming that all psychopathology can be explained by intrapsychic conflict. Currently we have an understanding of the etiology of psychopathology not possible in Freud's time, and I believe that such knowledge enables us to move beyond a monolithic view of symptoms as signifying a single dynamic and requiring a uniform indirect treatment method to a view that is multifaceted and individualized. As Westen (2002) has stated:

> The mind is a very complex thing, and we are unlikely to honor its complexity if we write as if any single cause explains most or all psychopathology. And we are unlikely to do optimal work therapeutically if we imagine that any single therapeutic aim and corresponding technical strategies . . . can address the many ways in which the hundreds of functions that constitute the mind could go awry [p. 866].

ACTIVE TECHNIQUES AND PSYCHOANALYTIC TREATMENT

Within the last few decades, various authors have considered whether more direct techniques have a place within psychoanalytic treatment. However, earlier figures in the history of psychoanalysis pioneered ideas that enlarged conceptions of psychopathology and treatment to include deficit as well as conflict, and suggested strategies of intervention not limited to interpretation. Ferenczi (1927) proposed that a certain "elasticity" of psychoanalytic technique might be required when patients fail to respond to the usual measures, and stressed the importance of adapting to the needs of particular patients through such modifications. He emphasized the impact of severe early trauma on development and believed that orthodox treatment might be inadequate in producing successful and lasting results for patients with such a history. Ferenczi (1931) suggested, for instance, that an analyst engage in a kind of play therapy as a participant in order to reach the child aspect of the adult analysand; he believed it necessary to provide some "child-like relaxation" in treatment, not merely the "educative frustration" of classical technique. From our current vantage point some of Ferenczi's ideas that were harshly criticized have been vindicated, while others (such as "mutual analysis") are still regarded as problematic, but he was influential in moving psychoanalytic technique in a more flexible direction (Hoffer, 2005).

The same is true for Alexander and French (1946), who coined the term corrective emotional experience to describe what they viewed as the need to expose the patient, under the more favorable circumstances of the treatment, to emotional situations that he had been unable to manage at an earlier time in life. Those authors considered the conditions of the analysis to be more facilitating because of the helpful, caring attitude of the analyst. Alexander (1950) wrote, "The treatment ultimately aims at changing the ego to enable it to resolve conflicts with which it could not cope before. The method by which this change in the ego is achieved is a kind of gradual learning through practice—by exposing the ego, step by step, to conflicts as they emerge in the course of treatment" (p. 262). He further noted the need to maintain the transference on an optimal level so that the integrative functions of the ego would not be overwhelmed and disorganized by overly intense affects, in which case the treatment would resemble the original problematic situation rather than providing an opportunity for mastery. Such graduated exposure to traumatic material and provision of assistance to the patient in titrating emotional intensity are significant features in contemporary theories, including the one I formulate in this book.

Some more recent theorists have explicitly proposed various integrations of psychoanalytic and behavioral or cognitive behavioral methods. Wachtel (e.g., 1977, 1987, 1997) has written a notable series of ground-breaking books and papers in the area of psychotherapy integration. A major focus in his writing is the importance of anxiety in a wide variety of problematic issues for patients. Wachtel (1977) points out that behavior therapists and analytic clinicians alike intervene in cases of anxiety and avoidance; behavior therapists are likely to use exposure and relaxation techniques, such as systematic desensitization, whereas analysts help expose patients to greater anxiety by interpreting their defenses and thus interfering with their usual means of avoidance. Using a psychodynamic framework influenced by such authors as Horney and Sullivan, a framework that he first termed interpersonal and later changed to relational, as that broad perspective evolved, Wachtel suggests that behavioral and cognitive therapies may be integrated to produce a new synthesis. He comments that, although both methods may be defined in ways that preclude integration, they have areas of compatibility that, when recognized, lead to an approach that is rich and effective.

Elsewhere (Johnson and Connors, 1987; Johnson, Connors, and Tobin, 1987; Connors, 1992) my colleagues and I described ways in which the integration of psychoanalytic psychotherapy with techniques of symptom management not only facilitated control of a problematic symptom but also furthered the analysis of the transference. We proposed that all events in treatment, including the introduction of cognitive behavioral techniques, will be experienced by the patient in ways that reflect the patient's characteristic perceptions of the self and of others, which can then be explored in detail. We suggested that inviting the patient to discuss her or his ongoing experience of the clinician and the therapy as symptom management techniques were employed could strengthen the therapeutic alliance. We reported that symptom management would not be successful with many patients in the absence of a strong therapeutic alliance and stated that clinicians would be in the most favorable position "to facilitate behavior change and to analyze resistance to behavior change" both by offering suggestions for symptom management and being committed to understanding the patient's experience of this offer (Johnson et al., 1987, p. 669).

Similarly, Frank (1990, 1992, 1993, 1999), in several lucid works on the integration of cognitive behavioral techniques and object relations based psychotherapy, notes that in a two-person psychology in which it is clear that the clinician's influence is always present, such techniques can be implemented "analytically"—that is, in a way that promotes understanding and consciousness. Frank (1999), anchoring his suggestions for the use of active techniques in a model of expanded psychoanalytic participation, states that attempts to minimize the analyst's activity, frustrate the patient, and avoid the impact of the analyst's uniqueness in favor of ideals of abstinence, neutrality, and anonymity actually hinder the psychoanalytic endeavor. He calls instead for making analytic use of the personal contribution and participation of the analyst, including a more active dimension than traditional theory endorses. Frank stresses the need to balance the traditional goal of analytic therapy, that is, structural change, with concern for the quality of life and the level of distress of the patient. He describes a psychoanalytic process oriented more around progression than regression in which the analyst makes an effort to assist the patient with her life goals.

Frank (1992), commenting on the traditional psychoanalytic opprobrium toward the use of active techniques, notes that action in psychoanalysis has been associated with resistance and acting out and that the relationship between action and intrapsychic processes has been relatively neglected in psychoanalytic study. Refraining from action at times is valorized. For example, Balint (1993) discusses a situation in which the patient was experiencing terrible distress. Although Balint recommended that it was important that the analyst not withdraw, she also suggested that the clinician refrain from attempting to relieve anxiety. She thought that the patient and the analyst must tolerate "not being able to be helped or to give help, to rescue or be rescued; and instead, having to stay there and not be terrified and so pushed into activity" (p. 122). Although it is entirely possible that in this particular case activity was inadvisable, the passage illustrates a common belief in psychoanalytic work that action obviates exploration. Moreover, the classical theory of technique was largely focused on prohibition and restraint, with much emphasis on what *not* to do (Gill, 1984; Mitchell, 2000).

Bader (1994) notes a tendency in psychoanalysis to focus too narrowly on process goals such as insight and to deemphasize therapeutic change and symptom relief. He states that we often seem more comfortable with understanding the dynamics of a case rather than with helping the patient get better in his or her outside life. Bader suggests that a variety of factors in the history of psychoanalysis have resulted in a subtle prioritizing of intraanalytic processes over therapeutic aims. He notes that, for a number of theorists, understanding and exploration constitute the analytic task, symptom relief being a relatively unimportant byproduct. Bader cautions that a theory encouraging an exclusive focus on the analytic interaction may result in a process that is overly theory driven and insufficiently responsive to the patient's actual difficulties.

This possibility was illustrated in a psychologist friend's description of a seminar she attended during her internship at a psychoanalytically oriented hospital. The seminar was led by a noted analyst, who asked anxious trainees in the first meeting to describe the appropriate role of the therapist. "To help people?" volunteered my friend. "No!" she was informed, in a response that she remembers as conveying withering scorn at such naivete. "Our role is to understand!" Such dichotomizing of the realms of "helping" versus "understanding" (as well as repudiation of the wish to help) does not further our doing either. It is notable that one review of the psychotherapy outcome literature reports that insight and self-exploration are associated with outcome only when specifically focused on the patient's presenting problem (Whiston and Sexton, 1993). A therapeutic focus on problem solving and mastery was much more related to positive changes than insight and self-exploration were. The authors comment, "For the practitioner, these findings would suggest that insight and exploration be purposefully related to understanding elements of the problem currently facing the client" (p. 48).

SUPPORT AND EXPRESSIVENESS IN PSYCHOTHERAPY AND PSYCHOANALYSIS

At this point I would like to clarify my terminology. I use the terms psychoanalytic and psychodynamic interchangeably. Westen (1990) commented that for some time the word psychodynamic was used "to characterize the ragtag army of the not-quite-analytic-enough" who rejected various elements of classical theory, but that such perspectives are now mainstream in contemporary psychoanalysis (p. 21). For the sake of brevity, I also abbreviate "psychodynamic" to "dynamic" when referring to symptom-focused dynamic psychotherapy. Moreover, I like the set of associations that "dynamic" conjures up—the rich history of the evolution of psychoanalytic thinking about internal states in flux, as well as more current models of nonlinear dynamic systems that are viewed as constantly changing rather than static or fixed (e.g., Piers, 2005).

I also want to comment on the distinctions that have been made between supportive and expressive psychotherapy, as well as those between psychoanalysis and psychotherapy. Supportive psychotherapy has typically been thought of as an appropriate treatment for patients whose internal resources are limited. It may have as a goal the restoration of a previous homeostasis and the reinstatement of the coping strategies that characterized the patient's previous highest level of functioning (e.g., Hollander and Ford, 1990). Supportive therapy often focuses on strengthening defenses and reducing anxiety. The positive transference is facilitated, and if a negative transference appears efforts will be made to eliminate it. Wachtel (1997) noted that the term supportive therapy carries negative connotations, implying therapeutic pessimism and the selection of limited goals only. He further stated that a somewhat moralistic stance may underlie a view of supportive therapy as lesser, and that an emphasis on change as exclusively caused by autonomous action may reflect an identification with overly individualistic values of capitalistic culture.

In contrast, psychoanalysis is characterized by the use of free association and more emphasis on the transference, including the cultivation of a transference neurosis (e.g., Solomon, 1992). Solomon, comparing psychoanalysis with psychotherapy, suggests that in psychotherapy a greater emphasis on current events prevails and that intense aggression in the transference is to be avoided. Gill (1988) stated that psychotherapy includes more suggestions to impel change, whereas analyzing the therapeutic relationship is the primary task of analysis. He distinguished between what he termed the intrinsic and extrinsic criteria of psychoanalysis, intrinsic referring to a commitment to understanding the meaning of events in the transference and extrinsic relating to the structure of the treatment, such as frequency of sessions and use of the couch. In a later work Gill (1994) described a kind of psychoanalytic psychotherapy that, while not meeting the extrinsic criteria of psychoanalysis proper, could meet the intrinsic criteria by establishing a "psychoanalytic situation" with much attention to transference.

Although the symptom-focused dynamic therapy that I conduct may have supportive elements, I do not see the provision of assistance with symptomatic difficulties as incompatible with ambitious goals for treatment. Complexity theory (e.g., Thelan, 2005) suggests that behavior is the result of numerous interacting elements and that in nonlinear dynamic systems small differences can produce substantial changes in a system, rendering outcomes unpredictable. Nor does aid with symptoms preclude thorough analysis of the transference, including negative transference. I believe that the historical distinction between supportive and expressive therapy reflects the continuing influence of the classical perspective and various efforts to modify it so that a more diverse patient group can tolerate treatment. In relying on more contemporary theory I see no need to retain such a dichotomy. As I discuss shortly, symptom-focused dynamic therapy is tailored to the individual patient and may include elements that have been termed supportive or expressive.

It may be possible to view psychoanalysis and psychotherapy on a continuum rather than as representing sharp dichotomies (Wachtel, 1997; McWilliams, 2004). Gill (1984), discussing the integration of analytic and behavioral techniques, suggested that they could be combined in psychotherapy but not in psychoanalysis. He stated that it was difficult to see how a treatment involving desensitization, for example, could be combined with an overarching emphasis on the patient's experience of the relationship; however, he did not proscribe activity in analytic treatment: "I remain convinced that a more active stance than many analysts employ would move things along much more quickly" (Gill, 1994, p. 76). Discussing the introduction of behavioral techniques into psychotherapy, he seemed to suggest that such a combination could be "psychoanalytic," based on the nature of the therapeutic interaction and the analysis of its meaning in the transference. When formulating my model of symptom-focused dynamic psychotherapy, I had psychotherapy rather than psychoanalysis in mind—but this decision probably resulted from my anticipation that analytic clinicians might experience less discomfort using active techniques in a treatment modality that historically has permitted more flexibility. Integration is not obviated on a theoretical level, especially if one thinks about treatment as on a continuum of intensity and remains committed to psychoanalytic exploration. On a practical level, some techniques are easier than others to integrate into a conversational treatment process in a fashion that enables the dialogue to continue. (Gill ([1984]) referred to systematic desensitization, which I do not use because it is too cumbersome and time consuming.) Although I focus on symptom-focused dynamic psychotherapy, some analysts might elect to try certain techniques with their analysands, using principles I outline for assessment and intervention.

DYNAMIC AND BEHAVIORAL PARADIGMS CAN CONVERGE

In contrast to the lack of emphasis on symptom amelioration in psychoanalytic writings, the literature from behavioral and cognitive behavioral perspectives primarily addresses specific symptomatic disorders and often describes empirical studies measuring the efficacy of one treatment technique versus another. Treatment "manuals" now exist for a number of disorders, and cognitive behavioral techniques predominate in the current writings on "empirically supported treatment." If addressing symptoms is often necessary, as I have posited, should patients with symptomatic problems be directed to a treatment that is exclusively cognitive-behavioral? I do not believe so; psychodynamic psychotherapy provides essential elements in a treatment that are quite different from those supplied by cognitive behavior therapy. The concrete, specific, problem-focused nature of the latter approach is unparalleled for effective intervention in certain situations, but such techniques are frequently insufficient for the long-term changes that patients deem important. Although persons suffering with problematic symptoms often want direct help with them, such help may not be as straightforward as some cognitive behavioral treatment manuals might suggest. Attunement might require less symptom focus and more exploration of other issues that the patient experiences as pressing, such as family and relationship concerns or aspects of the therapy relationship. I have argued for the importance of attending to symptoms, but these symptoms, part of a person's whole self and subjective world, are inseparably linked to one's defenses, interpersonal style, and other concepts stressed by psychoanalytic authors. A recent study of the efficacy of short-term, action-oriented treatments found that most problems do not remit in a brief treatment, and the authors note that symptoms are inextricably interwoven with personality characteristics and are not very malleable (Westen, Novotny, and Thomson-Brenner, 2004). Behavioral approaches often err in being mechanistic, narrow, and naive about the tenacious nature of psychopathology and patients' resistance to change. As Wachtel (1997) states, "Treatment that tries to remove symptoms without understanding their basis is not likely to be free of complications" (p. 122).

Blagys and Hilsenroth (2000) conducted a review of psychodynamic and cognitive behavioral treatments in order to understand the techniques and processes that distinguish between the two approaches. The investigators identified seven elements of consistent difference. Compared with cognitive behavioral clinicians, dynamic therapists tend to focus more on access to and expression of emotion, to emphasize the identification of patterns in patients' behavior and internal states, to focus on the past as an important determinant of present experiences, and to stress investigation of blocks and resistances to patient engagement in treatment. Dynamic therapists also place more emphasis on patients' interpersonal experiences, with particular focus on the therapeutic relationship, and explored dreams, wishes, and fantasies to a greater degree. I suggest that, in a type of integration referred to as assimilative (e.g., Messer and Warren, 1995), it is possible to do all these things *and* attend to particular symptoms as well; that is, a psychodynamic focus is maintained while additional techniques are assimilated into the basic model. The psychoanalytic attitude is characterized by respect for "the complexity of the mind, the importance of unconscious mental processes, and the value of a sustained inquiry into subjective experience" (Mitchell and Black, 1995, p. 206). No aspect of this stance is incompatible with direct attention to symptoms.

Moreover, some current models of cognitive behavioral treatment may be seen to converge with those of relational psychoanalytic theory because of a mutual focus on internal states, regulation of affects, and anxious avoidance. Since Wachtel (1977) noted the similarities between the ways in which psychodynamic treatment "exposed" patients to anxiety-provoking experiences and behavioral therapy's emphasis on actual exposure to feared situations for phobic patients, other theorists have similarly bridged the usual analytic–behavioral divide. McCullough and Andrews (2001) describe a model of short-term dynamic psychotherapy that conceptualizes neurotic psychopathology as resulting from what they term "affect phobias," or fears and conflicts concerning feelings. Their treatment plan includes gradual exposure to the frightening affects and prevention of the usual avoidant responses. Similarly, recent trends in behavior therapy particularly emphasize the difficulties that result from what certain authors term experiential avoidance (e.g., Hayes, Strosahl, and Wilson, 1999), referring to a tendency to avoid disturbing thoughts and feelings. Clinicians who take that position suggest treatment approaches that foster greater acceptance of various internal events. Empirical studies have documented the way in which attempts to suppress particular thoughts instead result in increased frequency of those thoughts (e.g., Wegner, 1994). Such issues have long been of concern to psychoanalytic clinicians observing defensive processes, and numerous psychoanalytic writings offer highly sophisticated exegeses of such phenomena, whose importance is now more recognized by cognitive behavioral theorists. In fact, the whole area of cognitive behavioral treatment has been expanding its boundaries to include attention to topics that historically were in the domain of psychoanalysis, such as the therapeutic relationship (Safran and Segal, 1990) and dreams (Rosner, Lyddon, and Freeman, 2004).

Dynamic therapy's focus on the therapeutic relationship, the nuances of the internal world of the patient, and the value of insight enable profound therapeutic work to proceed. Moreover, other elements of psychoanalytic theory, such as its emphasis on the impact of early development and the importance of unconscious processes, can illuminate intrapsychic and interpersonal phenomena in a unique fashion. Finally, the psychoanalytic tradition of free association facilitates attention to the agenda of the patient in a less structured fashion than is often the case in a cognitive behavioral treatment. As London (1986) has commented, "For purely symptomatic problems, people need a doctor. For problems of existence, at the other pole, they need a priest, or someone who can fulfill the role for which, in other times or places, they would seek a priest. In between, where most of us may fit, they need both" (p. 151).

In my view, analytic and cognitive behavioral perspectives, in isolation, can be misattuned to patients' real needs. An integrative approach, however, enables the clinician to attend to specific problems effectively while at the same time appreciating the intricacies of the entire self-system in which they are embedded. The incorporation of symptom-focused techniques into a relational psychotherapy fosters an inclusive approach in which neither present difficulties nor past etiological influences are neglected, and the focus can oscillate between concrete specific issues and more global themes. Atwood and Stolorow (1984) describe psychoanalytic treatment as a method by which a patient acquires reflective knowledge of unconscious organizing and structuring activity. The use of active techniques may, in fact, facilitate this process by assisting patients to focus on their internal states and interpersonal interactions.

Moreover, if we return to our earlier discussion of respective goals of treatment in the two perspectives, we might consider that perhaps accomplishing some measure of what each perspective views as a worthy goal of treatment has the potential to facilitate goals valued by the other. Frank (1992) suggests that behavior change can facilitate structural change and that insight and adaptive behavior form a dialectic in which behavior change may lead to increased insight, and vice versa. For example, a patient who makes some discernable progress in overcoming compulsive behavior may then be less defensive about his conduct and more able to reflect on himself; his increased insight permits further problem solving from an enlarged perspective. It is possible to shift back and forth, often rather rapidly, between a symptom focus and analysis of other material in which each discussion can advance the other. A perspective that begins on the "outside," that is, with cognitive and behavioral aspects of symptoms, can interpenetrate with work that commences on the "inside," with analysis of self-object needs, defenses, and so forth.

Wachtel (1994) notes that, although this is an era in which psychotherapy integration is proceeding rapidly, the existence of "separate and bifurcated cultures" remains pervasive for psychoanalysis and behavior therapy (p. 122). As Stolorow and Atwood (1979) point out, subjective preferences play a large role in one's adherence to any personality theory. Moreoever, such allegiances are often suffused with passion and a sense of identification that goes well beyond a reasoned and informed understanding of one's choices. I am reminded of a graduate school classmate who inscribed the words "Behaviorism Sucks!" on a sign at a behavior therapy conference, and of the colleague who heatedly announced to a group of us who were all in analysis, "I don't believe in analysis!" Although I believe that both behaviorism and psychoanalysis will survive such derision, it is worth considering ways in which aspects of each may benefit from an infusion of the values and methods of the other. Postmodern thought suggests that our notions of inner–outer, self–other, interpretation–new relational experience, and action–insight as rigidly demarcated dualities do not accurately represent the infinitely more complex reality of intricate interrelationships. I hope that, as our understanding of these false dichotomies grows, it becomes more possible to practice in a way that integrates the insights drawn from long-term immersion in patients' subjective worlds with those emerging from research studies into a seamless whole.

CHAPTER TWO

Active Techniques in a Context of Integrative Possibility

IN AN EXTREMELY INFLUENTIAL WORK, Mitchell (1988) described Freudian drive theory as outdated, stating, "we have been living in an essentially post-Freudian era" (p. 2). Mitchell noted that for the first half century of psychoanalytic thought, the guiding vision of treatment was one of the exploration and eventual renunciation of infantile instinctual drives, but that a revolution has occurred over the past several decades. Greenberg and Mitchell (1983) coined the term relational model to characterize a perspective that focuses on relations with others rather than on drives. Contributions from relational thinkers are quite diverse but tend to focus on the individual as a participant in a matrix of relationships rather than as an isolated figure experiencing internal pressures. Moreover, as Stolorow et al. (1987) postulate, a focus on affects rather than drives is central to relational psychoanalysis. The shift to a relational model has invigorated psychoanalytic thinking. It also enables a kind of integration with other theoretical frameworks that was not possible with drive theory's view of

I would like to acknowledge the very substantial contribution made to the chapter by Roger Thomson, Ph.D.

the individual as a relatively closed system and its focus on invariant stages and the primacy of fantasy. Gold and Stricker (2001) similarly assert that relational psychoanalysis provides a foundation for assimilative integration. Mitchell (1988) declared that mind "is composed of relational configurations" (p. 2) and Stolorow and Atwood (1992) critiqued what they term the "myth" of an isolated individual mind, which they believe characterizes Western culture, including psychoanalytic thinking. The nature of such relationally oriented mental processes, their genesis, and their potential transformation in treatment may be illuminated in diverse ways, including, I believe, some of the nonpsychoanalytic methods that I discuss in this book.

Other authors have emphasized the need for a historically grounded psychology. Cushman (1990) argues that the study of the self cannot be decontexualized and that each era produces a particular configuration of self as well as corresponding types of psychopathology. Freud's Victorian period was characterized by polarized and constricted gender roles, strong beliefs in empiricism and rationality, and a notion of the interior self as primitive and potentially dangerous. Freud's concept of a self whose sexual and aggressive drives must be restricted if normal bourgeois society is to function derived from an era very different from ours. Cushman cites the observations of cultural historians that Americans have slowly changed from a Victorian people with deeply felt needs to restrict their sexual and aggressive impulses and to save money and notes that Americans now seem to have intense needs to indulge their impulses and to spend money. Lasch (1978) describes the late 20th century as an era of diminishing expectations and a culture of narcissism. Cushman (1990) observes that the post–World War II self in America is an "empty self" unmoored from tradition and community and eager to fill itself up with consumption and acquisition. This modern "configuration of self" may require a treatment approach more specifically tailored to its particular needs than classical psychoanalysis; for instance, the empty, alienated self may seek connection and guidance more than the Victorian self did.

The character of American psychoanalysis adds to the possibilities for integrative theorizing. Mitchell and Harris (2004) have commented that American psychoanalysis has a distinctively optimistic tone in which possibilities for change have been discussed more than in European writings (which at times have dismissed such notions as behavioristic or lacking appreciation for the importance of the unconscious and of psychic structure). Gedo (1991) similarly notes the character of American psychoanalysis as optimistic and pragmatic. Spezzano (2004) underscores the importance of pragmatism in America, with the notion that "people are more important than ideas about people" (p. 205). Layton (2004), contrasting trends in American psychoanalysis with those in Europe, states that many Kleinians do not feel that analysis should be about cure and that Lacanians tend to see analysis as something other than a method for alleviating suffering and are critical of American "therapeutics."

Havens (2004) has issued a call for us to direct our attention to the future, including asking the patient his aspirations. Havens predicts that in the future psychoanalysis will include attention to the psychological resources required to achieve a certain sort of personal outcome. "It would be a very American orientation to call attention to the conditions of success" (p. 263): Havens's prediction contrasts with Thompson's (2004) characterization of a tradition of psychoanalysis since Freud as more focused on managing frustration and loss than with fostering success. Finally, Reis (2005) suggests that the American relational psychoanalytic notion of the self is one of abundance and multiplicity, with ideas of subjectivity that include historicity, gender, race, culture, class—not the fragmentation and alienation common to European postmodernism, but with a sense of expanded rather than contracted boundaries and a broad perspective of social context. Such explicit attention to pragmatism, optimism, and breadth of perspective in American psychoanalytic writings suggests that incorporating additional change techniques into theory and practice should be possible.

A distinctive feature of postclassical analytic literature is its tone of emancipation and liberation (Mitchell, 2000). Whereas classical writings have tended to emphasize restraint, recent authors have focused on the beneficial impact of more expressive phenomena such as self-disclosure and the deep affective engagement between analyst and patient. These shifts have been occurring among self psychologists, object relations theorists, interpersonalists, and others, and this increased emphasis on the legitimacy of noninterpretive interventions provides support for the inclusion of a variety of responses in the clinical situation. In this chapter I develop a theory of therapeutic interaction in which the proffer of active techniques is seen as an entirely natural development in response to the clinician's experience of the needs of a particular patient. In constructing my model of symptom-focused dynamic psychotherapy, I draw on empirical research on development, psychopathology, and treatment, in addition to theory derived from clinical experience. My analytic perspective is broadly relational, and I elaborate on the particular aspects of postclassical approaches that I find most compatible. I strive to be attentive to social context and to the ways in which social forces prompt and perpetuate certain types of difficulties, such as internalized homophobia or preoccupation with thinness. I also know that my subjectivity is ineluctably shaped by my membership in 21st-century American culture and that such embeddedness produces views that are often relevant in a transitory and local fashion only.

DEVELOPMENT, PSYCHOPATHOLOGY, AND THE IMPACT OF ACTIVE TECHNIQUES

Ideas about development and psychopathology continue to be diverse and contentious among clinicians. Some current analytic authors focus little on such issues (e.g., interpersonalists); instead they concentrate on such here-and-now topics as self-disclosure and authenticity in the analytic relationship. Any proposal for an integrative treatment method, however, must offer an understanding of the processes involved in the origin and maintenance of the pathological conditions to be treated. I take the approach of developmental psychopathology, in which normal and abnormal behaviors are understood together. In chapter one I described some possible pathways to formation of a particular symptom. Here I discuss some of the concepts from two areas of relational psychoanalysis writings that inform my view of development and symptomatology: self psychology/intersubjectivity and attachment theory. Self psychology highlights the development of an integrated and consolidated self; attachment theory, the need for a secure tie to the other. I use ideas from both models, inasmuch as relational security and self-cohesion are intimately associated with one another. A self is always a self-in-attachment.

SELF PSYCHOLOGY AND INTERSUBJECTIVITY THEORY

Kohut held that the self is the supraordinate structure of personality, "an independent center of initiative and perception" (Kohut and Wolf, 1978, p. 414). The development of this self over time is tied to the provision of certain kinds of experiences, which Kohut called selfobject experiences. A selfobject experience is "any experience that functions to evoke or maintain a structured, cohesive self-experience" (Wolf, 1998, p. 52). In Kohut's final, posthumous work (1984) he defined selfobject as "that dimension of our experience of another person that relates to this person's functions in shoring up our self" (pp. 49–50). Wolf (1988) noted that the selfobject is neither self nor object but, rather, refers to the intrapsychic function served by others whose responsiveness assists one's experience of a cohesive self. This concept of the selfobject holds a central place in self psychology. Ornstein (1991) characterizes the selfobject concept as the single element of decisive difference between self psychology and other psychoanalytic models; it is generally agreed that the selfobject concept is the "cornerstone" of the self-psychological perspective (Bacal, 1994).

Chronic failure to respond to a child in an attuned fashion can result in derailments of self-development. Kohut (e.g., 1977) described three important types of selfobject experiences as developmental necessities. Mirroring experiences refer to a need to feel affirmed, truly seen and understood, even admired, especially when one is displaying oneself. The child who shouts to a parent, "Look at me! Watch me!" as she executes a physical feat on the playground is displaying mirroring needs. Kohut also identified what he called idealizing needs, which are needs to be connected to a calming, wise other who is seen as more competent than oneself. The upset child whose distress abates after a hug from a parent has had an idealizing selfobject experience. Finally, Kohut described what he called alterego or twinship needs, which refer to needs to experience alikeness, belonging, and kinship with others rather than feeling isolated and singular. Wolf (1988) has suggested two additions to this enumeration of selfobject needs: adversarial needs, which refer to a need to experience assertiveness and confrontation without the loss of acceptance from the selfobject; and efficacy needs, to experience being able to affect the selfobject and to secure needed experiences.

Significant consequences for the state of the self ensue, depending on the adequacy of selfobject experiences. Sufficient mirroring experiences facilitate self-esteem, assertiveness, and an ability to sustain interests in pursuits and enjoy one's successes. Idealizing experiences foster one's ability to self-soothe and regulate affects. Other selfobject experiences contribute to a sense of belonging to the human community, viewing the self as an active agent, and feeling that one can have one's needs met within the context of important relationships. Essentially, the state of the self should be relatively cohesive, that is, having a sense of wholeness, firmness, inner harmony, strength, vitality, and worth. Inadequate selfobject experiences, especially when chronic and pervasive, are seen as the major determinant of adult psychopathology.

Insufficient selfobject experiences lead to a self that is vulnerable to fragmentation, a distressing affective and cognitive experience referred to in such phrases as "coming unglued" or "falling apart." Fragmentation experiences may include such phenomena as increased desperation, rage, poorly modulated affects and actions, inefficiencies in functioning (such as memory or motor coordination), confusion, and loss of the feeling of continuity over time. Fragmentation experiences range from dysphoria to a panicked sense of impending annihilation or disintegration. Mild fragmentation experiences are common and normal, as anyone who ever had a day when one lost the car keys twice, spilled coffee all over oneself, and forgot to accomplish a few vital tasks can attest. Severe fragmentation, however, is a highly aversive experience, and as I noted in chapter one, it produces such symptomatic manifestations as addictive behavior in an effort to stave off this painful state.

The selfobject concept, useful in illuminating etiological factors in the development of the self, also has ongoing relevance. Self-psychological theory holds that selfobject needs continue throughout life, although they mature in form; for example, one might feel mirrored by reading a book whose author captured some element of one's own experience. A highly "relational" aspect of Kohut's theory is that the individual is seen as existing within a matrix of selfobject experiences all through life, rather than reaching some endpoint of putative autonomy. An important implication of the continuation of selfobject needs throughout adulthood is that selfobject experiences, both in a patient's life outside therapy and in treatment with the therapist, may affect the integrity of the self. For example, receiving a rejection letter from one's desired academic program (a blow to one's wishes for mirroring) might result in some degree of fragmentation, but the experience of feeling carefully listened to (mirroring) and connected to the calm therapist (idealizing) could restore self-cohesion.

Over the last few decades Stolorow and his colleagues (e.g., Stolorow et al., 1987; Stolorow and Atwood, 1992; Brandchaft, 1994) have formulated what they term a theory of intersubjectivity. The appropriate study for psychoanalysis is not an individual mind, but a larger system, the intersubjective field—"the field constituted by the reciprocal interplay between two (or more) subjective worlds" (Stolorow, 1992, p. 247). As I have already mentioned, the concept of the selfobject is of primary importance in self psychology, but I believe that the critique of the construct offered by those authors makes possible a more accurate conceptualization of complex dynamics. Stolorow and his colleagues suggest that the concept of an intersubjective field possesses a higher level of generality than does the notion of a self–selfobject relationship. This intersubjective field includes dimensions of experience other than the selfobject dimension. Selfobject longings are one of several types of principles that unconsciously organize subjective worlds (Stolorow, 1995). Stolorow suggests that selfobject and other dimensions of experience oscillate between figure and ground in a constantly shifting intersubjective context.

Intersubjectivist writings refer to the large body of developmental research that suggests the existence of a child–caregiver system of mutual regulation. Recurrent patterns of transactions and mutual influence in this system eventually give rise to what Stolorow et al. (1987) term invariant organizing principles. On an unconscious level, these principles organize the child's interpretation of subsequent experience, so that personality development is codetermined by the child's preexisting principles and the ongoing relational milieu. Regulation of affect within the child–caregiver system is a major focus. Stolorow et al. cite the work of Krystal (1988) on affective development processes. Krystal proposes that early affects are experienced as physical sensations and gradually become desomatized. Early undifferentiated basic affects of pleasure and unpleasure gradually evolve into more nuanced emotions. Affect differentiation and affect tolerance are aided by the ability to symbolize and articulate. The unfolding of this process, however, rests on the responsiveness of caregivers to the child's emerging affect states; ideally, parents should permit the child to experience and express a range of affects but intervene and comfort the child before affects become overwhelming and traumatic. Chronic failures of attunement may result in a variety of difficulties in later life, including alexithymia, bodily complaints linked to insufficient desomatization of affects, and addictions.

Intersubjectivist concepts of unconscious processes are similarly linked to validating responsiveness in the interactional world. Stolorow and Atwood (1992) have proposed the existence of three interrelated forms taken by unconscious processes. The first they term the prereflective unconscious, which consists of the organizing principles that shape subsequent interpretation of experience. The second is the dynamic unconscious, consisting of unintegrated affect states that have been defensively split off and are experienced as threatening to one's psychological equilibrium and needed relational ties. These contents connote unbearable conflict and danger. Finally, the invalidated unconscious contains experiences that could not be articulated because of an absence of confirming responsiveness.

Intersubjectivity theory postulates the existence of an additional selfobject experience, the self-delineating selfobject function; this refers to the need to have one's affects and perceptions sufficiently validated by caregivers as to engender a sense of their realness. Patients who lack this experience may develop a self-delineating selfobject transference within which the clinician's attunement to their inner experiences eventually leads to a more articulated, grounded, and confident self. The realm of the invalidated unconscious shifts in the context of this responsiveness. Analyst and patient also attend to the two other types of unconscious contents, illuminating the patient's prereflective unconscious largely by examining ways in which the analytic relationship is patterned according to the patient's organizing principles. The dynamic unconscious is revealed and transformed primarily through exploration of the patient's fears that revelation of his or her true feelings will result in retraumatization; the patient anticipates that the analyst will respond in the same critical and rejecting ways as early caregivers. Stolorow et al. (1987) propose that careful exploration of these anxieties not only reveals unconscious patterns but also restores the disrupted selfobject tie, enabling arrested developmental processes to continue.

SELFOBJECT EXPERIENCES AND ACTIVE TECHNIQUES

Because Freud (e.g., 1917a) considered needs to be primarily sexual, gratification has traditionally been considered regressive and antitherapeutic, and frustration became associated with moral purity and righteousness (Terman, 1988). The analyst must of necessity thwart the patient's wishes because the patient is seen as a hopeless dreamer who must accept the reality of unrequited (oedipal) love (Thompson, 2004). In practice, this stance tends to mean that whatever the patient seems to want in response from the analyst must, on principle, be denied (Basch, 1995). Bacal (1985) concurs that Freud's directive to frustrate patients' wishes for libidinal gratification has unfortunately been taken as a mandate to obviate all patient satisfaction within the treatment situation.

Current trends in psychoanalytic theory are more focused on the legitimacy of patients' needs and clinicians' responses to those needs. This shift has been particularly apparent in self psychology. Treatment from a self-psychological perspective entails engaging in an empathic relationship that permits the reemergence of thwarted developmental strivings, interpretation of environmental failures in the provision of selfobject experiences, and a focus on strengthening the self (Kohut, 1971, 1977, 1984; Wolf, 1988). Kohut recommended "empathic immersion" in a patient's experience, so that we consistently understand from within the patient's perspective. "The hallmark of empathy is the sense of a direct grasp of the subjectivity of the other" (Bacal, 1998, p. 289). Bacal points out that, although one of Kohut's major contributions was that empathy constitutes the fundamental means of gathering data in clinical work, it has often been more implicit that empathy is also one of the most powerful and curative elements offered in treatment.

Bacal (1985) suggests that the concept of "optimal responsiveness" might better describe a growth-enhancing interpersonal milieu than does Kohut's (1971) "optimal frustration." Satisfaction of important needs, rather than frustration, seems to lead to the development of internal structure (Terman, 1988). Lindon (1994) commented on the deleterious effects that the "rule of abstinence" has had on psychoanalysis, and proposed, instead, "optimal provision," or that which meets a mobilized developmental longing and advances the analytic process, as a replacement.

More specifically, one aspect of this debate within self psychology relates to the concept of selfobject experiences. Kohut (e.g., 1977) suggested that the appropriate role of the clinician vis-à-vis selfobject experiences is to interpret deficits in previous responses to these needs and the impact of these failures, but not to attempt to meet selfobject needs in the present. Likewise, Goldberg (1978) states that the analyst does not actively soothe or mirror but, rather, interprets the analysand's yearning for such responses. Goldberg further notes that, although it is soothing to be listened to and understood, this wish is interpreted, and "the whole analytic process in this way blocks exploitation for mere gratification" (p. 448). Wolf (1983) cautions against an analytic milieu that is overly cold and depriving, but also warns that an ambience of gratification and need-filling can prevent a true analytic process in which selfobject transferences are mobilized.

Fosshage (1997) comments that Kohut, faithful to his roots in classical theory, viewed interpretation as the principal form of intervention, in contrast to "gratification." Fosshage considers this dichotomy a legacy of classical theory that did not encompass the idea that the clinician might respond and explain at the same time. He points out that Kohut (1984) did state that ongoing selfobject experiences with the analyst are structure producing. Kohut was undecided for some time whether interpretation or relationship is the fundamental therapeutic element in psychoanalysis; he emphasized the curative aspects of the relationship with the analyst in some discussions of transmuting internalization related to the functions of the analyst as a selfobject (Bacal, 1985).

Some authors (e.g., Bacal, 1990; Stolorow and Atwood, 1992) have suggested that supplying selfobject experiences to patients is vital in treatment. Wolf, in a more recent work (1998), stated that the goal of treatment is to strengthen the self, which occurs when the analyst "is experienced as an understanding other who provides needed recognition and is available for idealizing, alter-ego, adversarial, vitalizing, and efficacy selfobject experiences" (p. 240). I believe that providing some selfobject experiences for patients in the present is inevitable as well as therapeutic, if clinicians are aware of limitations in their ability to compensate for past deficits.

Moreover, it should be recognized that the intention of the clinician to provide a particular selfobject experience (or not) does not determine whether or not the patient actually *has* a selfobject experience. The clinician is placed in the role of a selfobject by the spontaneous transference of patient need, rather than by the clinician's active seeking of this role (Tolpin, 1983).

If thwarted developmental needs are remobilized in treatment, as self psychology suggests, it is useful to consider what might constitute optimal responsiveness to them. Patients' requirements for various selfobject experiences are often readily accommodated by a relatively traditional therapeutic style. Yet there may be occasions when the therapist's attempt to understand is not a sufficient response. I agree with such authors as Fosshage (1995) and Shane, Shane, and Gales (1997) that, to create with patients new and developmentally necessary experiences, clinicians must be willing to be shaped by the needed interactions. An analytically informed treatment that also offers patients specific help with disturbing symptoms provides a unique combination in which special expertise is offered in the context of a transformative relationship.

Important selfobject functions are served by the provision of active help with symptoms, most notably idealization (Connors, 2001a). A patient feels calmed and soothed when the therapist seems to possess sufficient competence, knowledge, and experience to help with particular problems. It can be intensely relieving for patients to begin discussing their symptoms (so often kept secret because of shame and embarrassment) with a therapist who has enough expertise to ask the right questions and eventually offer a few suggestions. Because symptomatic problems frequently surface from a somewhat fragmented self-state, patients often feel overwhelmed by dealing with symptoms; their self-cohesion can be improved considerably if they feel attached to an idealizable therapist who knows just what to do. Many, if not most, patients lacked attuned and competent parental care when they had a problem because their parents were fragile, preoccupied, or limited in one way or another owing to their own psychopathology and stressors. A therapist who provides useful help with a specific problem in the context of a warm relationship, like the good-enough parent who bandages the scraped knee, is doing no small thing.

Mirroring functions are served as well in the offering of symptom management (Connors, 2001a). Patients may feel that the clinician really understands and is attuned to their unique problems. Twinship needs may be met as patients come to understand that other people with problems similar to theirs have been helped. This is not to suggest that clinicians regale patients with tales of former patients who are now "success stories," but, rather, that therapists communicate that, in their experience, as well as in the literature, symptoms similar to those of the patient can improve. Meeting such twinship needs inspires hope and a sense that one is part of the human community of people with troubles rather than an isolated and singular sufferer. This selfobject function is probably responsible for much of the success of self-help groups for people with specific problems. Finally, patients' efficacy needs may be met as they perceive that they are having sufficient impact on the therapist in that she offers an individualized plan designed to respond to their particular concerns.

As we thought about the selfobject experiences sought by patients in therapy, Thomson and I identified a selfobject need not previously discussed in the self-psychological literature. We termed this need "instructional selfobject experience" (Thomson and Connors, 2001). We noted that Kohut had identified a sector of the self relating to the development of talents and skills, and the selfobject experience we are describing enhances a person's sense of well-being by directly participating in the growth of talent and skill. Many authors have seen this drive toward the development of competencies and skills as fundamental in human functioning. Decades ago White (1959) identified the search for competence as the basic motivation for behavior, a position echoed by Basch (1988) much later. Bowlby (1969) discussed the young child's need to explore and master the world and to use the attachment figure as a safe base for doing so, and Lichtenberg (1989) has identified needs for exploration as a major component of a motivational system. Lichtenberg (1990) further states that the pleasure of competence and efficacy is inherently self-enhancing, which suggests that acquisition of competencies involves selfobject experiences. Ghent (2002) asserted that individuals develop what he termed functional capacities, by which he meant capabilities or skills, and proposed that needs to execute and further develop capacities will emerge to the extent that such capacities promoted satisfaction and decreased distress.

INSTRUCTIONAL SELFOBJECTS

In the relational model I am proposing, it is ineluctable that the development of competence requires the responsive relatedness of an environment that is ready to accept, nurture, and encourage its growth. The task is not simply to value the accomplishments of the self (mirroring experiences) or to provide models and values to guide its development (idealizing experiences) but to aid directly in the development of competency in dealing with the intrapsychic, interpersonal, and practical problems one faces. It is this activity that we identify as an instructional selfobject experience. When adequately provided, the instructional selfobject function is experienced as an effort to assist the patient in learning to be who he or she wants to be; it focuses on the acquisition of pragmatic, interactional, and self-management skills. Along these lines, Tolpin (2000) has made a brief reference to a "coaching transference," which nicely expresses the essential instructional element of offering knowledgeable guidance.

Most societies recognize that children require a great deal of instruction, and this belief is reflected in numerous cultural institutions, including our establishment of compulsory education through the teen years. It is taken for granted that children need to be taught skills ranging from shoelace tying to long division and that, although at times mastery may be achieved through observing others, typically verbal instruction or step-by-step physical demonstration is employed. Parents constantly serve an instructional function for their children, and it is important to note the experience of pleasure and vitality displayed by children who are learning skills in a secure relational milieu. In many ways learning is the task of childhood, and the child whose parents and teachers teach well and with attention to his or her cognitive and affective development will thrive on the experience of gaining mastery. We propose that children have needs for direct instructional experiences, and, just as children's frequent expressions of "Watch me! Look at me!" signal their needs for mirroring, so too do such pleas as, "I want to do it—show me!" suggest children's requirements for instructional selfobject experiences.

In addition to its obvious fostering of adaptive functioning, the instructional selfobject experience and the talents and skills it sustains play an important developmental role in harmonizing conflicts in the maturation of mirroring and idealizing needs. A child's need to feel strong and powerful is not always affirmed by his awareness of the immensely greater competencies of the adults in his world. If a prematurely realistic view of the power of self-in-relation-to-adult others were to develop, the child's evolving sense of strength and value might be compromised. One way the adults can protect against such traumatic realizations is to be available to help the child bridge the gap between immature and mature levels of skill. By taking an appropriately attuned instructional relationship to the child, parents can support his or her sense of growing toward the competencies of the idealized other and thus firm up the still-fragile grandiose self while also realistically strengthening the area of talents and skills. The protection against fragmentation that is thus provided is one reason we consider these commonplace instructional interactions to have selfobject qualities.

Through our observations in clinical practice, Thomson and I realized that these instructional needs are retained in adulthood, although, of course, as with other selfobject needs, they mature in form as development progresses (seeking a mentor who can teach needed professional skills is one example from adult life). However, despite the fact that our culture values education in adulthood and adults are offered an array of opportunities to learn new skills, concepts of learning and the need for instruction have been largely absent from psychoanalytic models of treatment. Although insight has been highly valued in psychoanalytic thought as a goal of treatment and accruing enough of it might traditionally be equated with cure, interpretation has been posited as the singular means by which insight occurs. Traditional concepts suggesting that the analyst must be neutral in his or her stance toward a patient's wishes, fantasies, and so forth have further contributed to the paucity of analytic attention to concepts of teaching and learning in a treatment situation, as has the view that the analyst must remain anonymous to enable the development of a transference thought to be uncontaminated by aspects of the real person.

A few authors have addressed teaching and learning from psychoanalytic perspectives. Wolf (1989) and Elson (1989) have applied self-psychological concepts to educational settings, and both emphasize that selfobject needs may emerge in a teaching and learning process. Wolf (1989) comments that teaching is, at least in part, a selfobject function. Elson (1989) discusses the unique vulnerability of the adult learner, who may feel great shame at not knowing things he or she feels should have been learned already. Elson further notes that learning in adulthood may reawaken a combination of hope, helplessness, and selfobject needs. Although neither Wolf nor Elson propose a new selfobject need to describe these experiences, their work conveys their sense that learning in childhood and adulthood can become imbued with salience and urgency and requires much sensitivity in response.

McWilliams (2003), noting the lack of explicit attention in psychoanalytic writings to the educative aspects of psychoanalysis, states that clinicians are always involved in teaching and that even the most classical interpretation or information-gathering inquiry conveys educative messages. McWilliams suggests that we educate our patients in several different ways, including instructing and socializing them about how to be patients. She comments that we also teach our patients about emotions, for instance, that talking about distressing affects is helpful and that feelings and behaviors are not the same. McWilliams further states that we often educate our patients about developmental issues, the impact of stress and trauma, intimacy, sexuality, and self-esteem. She concludes that, by helping patients discover how they want to live their lives, "we inevitably educate them more actively than our mainstream theories of practice have acknowledged" (p. 258).

Gedo (1979, 1988, 1991) has made a unique contribution to the analytic literature by elaborating the importance of learning in psychoanalysis. He describes "apraxias" as the deficiencies caused by failures to learn such adaptively essential skills as tension regulation, and noted that such difficulties are common. Gedo and Goldberg (1973) discuss apraxias that include difficulties in tension regulation and in developing a coherent program of goal-directed action. Gedo (1988) postulates that certain characteristics of caregivers, as well as vulnerabilites of the child, can lead to interferences in the child's capacity to learn appropriate skills. For instance, a child could acquire strange beliefs about the world by identification with a disturbed parent. Gedo (1991) holds that psychological maturation requires competencies in mental and behavioral skills and that failure to attain such skills interferes with future development. In fact, he states that all psychological problems may be considered learning disabilities.

Gedo (1988) comments that successful interventions to aid patients with apraxic difficulties are seldom reported in the literature or are dismissed as countertransference errors; he suggests that helping patients to identify their apraxias and initiate a process of new learning is vital. Gedo and Goldberg (1973) propose that patients with more regressed mental functioning may require measures involving "pacification," that is, tension regulation, or "unification," by which the authors mean reintegration for disorganized states and help in formulating a coherent program of goal directed actions. Gedo (1988) asserts that helping patients to gain such skills is very important and can occur through direct instruction if necessary. He recommends (1991) active collaborative efforts to assist patients to learn skills, including by noninterpretive means, and notes that such interventions should not preclude exploration and resolution of transference: "Permitting such patients to borrow missing skills through explicit instruction . . . does not interfere with the subsequent development of transferences" (p. 102). Gedo highlights the importance of the patient's identifying with the analyst's competence as the analyst provides a model to emulate and that clinicians require further specification of the processes by which patients acquire new skills and new information. We believe, with Gedo, that one of the cornerstones of psychoanalytic treatment is (and should be) a process of learning self-regulatory and interactional skills. One way this process occurs is the mobilization of a selfobject transference that is, at least partially, organized around needs for instruction that the clinician provides.

Therapist Caution Regarding Instruction

Instructional selfobject needs arise in therapy in a variety of ways; for instance, patients request advice in managing problematic interpersonal situations, or they seek strategies for minimizing disturbing symptoms and affects. Clinicians often deflect these requests because of the fear that they will be inappropriately involved in their patients' lives, derail the exploratory work, or compromise the patient's autonomy. Remnants of classical theory's admonitions to forbid patients' gratification and Freud's (1919) devaluation of "the copper of direct suggestion" (p. 168) can lead clinicians to feel that they are failing to uphold appropriate analytic ideals if they accede to patients' wishes for guidance and suggestions. As Renik (1992) writes, "neutrality, the effort to avoid suggestion and compromise of the patient's autonomy, is at the core of classical technique" (p. 75). Clinicians may feel that there is something wrong with patients' wanting guidance from us and something very transgressive about providing it.

The typical prejudice against directly instructive interventions has penetrated so far into common cultural stereotypes about psychotherapy that patients feel required to preface their wishes for advice or instruction with such statements as, "I know you can't tell me what to do, but . . ." The attitude of an overly cautious therapist against "intrusiveness," and a deliberate shunning of advice giving, teaching, or instructive interactions, although it may serve to protect the patient from a traumatizing reenactment of a relationship with an overly controlling parent, is not without cost: the drawback of this stance comes from the potential failure of the therapist to respond to real selfobject needs that are not recognized as such.

One patient reported that, although she had received some help from a previous therapist, he had a very annoying feature: he would not respond to certain direct questions she had, but instead invariably directed her back to her own ideas and inclinations. The patient felt very put off by this reaction and persisted in trying to find a way to elicit the responses she wished for from him. She found that, if she phrased her questions in certain ways, she could persuade him to provide the information she wanted. She thus modified her method of relating to him, but she resented having to mold herself so awkwardly to achieve her goals. To this day, the therapist's contribution remains diminished by the patient's feeling that she was not acceptable as she was and that her needs had to be disguised to be tolerable to him. His unwillingness to respond to some needs had a far-reaching effect on multiple sectors of her personality; mirroring needs in particular were frustrated by his efforts to be "empowering," but in addition, her needs for an idealizeable other were also thwarted.

We have found that many patients will attempt to disguise their wishes to engage the therapist in an instructional dialogue because they believe that doing so would be unwelcome. The risk presented by an overly conservative attitude toward interactions such as direct behavioral suggestion is that we may be inadvertently frustrating an expression of the very needs that we seek to revive in treatment, perhaps even the one aspect of genuine self that the patient is willing to share with us at a given point. We believe (like some of our patients) that much therapeutic practice is unnecessarily dominated by an insistence that the patient must find the answers within herself or himself, with a corresponding dismissal of the assistance that the relationship might afford.

This sort of frustration should play a lesser role in psychodynamic treatment than it currently does. Freud (1940) himself did not eschew the role of the analyst as educator: "We serve the patient in various functions, as an authority and a substitute for his parents, as a teacher and educator" (p. 181). Freud (1917c) also wrote that psychoanalytic treatment "has justly been described as a kind of after-education" (p. 451). Clinicians who are concerned that offering more active guidance involves "imposing" their values and judgments on patients might consider that all their actions and all refusals to act are "imposing" in that they reveal the self of the clinician. Gill (1994) cautioned that the therapist must accept that whatever he does or does not do is an action that will have some sort of interpersonal meaning. Gill pointed out that it is the responsibility of the therapist to search for this meaning. In an earlier work, my colleagues and I noted that all therapists and analysts offer (implicitly or explicitly) suggestions to patients for proceeding in a manner they hope will be helpful, including free association, meeting a certain number of times per week, and so forth (Johnson et al., 1987). We may reveal more about the way we think about things when we offer suggestions, but I do not see this as problematic if it serves the needs of patients and if their responses to such activity can be explored.

Renik (1995) asserts that we are mistaken in our belief that, by imposing inhibitions on ourselves in the clinical situation (for instance, remaining silent rather than making a comment) we are reducing the degree to which our personality is felt; we are merely altering it; "we can put our hands over our eyes if we want, but we will not disappear" (p. 469). Gill (1994) noted that the analyst's passivity can be mistaken for neutrality, and stated, "the silent analyst is not doing nothing. Omission of what needs to be said is as crucial a matter as what is said" (p. 76). It is impossible for the analyst to focus on the patient's inner reality from a position of analytic objectivity that is free of personal biases, even for an instant (Renik, 1993).

Hoffman (1998) has written of what he terms the "intimate authority" of the psychoanalyst's presence and suggests that we are inevitably involved with our patients in a mentoring role, whether we wish it or not. He states that "in trying so hard to stay out of it, we can really *be* 'out of it'" (p. 73). Hoffman underscores that every action of the clinician leads the patient in some direction and that we are involved in the construction of the patient's internal reality, not merely the discovery of it. He proposes that clinicians would do well to embrace the reality of their role as a particular kind of authority in the patient's life and do their best to act wisely, rather than thinking that somehow there is a safe position of noninfluence to which we can retreat. Pizer (2003) discusses ways that ideas about technique constrain clinicians and lead to what she terms relational (k)nots, modes of relating that are limited and distorted. She recommends that "we remain mindful of how unexamined elements of training and technique can engender relational nots . . . once we set our own behavior to a standard of 'too therapeutic' or 'insufficiently analytical' —we have seriously curtailed the relationship with the person we are trying to talk to" (p. 179). She proposes that tradition not be privileged at the expense of patients' real needs.

We might all agree that encouraging patients to employ all their resources in problem solving can often be productive. An intervention such as, "Yes, I do have some ideas about what might help you with that," when a patient requires more resources than she currently possesses, may be more useful still. Although interpretation may be central for resolution of conflict, patients require various forms of support, including educative measures, when deficit is the issue (Markson, 1992). Many patients in need of skill acquisition experience interferences in their ability to learn because of such problems as identification with maladaptive parents, grandiosity about the need for perfection without learning, and rejection of authority in the interest of preserving autonomy (Gedo, 1988). The complexities of psychopathology are such that many patients probably experience intricate blends of internal conflict and true deficit. Some of the deficits may be ameliorated with the use of active techniques, but whether or not these efforts are effective the issues to which Gedo refers may be more sharply delineated in the attempt. He recommends (1991) offering a therapeutic trial that may address the apraxic difficulty if it is unclear whether a patient has an apraxia or some sort of repetition: "When we neglect to offer needed assistance of that kind, our insistence on a technical approach predicated on dealing exclusively with unconscious intrapsychic conflict can only lead to therapeutic failure" (p. 112).

The importance of instructional selfobject experiences is illustrated in the case of Ellen, who sought therapy in her late 20s because of chronic depression. She complained of poor self-esteem, lack of zest for living, and feelings of isolation and estrangement from others. It became apparent that both parents had suffered a series of unresolved and tragic losses during their lives and had been too depressed themselves to provide her with many needed selfobject experiences. Her parents had been unable to take an authoritative role when she looked to them for guidance and structure and she had always felt she was alone with her problems. She discussed painful experiences of wishing to have her parents teach her things and said that when they failed to respond she concluded that she was bad for desiring this.

Ellen did not want to take medication and requested that psychotherapy provide her with some concrete and practical help. I believed that an optimally responsive treatment should accommodate her wish and thought that engagement with Ellen would be facilitated if I framed some of the treatment as instructional, in accordance with Ellen's request for practical assistance. Ellen's lack of regard for her own needs resulted in her often being taken advantage of in relationships, and she eagerly agreed to work on learning how to set limits with others.

We discussed in detail the many situations in which Ellen felt compelled to take care of others and accede to their requests. I helped Ellen to understand some of the childhood determinants of this anxious caretaking in her relationships with fragile family members and gave her some guidance and suggestions for handling this issue differently. Tentatively Ellen began to be able to say she needed to "think about" it instead of giving automatic assent to someone who wanted her to do something. Although it was anxiety provoking to assert her own needs in a way that had been prohibited in childhood, she had the opportunity to see that no catastrophic consequences ensued, and she felt more empowered and free of the constant obligations that had sapped her energy.

Many themes in Ellen's psychotherapy related to frustrated wishes for teaching and learning. Ellen described having always thought of herself as deficient, someone who simply did not know how to live life as others did ("I never got the instruction manual"). She told of a visit to her mother during which she noticed that under her mother's care a recently acquired plant had died and that she understood something about why she herself couldn't take care of plants—she had never been taught. She stated that she was realizing that so many bad feelings about herself that she thought she must have had from birth related to not having been taught how to do things, and feeling anguished about not knowing. She was able to arrive at this insight only after a number of experiences in the treatment in which she found that she could, in fact, learn to do new things, rather than considering herself hopelessly defective.

Ellen's treatment took several years and continued to interweave instructional interventions with more standard elements of an intensive psychotherapy. It is unlikely, however, that Ellen would have remained in a long-term treatment if her instructional selfobject needs had not been attended to, both by interpretation of past failures in this area and by provision of a new experience in the present. Her history had resulted in her being quite dubious about the possibility that anyone would be interested in taking her needs seriously, and trust was built very slowly. Even after a few years of treatment, when I asked about Ellen's experience of my trustworthiness, Ellen responded, "You've been OK—so far!" Ellen's readiness to engage in consultation concerning instruction ultimately resulted in a gradually deepening involvement that included mirroring and idealizing needs as well, and the treatment process resulted in substantial transformation. Our treatment ended when Ellen's increased confidence in herself as a learner resulted in her relocating to pursue graduate study at a prestigious institution.

Terman (1988) has highlighted the importance of our active participation in a "dialogue of construction" that involves communication, affectivity, and the generation of structure-building pattern (p. 125). Selfobject functions served by the provision of active help may enable patients to be more trusting in the therapeutic relationship, as was seen in the case of Ellen. Moreover, aiding a patient in achieving mastery over and relief from a significant problem inspires hope and releases energy to work on other issues. When patients are attempting to solve problems that are too difficult for them, they become hopeless and frustrated, but people confronted with problems that they are capable of solving with concerted application and appropriate help experience a sense of efficacy at doing so. Patients such as Ellen, who experience symptomatic improvement in the context of a relationship in which long-suppressed selfobject needs are attended to, have enhanced self-esteem, greater vitality, and a more harmonious self-experience, all indicative of improved self-cohesion. Moreover, Seligman (2005) stresses the self-organizing nature of complex dynamic systems: one progressive development tends to lead to other positive changes.

The question may be raised whether phenomena Thomson and I call instructional selfobject needs really require this new term, rather than one of our previously delineated selfobject functions. The developmental needs that Kohut termed mirroring, idealizing, and twinship are in need of further refinement and elaboration, including the discovery of new configurations (Ornstein and Ornstein, 1995). We echo Rowe's (1994) statement that our ability to perceive and understand selfobject needs depends on our commitment to Kohut's "experience-near" mode of observation, and it is from this dedication to listening to our patients that we derive these ideas. Moreover, we believe that what we term instructional selfobject needs do require elaboration, primarily because recognition of them as selfobject needs may help clinicians to respond to them.

ATTACHMENT THEORY

You and I might well be pursuing different career paths if not for the profoundly important discoveries of Freud, who posited that "the talking cure" might ameliorate psychological ailments. Inevitably, many of Freud's ideas reflected the era in which he lived and the knowledge base of that period. Advances in scientific methods now enable us to have access to information about development and psychopathology that was completely unknown in Freud's time—brain imaging studies, genetic epidemiology research, and microanalysis of transactions in early infancy. Historically and in the present day, psychoanalysts have been skeptical about the value of information originating outside the psychoanalytic consulting room (Safran and Aron, 2001). For example, Orange (2003) has termed neurobiology and cognitive neuroscience reductionistic and writes that they have no place in psychoanalytic discourse. Even

Mitchell (e.g., 1997), who was fearless in his trenchant explication of theory, has been criticized for placing insufficient value on empirical data that would have buttressed and helped correct various points he argued (Masling, 2003). Westen (2002) noted that analysts commonly believe that being empathic and being scientific are incompatible.

However, many analysts now decry the regrettable split between the worlds of clinical work and of research. Kernberg (2004) discussed the deep ambivalence about research in the psychoanalytic community, noting the conflict between our awareness of the importance of research findings and our fears of how such data will affect our traditional assumptions. He argues strongly for "radical changes" in the current educational system in order to train research scientists. Safran (2001) suggested that the current movement toward empirically validated treatment offers a needed corrective to some overly insular elements within psychoanalysis, and Fonagy (2001) proposed that analytic clinicians use research findings to help excise the "one size fits all" approach that he believes is often applied in analytic work. Westen (2002) recommends that authors of psychoanalytic papers conduct searches of relevant empirical research papers as well as of analytic literature when writing on such topics as emotion and development. Incorporating recent neurobiological data into psychoanalytic thinking can help solidify the status of analysis as a demonstrably effective treatment (Pariser, 2005). For Gedo (1999), all the traditional psychoanalytic beliefs about early childhood development have now been invalidated, and it is crucial to include data from cognitive science, neuroscience, and observational studies of young children into psychoanalytic theory.

The status of attachment theory within the psychoanalytic literature illustrates the conflictual but shifting attitudes toward empiricism over the last several decades. Although Bowlby was trained as a psychoanalyst, his theory emphasized the importance of such external events as separations and losses at a time when psychoanalysis was focused on the primacy of internal fantasy. For this and other reasons his work did not find acceptance within the psychoanalytic community (see Fonagy, 2001, for a full discussion). It did, however, become very influential in developmental psychology. More recently, paralleling the turn to relational issues rather than drives within the psychoanalytic community, interest in attachment theory has grown.

Attachment theory centers on the idea of a bond between infant and caregiver that promotes the protection and survival of the infant. Incorporating concepts from ethology and evolutionary theory, Bowlby (1969) postulated that the prolonged period of relative helplessness that characterizes early childhood necessitates a system for maintaining proximity between child and caregiver. The infant uses the attachment figure as a secure base from which to explore and will seek greater proximity under conditions of danger, stress, or novelty. Although early theory focused on the need for actual physical proximity, later conceptualizations proposed that the goal of attachment seeking was "felt security" (Sroufe and Waters, 1977) and the maintenance of the caregiver's accessibility and responsiveness (Kobak, 1999). Because attachment represents the infant's primary mechanism for ensuring survival, the attachment system is viewed as continually operating; at some level (which may be out of awareness) the relative balance of safety versus threat in the current situation is being monitored (Main, 1995). The infant or child actively organizes information concerning the attachment figure's availability and regulates her or his own behavior accordingly to maximize security.

Although Bowlby's emphasis on observable events such as disruptions in the parent–child relationship was frequently disparaged within psychoanalytic circles, he also highlighted the importance of internal representations of self and other. Bowlby suggested that, drawing on his caregiving experiences, the infant gradually develops "internal working models" of the self as worthy of attention and care or not, and of others as trustworthy or not. Bowlby (1973) wrote that individuals develop varied expectations of the availability and responsiveness of attachment figures that are "tolerably accurate reflections of the experiences those individuals have actually had" (p. 202). These expections guide future behavior. Although the term internal working models is a bit clumsy, it was intended to convey that these internal representations become relatively firm but are still subject to revision on the basis of new attachment-related information.

I believe that a good deal of overlap exists between Bowlby's concept of attachment needs and self-psychological conceptualizations of idealizing needs, in that both stress the requirement for connection with another who is seen as stronger, wiser, and more competent than the self and who can provide soothing and comfort. Criteria for an attachment relationship include the following: the bond is persistent, emotionally significant, involves wishes for proximity to the other, and takes place in a very specific fashion with a particular individual (Ainsworth, 1989). Moreover, the person seeks security and comfort in the relationship and suffers distress at involuntary separation when proximity is desired. Thus, attachment theory places more emphasis on the provision of a sense of safety and security and the need for a particular attachment figure. The specificity of the attachment bond is obvious to parents whose distressed child is crying for "Mommy!" or "Daddy!"; at times the other parent's attempts to comfort simply will not do.

Attachment researchers have identified some relatively stable configurations of behavior in children that are associated with varying types of behaviors in parents, although maternal sensitivity is an important, but not an exclusive, factor in the development of attachment security (Belsky, 1999). Securely attached children seem to have parents who are consistently available, sensitive, and responsive. These children show discomfort upon separation from an attachment figure but are quickly comforted upon reunion (Ainsworth et al., 1978) and seem to be able to use the caregiver as a safe base from which to explore. Psychologically healthier parents are more likely than parents who are less emotionally robust to have children who are securely attached to them (Belsky, 1999).

Researchers have also identified patterns of attachment that they term insecure. One group of infants had mothers who were inconsistent, unpredictable, discouraging of autonomy, and insensitive, although they did display warmth at times (Ainsworth et al., 1978). These infants were observed to be preoccupied with their mothers when they were present and unable to focus on exploration. The infants exhibited great distress at a brief separation and at reunion alternated intense proximity seeking with displays of anger. This group has been termed ambivalent or resistant. They seem to be organized around having a single attentional focus on the attachment figure (Main, 1995).

Another group of infants displayed a very different pattern. Infants termed avoidant were observed to have mothers who were consistently rejecting and who rebuffed their infants' bids for responsiveness. These mothers seemed to avoid physical contact with their infants and withdrew from them when the infants showed distress (Ainsworth et al., 1978; Grossmann and Grossmann, 1991). In laboratory playroom settings these infants showed no response to brief separations from their mothers, interacted as readily with strangers as with their mothers, and, often busying themselves with toys, ignored their mothers upon reunion. Attachment behavior was absent, replaced with active avoidance of the attachment figure and a focus on the environment, but high levels of physiological arousal suggested that these infants were indeed stressed by separation (Main, 1995).

More recent research has identified another insecurely attached group whose behavior does not seem to fit any organized pattern. These "disorganized/disoriented" infants (Main and Solomon, 1986) seem to display incoherence in their attachment-related behavior, including freezing, displays of fear, and disorientation. Such infant behavior has been linked to child maltreatment and unresolved trauma in the parent. Main and Hesse (1990) have proposed that such infants experience the parent as frightened or frightening, and the parent is at once the source of security and the source of danger. These mothers arouse strong affect in their children and, failing to terminate it, frequently behave in alarming and punitive ways (Solomon and George, 1999). Solomon and George report the response of a mother of a distraught kindergarten-age child who was grieving over her dead hamster and wished to have the pet back. The mother said, "I showed her a dead skunk in the road . . . and I said . . . this is what dead is. And if this happens to you, you'll never come back" (p. 20). These authors suggest that disorganized attachment behavior may represent a severe failure to integrate attachment-related thoughts, feelings, and behaviors, probably related to parental behavior that exacerbates attachment-related distress rather than alleviating it.

Securely attached infants are able to use the attachment figure to help them regulate distress. They turn to the attachment figure, are comforted, and may resume exploration. Insecurely attached infants, however, must find a way to modulate affect in the absence of a secure bond to a regulating other. They have to evolve conditional strategies that enable them to preserve some degree of proximity to a problematic attachment figure (Main, 1995). Ambivalent infants attempt to manage this situation by constant activation of the attachment system; they are hypervigilant in attending to the caregiver's whereabouts and states of mind. Since these parents do respond to their children at times, the children seem to engage in intense displays of neediness and emotionality in attempts to obtain nurturance from inept or self-preoccupied caregivers. Avoidant infants, whose mothers are consistently rejecting, attempt to minimize distress by defocusing from the attachment figure whose rebuff is so expectable. They regulate the level of need that they display to an unavailable caregiver and distract themselves with attention to the nonrelational world. Attachment disorganization, in which children have no coherent strategy for dealing with overwhelming affects and frightening caregivers, has been linked to dissociation, overcontrolling behavior, aggression, and interpersonal incompetence (Solomon and George, 1999; Fonagy, 2001).

Although Bowlby (1969) emphasized that attachment security is important "from the cradle to the grave" (p. 129), a focus on attachment processes in adults is relatively recent. In the 1980s such researchers as Hazan and Shaver (1987) began conceptualizing romantic love as an attachment process. They suggest that the secure, ambivalent, and avoidant styles are manifested in adult romantic relationships. Main and her colleagues (George, Kaplan, and Main, 1996) developed the Adult Attachment Interview (AAI), an extremely sophisticated interview designed to assess a subject's state of mind regarding attachment by requiring her or him to produce and reflect on attachment-related memories while simultaneously maintaining coherent and collaborative dialogue with the interviewer (Hesse, 1999). Adults rated as secure seem comfortable with intimacy and with their own emotions (Main, 1995). Adults classified as insecure/ambivalent are termed preoccupied in adulthood because they display excessive preoccupation and entanglement with parents (Main, 1995). Intimate love relationships of this group are characterized by idealization, jealousy, dependence, and intense reliance on partners (Feeney and Noller, 1990). Avoidant adults are also termed dismissing because they minimize the importance of relationship, are uncomfortable with intimacy, and become very involved with work pursuits (Feeney and Noller, 1990; Hazan and Shaver, 1990). They report that they do not remember much about childhood, assert their normality, and minimize the impact of relational experiences (Main, 1995). Disorganized attachment is the subtype most clearly associated with significant psychopathology in adulthood, including dissociative disorders, violent behavior, criminal convictions, and manifestations of borderline personality disorder (Carlson, 1998; Fonagy, 2001).

ATTACHMENT SECURITY AND USE OF ACTIVE TECHNIQUES

Although the clinical implications of attachment theory are very salient, most of the literature about attachment processes is developmental rather than clinically oriented. Bowlby (1988) did suggest several key ideas for treatment, however. He proposed that the therapist, typically sought when an individual is in distress, would become a new attachment figure. Two major elements in treatment are seen as curative: first, the patient gains a new perspective on the development of her working models of self and others by regarding childhood events with the reflective capacity of an adult; and, second, the patient has a new and positive attachment-related experience with the therapist. Using the therapist as a safe base, the patient is able to explore internal events with less need for what Bowlby termed defensive exclusion of information, which may have been required in childhood. The particular attachment style of the patient (and of the therapist) will have much bearing on the course of therapy.

Using attachment concepts can illuminate a great deal about our patients' strategies of affect regulation and the ways in which they use relationships (or eschew using relationships) to help in this process (Connors 1997a, 2000). Secure individuals are able to internalize some affect-regulation capacities, but more avoidant persons may try to decrease and suppress affects (or "down-regulate"), whereas others (with a more ambivalent style) may amplify affects ("up-regulate") in the hope of a positive response (Sroufe, 1996). It is likely that different therapeutic strategies will be helpful with these contrasting styles. Moreover, some recent clinically related work in attachment is less centered on particular attachment categories and more oriented toward helping insecure person develop what Fonagy and Target (1997) term "the reflective function," referring to an ability to reflect on states of mind in oneself and others.

Becoming a Usable Object for Avoidant Patients

It is very easy for us to misunderstand which experiences are distressing to others if we ourselves are not affected similarly. This discrepancy was vividly illustrated in some video clips I saw on television recently purporting to be America's "Funniest," although I did not find these two amusing. The first involved a toddler with an expressed fear of heights, whose grandmother was pushing him higher and higher on a swing, despite his vociferous protests. When the swing finally stopped, the shrieking toddler jumped off and angrily flung the swing at the laughing grandmother. The second video showed a children's party at which one child was breaking a pinata that was rather realistically shaped like a dog. The sensitive sister of the birthday girl began sobbing and screamed, "You're breaking his butt. Stop it! Stop it!" and finally collapsing in a heap cradling the broken pieces, bitterly declared, "This is the worst day of my life!" In both situations the adults were amused (and in the first incident may have enjoyed indulging some sadistic impulses) while the children were deeply distressed.

There are patients for whom the process of psychotherapy might be reminiscent of these situations in which allegedly child-oriented activities felt traumatic for the children. As I described earlier, adults with a dismissive attachment style have adapted to consistent rejection by developing a defensively nonrelational stance. Even if the therapist does everything possible to establish an atmosphere of safety, sensitivity, and respect, the internal working models of these patients will be signaling danger and threat. And, although it is hoped that mental health professionals would not find this amusing, we ourselves may have such a high degree of comfort with the process of disclosing, remembering, relating, and so on that we may not fully appreciate the horror that some people experience at such a prospect. Newman (1998) has elaborated on Winnicott's concept of "usability" by suggesting that the clinician must find ways to become a "usable" object for the patient whose character defenses have been shaped by significant deficits in caregiving responsiveness. I propose that one way might be by providing instruction in symptom management.

Some findings from attachment research clarify the internal world of the insecure avoidant patient. Haft and Slade (1989) identified attachment styles in a group of mothers and then observed their interactions with their infants. The secure mothers responded to a broad range of affective experiences in their infants, but the dismissing group consistently distorted and misattuned according to the type of affect their babies displayed. These mothers seemed most comfortable attuning to their infants' exuberance and mastery in play involving separateness and autonomy. The mothers consistently misread their babies' negative affect and rejected their bids for comfort and reassurance, often with sadistic overtones. According to Haft and Slade, the transmission of insecure attachment styles from parents to children relates to experiences of discovering that some emotional states are acceptable and shareable with parents and others are not. The defensive strategy most available to the child is the one that the attachment figure habitually uses in response to distress, which is then internalized (Fonagy et al., 1995), and research, including studies in which parents were interviewed prior to the birth of their children (Hesse, 1999) confirms the intergenerational transmission of attachment style. Avoidant persons live in a world where negative affect is not tolerated, and so they come to find it intolerable themselves.

Bartholomew (1990) notes that one way to titrate the distress of rejection by attachment figures is to develop a model of the self as fully adequate and thus invulnerable to negative feelings. Other findings support this notion that dismissive persons hold a defensively positive view of self. Cassidy (1988) has found that avoidant children tend to describe the self as perfect. Cassidy and Kobak (1988) reviewed evidence suggesting the link between avoidance and idealization of parents and posited that defensively idealized models of parents may be related to defensively idealized self-representations. Mikulincer (1995) researched the view of self held by avoidant individuals and reports that it was lacking in balance, coherence, and integration, with much discrepancy between domains. He suggests that this view of self may not imply true high self-esteem but, rather, self-esteem so fragile that no flaws can be tolerated; the self is idealized as a defense against the rejection anticipated from others if one is not perfect.

Because avoidant persons are inclined to invest in work instead of relationships and may be very successful in professional endeavors, they likely never come to the attention of clinicians. Research suggests that avoidant attachment is usually not associated with emotional breakdown except in highly threatening or extreme circumstances (Shaver and Mikulincer, 2002). The autonomy of the dismissing style, unlike the obsessive clinging and overt dysfunction that may characterize persons with preoccupied or disorganized attachment, is admired in our culture. As we might expect from the elevated heart rate noted in avoidant infants, these people are prone to increased somaticizing when under stress (Mikulincer, Florian, and Weller, 1993). They may be vulnerable to such sequelae as muscular tension, high blood pressure, cardiac difficulties, and anxiety disorders. Avoidant persons have also been found to use alcohol to relieve tension (Brennan and Shaver, 1995). When they seek treatment, they may express a wish for "stress management" to help alleviate their symptoms.

As I have suggested, however, the treatment process poses considerable challenges. Dozier (1990) used the AAI to classify the attachment styles of young adults in treatment for serious psychopathology. Clinician ratings suggested that persons with strong avoidant tendencies were less likely to seek out treatment and were more prone to reject it than were patients with preoccupied strategies. Further, avoidance was inversely related to disclosure in treatment. Another study similarly found that avoidant persons self-disclosed less than did those with other attachment styles (Mikulincer and Nachshon, 1991) and seemed unaffected by level of partner disclosure, which suggests a lack of flexibility in articulating subjective experiences. Moreover, psychotherapy entails a consideration of past events, but avoidant participants show less access to memories involving anxiety and sadness than do other groups, and they rate these memories as less emotionally intense (Mikulincer and Orbach, 1995). Mikulincer and Orbach suggest that avoidant persons employ a strategy of undifferentiated defensiveness and display distance from their own inner worlds as well as from other people.

People who have had to structure their cognitive and affective life around avoidance of attachment-related information are better organized than are other insecure groups and are anxious about threats to their organization, including the threat emanating from a focus on attachment processes. The idea of relying on a new attachment figure in therapy will be strenuously resisted by those who were consistently rebuffed and treated harshly in the original attachment relationship. Therapist injunctions to speak freely about what comes to mind and inquiries into emotional states will be puzzling and foreign to patients whose caregivers discouraged expression of negative affects and may signal potential retraumatization. Main (1995) has described ways in which dismissive persons resist the tasks presented by the AAI interviewer—cutting the interaction short with brief replies, insisting on lack of recall, and portraying the self as invulnerable.

Therapeutic work on techniques of symptom management can be conducted in a more structured and less ambiguous fashion than typical psychoanalytic psychotherapy, and avoidant patients may find the former approach more tolerable. They will be more comfortable if they can view the therapist as a consultant whose expertise may be employed in an impersonal fashion that minimizes vulnerability. Patients may entirely repudiate any suggestion of being in distress. When one patient called for an initial consultation and I asked why he was seeking treatment, he informed me that he preferred not to think of himself as someone with a problem needing help, but that perhaps he could use some coaching. The active techniques of symptom management can be described to an avoidant patient and offered in a more or less distant and cognitive fashion if the therapist believes that the patient would find this less threatening. For instance, a woman with a dismissive style was interviewing potential therapists. In response to a question about therapist technique, the first clinician she consulted discussed using the therapeutic relationship to understand her better. The patient next consulted with me and, describing that meeting, stated that at that point in the interview she no longer had "felt safe" and would not return to the first therapist. When I explained therapeutic work in less relational terms, such as her learning certain patterns as she grew up and developing skills to change things in the present, the patient was much more comfortable and chose to begin a successful treatment.

Dismissive patients often have considerable intellectual strengths and interests resulting from their focus on nonsocial domains and may have received some positive parental response for achievements in the cognitive realm (Bartholomew, 1990; Crittenden, 1995). A therapist may be able to engage such patients' intellectual interest in and curiosity about some of the less threatening aspects of their development, particularly if the discussions can incorporate terms, references, and analogies that relate to areas of interest and expertise of the patients; for example, patients in information technology may relate to discussions of operating systems, programming, and tech support. I have found that a slightly matter-of-fact attitude and a focus on early learning and current skill-building are more likely to facilitate trust than any overt display of empathy for suffering. These patients easily feel condescended to and pitied when they have the unfamiliar experience of another person's focus on their pain; they may even advise the therapist that they wish none of "that empathy stuff!" (Thomson and Connors, 2001). Avoidant patients' previous experiences have led them to believe that relationships are useless at best and dangerous at worst. However, if therapists who appreciate their patients' disavowal of relational needs can help in concrete and cognitive ways, eventually avoidant patients may come to believe that other people have something to offer after all. Providing such aid for a troublesome symptom early in treatment may promote trust in the clinician as a competent expert and enable an uncomfortable patient to remain in therapy long enough so that ultimately the defensive avoidance can be addressed.

Increasing Self-Regulation in a Disorganized Patient

Although the therapeutic challenge with an avoidant patient is to attempt to build trust in someone who has essentially renounced reliance on others, working with preoccupied and disorganized patients often requires ensuring that the demands on the therapist do not become overwhelming. Preoccupied patients had to overfocus on the attachment figure and escalate their displays of distress to get through to a self-absorbed parent. Preoccupied attachment status has been strongly associated with borderline personality disorder (Fonagy et al., 1996) and with suicidal behavior (Adam, Sheldon-Keller, and West, 1996). Disorganized patients were required to accommodate to a frightening caregiver, and they display the most impairment of any group in adult life. I am discussing these two groups together at this time because both kinds of patients may have great difficulty in self-regulation as adults, as well as a tendency to display excessive dependency on others. These patients may be prone to quickly forming an intense attachment to the therapist, often with much idealization. They may have relational histories involving overinvestment in others and underinvestment in the self, along with a concomitant lack of

instrumental and self-regulatory skills. Such patients can be difficult to treat because they may regularly experience affect states
that overwhelm them, and they seek high levels of contact with
the therapist, including frequent telephone calls. The burdensome
nature of such contact is exacerbated for the therapist when much
of it relates to suicidal ideation and potential suicidal behavior
that the therapist must manage. Many of the techniques I discuss
involve increasing a patient's ability to self-regulate, which I believe
has numerous potential benefits, but the one I focus on here is the
impact on the therapeutic relationship in a situation of high
demand.

To illustrate: when Sandy entered psychoanalytic psychotherapy with me, she reported a history of severe depression that
included one suicide attempt, a hospitalization, and several years
of psychotherapy. She also described severe anxiety, panic attacks,
numerous physical problems, and difficulty functioning at her job.
Eventually it became clear that she had an extensive history of
sexual abuse and a dissociative disorder. (I discuss this case more
thoroughly in Connors, 1997b.) Many of Sandy's symptoms cor-
responded primarily to the category of symptom formation related
to trauma and defensive compromise; she used dissociation to protect herself from unbearable knowledge and affects.

Sandy had to be hospitalized when her suicidal impulses could
no longer be managed on an outpatient basis. A complex regimen
of medications was only mildly helpful. In the hospital, Sandy had
continuous access to staff to help her handle panic states induced
by emerging memories and rageful affects. She expressed great
anxiety at the prospect of leaving the safety of the hospital and
having to manage herself more independently. Sandy was also
experiencing much distress in her relationship with me, castigat-
ing herself for having become so dependent on me and fearing my
rejection. I, too, was very concerned about our posthospitaliza-
tion relationship. For months prior to her inpatient stay, Sandy
had called me daily outside of our three sessions per week because
she was panicked or suicidal. These calls often took place late at
night, and were quite disturbing and anxiety provoking for me,
despite the help I was receiving from extensive consultation on her
case. After a 2:00 A.M. call in which Sandy informed me that she
had all her pills arrayed on a plate and was trying to decide
whether to swallow them, I hospitalized her, but limitations on

her insurance coverage were such that I knew I must reserve hospitalization for the most serious suicidal crises. I felt it would be
beneficial for both of us if Sandy became more able to moderate
her intense states of distress without requiring immediate contact
with me each time.

Late evening hours were the most disturbing for Sandy, as she
usually was unable to sleep until early morning and would anx-
iously lie awake, feeling isolated with her tormenting thoughts. I
proposed making her a relaxation tape that she could listen to at
such times, for I believed that she would benefit from being able
to focus on doing something distracting in the midst of her misery, as well as from the relaxation itself. I also thought that having a tape of my voice that she could use at any time might help
her to feel more secure. Sandy expressed great enthusiasm about
having a tape. She responded well to an in-session relaxation exercise, but it was her use of the tape at home that proved most significant. She said that the tape helped her feel that she was still
connected to me even when I was not with her and that she felt
calmer and less alone. Listening to the tape assisted her considerably with her insomnia and management of affects, and her profound fragmentation gradually began to improve.

Sandy still called me outside of session, but calls became more
infrequent, which helped me to feel less burdened by this difficult
treatment. She also reported a sense of greater comfort in our relationship, and she worried less about feeling desperate and being
rejected. A theme throughout Sandy's life had been a level of neediness and preoccupation with a friend or intimate that ultimately
the other found intolerable. The result always was termination of
the relationship and Sandy's intense pain about yet another rejection. Listening to a relaxation tape enabled this distressed patient
to use the therapy relationship with me while simultaneously maintaining some self-sufficiency, and this use of me by proxy at times
was considerably easier for me than were constant late night emergency calls.

This technique did not obviate the importance of processing
the larger issue of Sandy's having more needs for me than I could
fulfill and the intense grief, rage, and shame that accompanied this
dependency for her; on the contrary, we had detailed discussions
of the impact of using the tape and of actually calling me in our
processing of the therapeutic relationship. These exchanges also

afforded many opportunities to explore genetic and life-history material concerning need and responsiveness in relationships. I believe that her treatment at that time included extremely complex repetitive transference and countertransference processes but was also affected by a genuine skills deficit on Sandy's part concerning self-management of painful affects. This deficit could be partially remedied by the external assistance of the tape in promoting relaxation. Sandy's intense transference wishes for round-the-clock care from me and equally intense anxiety and rage that such care would not be forthcoming, deescalated enough so that this material could be processed in a more manageable fashion. Sandy found the inevitable limitations on my availability easier to tolerate as she became a bit more able to calm herself. She used the relaxation tape regularly for the next few years and ultimately found that she no longer required it. Treatment continued to a successful conclusion, with Sandy's occasionally making a reference to those "terrible times" in her life and how helpful it had been to know that she could calm herself down by using the tape. That a tape providing instruction in relaxation can also function as a transitional object illustrates the inseparability of active techniques from the overall therapeutic relationship.

A SELF IN ATTACHMENT

Self psychology and attachment theory have essentially focused on different, although related, phenomena. Self psychology's supraordinate emphasis on the development of the self, although extremely helpful, might lead to a generic view of the multiplicity of experiences occurring in relationships, because theory has remained so focused on the selfobject concept (Connors, 2000). Attachment research suggests that objects are not interchangeable, that it is responsiveness from a particular other that is desperately sought, and that historically one's very survival depended on securing it (Bowlby, 1969, 1973, 1988; Ainsworth et al., 1978). Although self psychologists might relate to such a term as "father transference," self psychology has not emphasized the dynamics of reenacted early relationships. Attachment theory's greater focus on the process of relating and the way in which early self- and object representations are carried forward into adult relationships clarifies phenomena not well accounted for by ideas about selfobject experiences, valuable as they are. Attachment theory might be seen as emphasizing more heavily than self psychology what Rapaport and Gill (1959) have termed the adaptive point of view: adaptation to one's particular environment at every point in life fosters survival and is seen as a determining factor in motivating behavior. Both theories stress the potentially pathogenic impact of real, rather than fantasied, experiences; the importance of parental sensitivity; and the continuation of needs for others throughout the life span. I draw on both paradigms in asserting that symptoms are manifestations of a vulnerable self in an interpersonal milieu that has failed to provide needed security.

The exact relationship of selfobject needs and attachment needs is probably quite complex, but we might speculate that they comprise two separate but overlapping dimensions of experience. Because the attachment system functions to ensure survival, a more primary motivation is unlikely. If a person experiences a threat to survival on some level, for instance, when the attachment figure is unavailable, needs for various selfobject experiences and self-development will probably remain subordinate until a greater degree of security is restored. This "pathological accommodation" (Brandchaft, 1994), which prioritizes the tie to the other and may require self-abnegation, is probably responsible for much self-pathology. The experiences of mirroring, idealizing, and so forth, vital as they are, may be usable only if a reasonable level of attachment security exists. When safety is not threatened, attachment needs remain in the background and selfobject experiences assume the paramount position. However, this is a relatively crude depiction of imbricated processes, and much of the sensitive parental behavior that fosters attachment security also meets selfobject needs.

LEARNING, SELF-ORGANIZATION, AND INFORMATION PROCESSING

Attachment theorists and intersubjective theorists have attended to ways in which people organize, understand, and find meaning in their experiences. The concepts of internal working models and invariant organizing principles refer to views of self and other in the present and expectations about the future based on experiences in a particular context. Bretherton and Munholland (1999) suggest that internal working models are part of a complex network of schemas in which information is represented at different levels of generality. These authors noted that internal models of self and other regulate an individual's relational behavior through interpretive and attributional processes that are both "reality-reflecting and reality-creating" (p. 107).

That description underscores the role of learning and organization of information in the construction of the self. As I noted earlier, an emphasis on learning processes is seldom seen in psychoanalytic literature, although learning is often implicit in discussions of development and pathology, for example, in the literature on internalization. I believe that concepts of learning are foundational for a coherent integration of active techniques into dynamic treatment and that aspects of learning, in addition to the notion of instructional selfobject experiences, are relevant. Moreover, a number of authors are currently applying dynamic systems, complexity theory, and cognitive science to self-organization and therapeutic interaction.

Weiss and colleagues (1986; Weiss, 1993; Sampson, 1994) also explicating the role of learning, propose that psychopathology is grounded in pathogenic beliefs about oneself and one's interpersonal world. They suggested that people develop these pathogenic beliefs in childhood by making inferences about various difficult experiences within the family. Typically a child will assume that parental behavior is justified and that neglectful or abusive treatment is warranted because of her own defects and badness. Weiss (1993) states that such pathogenic beliefs reflect the fact that a child is highly motivated to view parents as wise and powerful because they are so essential to the child's survival. If the child, for instance, attempts to attain a goal and infers that this behavior threatens his ties with his parents, he will conclude that such behavior is dangerous (whether or not such a conclusion is warranted). Weiss noted that such inferences reflect the child's lack of understanding of causality, his egocentricity, and his proneness to take responsibility for parental behavior. Pathogenic beliefs are acquired by direct instruction from parents about the child and their response to him and by accidental events such as a death, in addition to the child's own inferences. Most if not all psychopathology is rooted in such pathogenic beliefs, and symptoms may express a patient's efforts to avoid the threats and dangers contained in the pathogenic belief system: "Pathogenic beliefs and the fear, anxiety, shame, and guilt to which they give rise provide the primary motives for the development and maintenance of repressions, inhibitions, and symptoms" (Weiss et al., 1986, p. 68). The work of Weiss and Sampson is compatible with aspects of attachment theory and intersubjectivity theory that stress the need to prioritize ties with caregivers and subordinate the self in the service of maintaining vital bonds. I have described this as one possible pathway to symptom formation.

The state of a system at any particular time depends on its previous states, and in a complex system many different interrelated factors have contributed to the present state (Thelen, 2005). Complex systems organize into patterns, and these patterns have varying degrees of stability and flexibility (Piers, 2005). To shift and reassemble, systems have to lose stability temporarily. Piers states that pathology is typically associated with excessive stability. Seligman (2005) commented that people who are more psychologically fragile paradoxically develop overly rigid functioning; these systems become repetitive, closed, and fail to adapt well to new environmental conditions (Seligman, 2005). In such a maladaptive style certain ways of relating and feeling are amplified while others are recurrently dampened, perpetuating the stable system.

Beebe and her colleagues (e.g., Beebe and Lachmann, 1992; Beebe et al., 2003a, b) have described what they term a dyadic systems model of interaction. Using infant research, they have examined self-regulation and interactive regulation within the dyadic system. These authors have used the concept of patterns of expectation, in which one member of the system anticipates the partner's pattern in relation to his or her own. They propose that this patterning defined presymbolic representation in the first year of life and suggest that infant and adult partners each generate patterns of expectation that are constructed through the sequence of their own actions in relation to the partner's, the result being patterns of coordination: "Moment by moment, each person 'influences' or coordinates with the other . . . moment by moment, each partner regulates arousal and inner state: threshold, intensity, activation, dampening, self-soothing" (Beebe et al., 2003a, p. 753). Beebe and Lachmann (2002) propose a "midrange model" of self-regulation and interactive regulation. They suggest that optimal development and social communication occur when partners in a dyad can move flexibly between self- and interactive regulation. At one pole of imbalance is hypervigilance and excessive monitoring of the partner, which interferes with self-regulation, while at the other pole is withdrawal from and lessened sensitivity to interactive regulation because of an overfocus on self-regulation. Both extremes suggest insecure attachment.

Bucci (1997) conceives of a psychoanalysis and cognitive science in which "emotion schemas" play a central role. She defines emotion schemas as "prototypic representations of the self in relation to others, built up through repetitions of episodes with shared affective states" (p. 195). Bucci views emotion schemas as the key elements of self-organization of personality. Emotion schemas are dominated by subsymbolic processing, such as patterns of visceral and somatic experiences of affect and arousal, and are resistant to change because of the salience and inaccessibility of these experiences. Pathological emotion schemas ensue when a person is faced with overwhelming painful affect. Bucci suggests that in such circumstances the person is likely to "desymbolize" or dissociate, that is, to cut the connection between symbolic and subsymbolic so that, for example, he or she could experience somatic arousal without knowing why (as in somatoform dissociation). Another possibility for coping with unmanageable emotion relates to psychoanalytic conceptualizations of defensive processes: the person will attempt to "resymbolize" by erroneously redirecting the experience, as in displacement.

Epstein (1994) describes what he terms cognitive-experiential self-theory, which integrates some psychoanalytic propositions with those of cognitive science by postulating the existence of two parallel but interacting modes of information processing. One is intuitive, affective, and is experienced passively and preconsciously, whereas the other is logical, analytic, and conscious. According to Epstein, people possess constructs about the self and the world in both systems, those in the experiential system being implicit beliefs or schemata that have evolved from making generalizations based on emotionally meaningful past experiences. Psychopathology can result when material cannot be assimilated and is dissociated; this can occur between the rational and the experiential system (corresponding to repression) and within the experiential system itself. "There is a fundamental motive to assimilate representations of emotionally significant experiences into a unified, coherent conceptual system" (p. 717). Material that cannot be assimilated or ignored will continue to emerge in various attempts at integration. Therapy is aimed at changing problematic schemata in the experiential system by such means as using the rational system to affect the experiential system, as in disputing irrational thoughts, and helping the patient learn directly through emotionally significant experiences and relationships.

Although a detailed review of the literature on neurophysiology, affect, and learning is beyond the scope of this book, it should be noted that such authors as Schore (1994) and Siegel (1999) hold that neurophysiological processes are affected by interpersonal experiences and that the maturation and organization of the nervous system is shaped by early dyadic relationships. Siegel notes that some people have difficulty modulating states of arousal because of ways in which traumatic experiences and insecure attachments have influenced corticolimbic functioning. Interpersonal interaction shapes the neuronal pathways responsible for emotion regulation.

PSYCHOPATHOLOGY AND COMPLEXITY

Each person's development occurs within a unique context that comprises a multiplicity of factors, including the personality and mental health of parents and other caregivers; their relationship with each other; their ethnicity, culture, religion, race, sexual orientation, health status, educational and financial resources; history of trauma and immigration; generational cohort; presence of siblings; and so on. Each child also possesses a unique set of constitutional variables and genetic potentialities. Interactions with caregivers, particularly those relating to attachment security and selfobject experiences, will shape the development of the self, including on a neurobiological level. Regulation of internal experience is a fundamental aspect of selfhood. An individual with a cohesive self-structure in a context of secure attachment will be conscious of affects, will be able to differentiate among a variety of affects and bodily states such as hunger and fatigue, and will experience internal states within a range of tolerability. Such people are able to modulate affects adaptively if they begin to get overly intense and to recover equilibrium relatively quickly. Spezzano (1995) notes that well-being is characterized by a feeling of confidence about being able to regulate one's affective life competently. The internal working models of a healthy self are characterized by a sense that the self is worthy and that others can be relied on. The person's relations with his or her own self and with others are sensitive, balanced, flexible, and positively toned.

We won't be seeing too many people like that in our clinical practices. Patients who consult us are more likely to suffer from fragmentation-prone selves in a context of insecure attachment. When efforts at self-regulation are insufficient to preserve adequate cohesion, as I discussed in chapter one, patients manifest various symptoms. They may experience affects as overwhelming and disorganizing, frequently reach states of arousal and dysphoria that feel intolerable, and may recover slowly from such disruptions. Patients with difficulty in affective regulation may be unable to differentiate various affects or physical states; such alexithymia has been linked to a broad range of pathological conditions (Grabe, Spitzer, and Freyberger, 2004). Emotion schemas may be desymbolized or resymbolized in maladaptive ways. Relations with the self and with others will be characterized by pathogenic beliefs and defensive processes, and the more extreme positions regarding self-and interactive regulation noted by Beebe and colleagues will predominate. Children growing up in insecure and traumatizing environments must find ways to handle affective experiences and organize themselves in the absence of optimal regulation from others and, in fact, may have to negotiate interpersonal situations that require suppression of their own affects and hypervigilance in favor of those of caregivers. In such situations apraxias, pathological emotion schemas, and pathogenic beliefs are likely to result. Persons may experience distress related to desomatized experiences that cannot be assimilated or accessed. Through a variety of processes that might include identification with the parent and the parent's view of the self and intergenerational transmission of insecure attachment styles, the child learns to view himself or herself negatively (possibly with a defensively grandiose overlay). Blaming the self rather than expressing anger at an abusive parent preserves the attachment relationship necessary for survival. Such conditional strategies help children to manage themselves and their relationships in nonoptimal environments, but such learned strategies for survival within a particular context may not be revised in adult life, particularly when they have been associated so strongly with intense affect. In essence, the child does her best to make lemonade with the lemons she is given, but at the cost of believing that she must be deficient because the world is not sweeter.

Pathology is rooted in the past with rigid pathogenic beliefs, emotional dysregulation, and restricted relational possibilities. Treatment offers hope that a self with more cohesion and security can come into being, and the American psychoanalytic tradition supports optimism about the potential for change: "Each occurrence of an emotion schema in a new interpersonal context has the potential to alter its form" (Bucci, 1997, p. 198); and even small shifts in a dynamic system can produce large effects (Seligman, 2005). Selfobject needs and attachment needs continue throughout life, and the therapy relationship provides a context in which they can be understood and altered.

SPECIFICITY AND THE INTERACTIVE CONTEXT

Although use of more active techniques may cause dynamically trained clinicians to worry that they are failing to uphold some higher standard of analytic purity, I argue that, in fact, use of these measures facilitates a dynamic psychotherapy by strengthening the treatment relationship as well as by assisting the patient in beneficial ways. Important selfobject needs that may have been long suppressed can reemerge in treatment and be well responded to through assistance with symptom management, including instructional selfobject needs. Moreover, use of such techniques may foster engagement with insecurely attached patients by engendering greater trust and comfort in avoidant patients and by reducing demand for contact with the therapist in more preoccupied or disorganized patients, who develop greater skill in self-regulation. An optimally responsive treatment process that facilitates self-cohesion and attachment security enables greater exploration of difficult material and self-reflective capacity.

Contemporary psychoanalytic writing reinforces a much broader range of interactive possibilities than was the case when drive theory was the dominant paradigm. Thompson (2004), noting the influence of the sceptic philosophers on Freud, suggests that their valorizing of equanimity and imperturbability affected Freud's concepts of neutrality and the technique of free association. Concerns that the "blank screen" of the analyst on which the patient projects transference fantasies would be contaminated by all but the most restrained and abstinent interpretive activity led to decades in which greater activity by the analyst was discussed in terms of "parameters" for more disturbed patients (e.g., Eissler, 1953), reprehended by the analytic community (e.g., Alexander and French's, 1946) "corrective emotional experience," or performed covertly (Bacal and Herzog, 2003). Since the mid-20th century, such innovations as Winnicott's (1960) recommendation that the analyst provide the patient with a "holding environment" and Kohut's (e.g., 1968) proposal of a noninterpretive approach for some patients have become widely accepted and have paved the way for the current focus in the literature on the clinician as a real person whose actions and inactions all affect the patient. In such a two-person model of interaction, much more consideration is given to actions of the clinician that could potentially be helpful, including self-disclosure (e.g., Ehrenberg, 1992), spontaneity and authenticity (e.g., Hoffman, 1998; Ringstrom, 2001), and the offer of a new relational experience (e.g., Summers, 1994; Mitchell, 2000). Frank (1999) suggests that interaction, intersubjectivity, and mutuality characterize the two-person model.

Another important contemporary development is an emphasis on the specificity of the therapeutic dyad and a move away from a "one size fits all" approach (e.g., Doctors, 1996; Bacal, 1998; Bacal and Herzog, 2003). These authors hold that each analytic couple comprises a complex and unique relational system and that what is optimal for one patient in terms of the clinician's responsiveness will not necessarily be ideal for another. "The specific characteristics of a particular therapeutic constellation will always centrally determine any therapeutically useful experience" (Bacal and Herzog, 2003, p. 639). Moreover, the particular type of responsiveness that is optimal for a patient at a certain time may change as the patient's self-development progresses. Similarly, from a dynamic systems perspective, the particular properties of the unique therapy dyad at a specific moment should prescribe technique (Seligman, 2005). Beebe et al. (2003a) state, "The advantage of working with a systems view of interaction is that all routes to self- and interactive regulation can be seen and held in mind. The broadest view is one in which all routes are potential pathways to therapeutic action, at different times, with different patient-therapist dyads" (p. 764).

Specificity theory postulates that there is not a single correct intervention for a patient that would be applicable by all clinicians. The therapeutic interaction will be unique to the particular dyad, and the potential for therapeutic action is related to the specific characteristics of each partner in the dyad. Bacal and Herzog (2003) recommend that the clinician must be open to his own and to the patient's experience in order to determine what is activated in the patient at any particular time and how he might respond most effectively. They propose that any number of interventions may be beneficial, as long as they do not interfere with the therapist's professional functioning or exceed the personal tolerance of either the therapist or the patient. Specificity theory "does not privilege or ignore any form of intervention . . . it rather reveals and legitimizes the diversity of responsivity that therapists actually proffer when they are working effectively" (p. 642).

Providing assistance with symptomatic difficulties might be viewed as a natural development in the current "widening scope" of therapeutic interaction: "The possible utility of such analyst actions seems much more acceptable with the recognition that interaction is constant anyhow and with attention to the analysis of such interaction" (Gill, 1984, p. 57). In such a context, specificity theory suggests careful attention to the unique properties of each therapeutic dyad to ascertain the range of activities that might be helpful. I suggest that such interventions may at times include the proffering of symptom-management strategies. In the next chapter I shall discuss characteristics of the therapeutic system to evaluate in considering such a possibility.

CHAPTER THREE

The Decision to
Use Active Techniques

DECIDING WHETHER TO USE SYMPTOM-FOCUSED techniques at any particular time is complex. Proffering such strategies may or may not constitute the optimal therapeutic intervention in a given situation. In considering this possibility, it is necessary that the clinician reflect on her understanding of her patient at this specific point. However, since therapy happens in real time, a balance of reflection and action is needed, including some openness to spontaneity and a willingness to try something different. Decisions must usually be made on the basis of incomplete information because it is so difficult to predict future events involving complex systems (Seligman, 2005). In this chapter I suggest several considerations that might indicate whether optimal responsiveness in a particular situation is best conveyed by traditional practices, such as empathic listening and interpreting, or by symptom-focused interventions.

TREATMENT PLANNING

It is useful to distinguish between an evaluation phase and treatment itself; in the evaluation phase a plan for treatment tailored to the individual patient can be formulated and the patient's consent can truly be informed (Peebles-Kleiger, 2002). Peebles-Kleiger suggests assessment of the nature of the patient's disturbance, his or her ability to form a collaborative alliance, functions served by the symptoms, the priorities concerning needed interventions, and the patient's relative strengths and weaknesses as well as learning style and expectancies. This information can be used to "cocreate" a plan with a shared focus. Peebles-Kleiger notes that a large collection of research supports the value of focus, defined as "mutually agreed upon goals, interventions to reach those goals, and ways to tell when the goals have been reached" (p. 25).

When conducting an evaluation and beginning treatment with a new patient, I inform the patient that I practice psychoanalytically oriented psychotherapy that can also include some specific techniques for symptom alleviation if that seems indicated. I have never observed a negative reaction to this information. Expressions of curiosity and sometimes relief are typical, and occasionally patients will refer to previous treatment in which bothersome symptoms received little attention and failed to change. I clarify that my treatment is tailored to the needs and wishes of the individual, and patients seem to appreciate the specificity and flexibility that I describe. As I gather the sort of assessment data to which Peebles-Kleiger refers, I begin to share my thoughts about possible frequency of meeting and whether or not I have a sense that symptom-focused work might be helpful. Aware that patients often reveal certain symptoms or symptom severity only much later in the treatment process, I also propose that we consider this eventuality at some future point should it seem relevant. I am careful to articulate that the use of any active techniques will be in accord with the patient's expectations, preferences, and priorities and that, should we employ such strategies, we would discuss in detail how the patient might be experiencing the process as well as the efficacy of such activity.

There are several major factors to be examined in the process of deciding whether or not to use active techniques. The first group of aspects pertains to patient variables. One concerns some sort of need on the part of the patient. I do not think that this need must be extreme before it is worth responding to, but there should be *something* in the patient's presentation of pain, trouble, dysfunction, and so forth that indicates difficulty moving beyond current strategies for managing affects and self states. Another factor is the usability of such interventions at this particular moment. Even in situations of great need, such as a highly destructive addiction, it does not necessarily follow that symptom-focused strategies will be usable; they may, in fact, be experienced as unwanted, intrusive, and irrelevant, and summarily rejected. Another set of variables relates to the therapist's countertransference and the particularities of the patient–therapist dyad at a specific time. I recognize that such organization fails to do justice to the complex ways in which therapist and patient are always mutually influencing one another, but I hope it will serve as a useful heuristic.

CONSIDERING PATIENT NEED

Need Over Time

As I noted in chapter one, some symptomatic patterns cause patients to experience physical distress or potential danger. This phenomenon is frequently seen in situations involving addictions; for example, patients may continue to drink despite worsening liver function, smokers create health problems for themselves and household members, and intravenous drug users risk AIDS by needle sharing. It is evident that self-mutilation and suicidal activity have dangerous consequences. Behavior that is a threat to others must be considered as well. Certain patients may inflict physical violence on partners, children, and pets; others may be sexually predatory. Addicted patients may pose a threat to public safety by drunk driving or impaired performance on a job involving the welfare of others. It is patently obvious that in all these situations change would be beneficial.

Other patients have symptoms that pose little risk to physical health but that endanger their self-esteem or lead to problematic life circumstances. Frequently patients who exhibit addictive or impulsive behaviors experience immense shame and self-loathing. Others, including many with depression, castigate themselves for what they perceive as their "weakness" in failing to just "get over it and be OK." I have heard many patients with symptomatic problems describe themselves in highly pejorative terms, such as "loser" or "baby," because of their difficulties in functioning. Moreover, behavioral strategies relied on by patients in an effort to contain symptomatic distress may, in fact, worsen and perpetuate it; examples are the binge eater who begins purging and the panic sufferer who becomes agoraphobic. Finally, some symptomatic patterns can lead to deleterious life circumstances, including loss of a spouse or partner who will no longer tolerate rage attacks or chronic depression; loss of child custody when parenting is impaired; and loss of employment and financial well-being when work performance is hindered or compulsions to spend or gamble are present.

In other situations, the symptomatic difficulties do not result in such overt dysfunction, but careful investigation reveals that they are interfering with a person's ability to live up to potential. Such symptoms as anxious avoidance are especially likely to thwart growth in this fashion. Socially phobic patients may avoid the interpersonal interactions that lead to relationship development or career enhancement. Their peers move on to committed relationships and positions of higher status and responsibility while avoidant persons eschew risk and prioritize familiarity and security. The result may be stalled adult development. Symptoms of poor organizational abilities, chronic depression, or difficulties in making decisions similarly may inhibit a person's capacity to find intimacy and to use talents and skills in a satisfying fashion. Patients may have some awareness that they are "underachieving" relative to their abilities but often lack perspective on how psychological symptoms hold them back (e.g., "I must just be lazy").

Immediate Need

So far I have been discussing the possibility that symptomatic behaviors may threaten physical safety, engender self-disgust, result in substantial losses, or interfere with satisfying adult development. I think it is clear that amelioration of symptoms in such circumstances is more likely than not to prove beneficial and that a need for symptom reduction exists. The problems I have been describing, however, generally are related to ongoing situations that over time have an impact on a patient's life. In addition, it is important to assess a patient's state within a particular session. I believe that occasionally a need exists for intervention in the moment, whether or not the patient is reporting much life interference outside of session. Here I am primarily referring to situations in which patients are feeling panicky or disorganized because of intense anxiety or are experiencing flashbacks to traumatic situations. Patients are often anxious and distressed in session, of course, much of which is an expectable response to processing painful memories and affects and is optimally responded to with empathy, careful listening, interpretation, and the like. As I noted in chapter one, however, there is probably an ideal range of physiological and emotional arousal for engaging in psychotherapy. Extreme arousal is likely to be experienced as a psychological emergency and typically connotes a state of fragmentation. Commonly this state is accompanied by decrements in ego functioning such that the patient's usual abilities to process information are attenuated. In short, conducting psychotherapy as usual in this circumstance may not be possible.

If a child were to become this overwrought, the good-enough parent would step in with some direct calming and soothing rather than letting the child exceed his capacities for self-regulation. At times a similar principle might apply in psychotherapy. Bacal (1985), noting the importance of taking the patient's state into account, asserts that a different type of response is called for when a patient is fragmented. The clinician's response to a patient's fragmentation, however, should not be unboundaried or infantalizing, and in this regard we might refer to Shane and Shane's (1996) proposal for "optimal restraint." They suggest that the clinician employ sufficient reserve so that the response provided is not in excess of what is really needed or desired by the patient. Peebles-Kleiger (2002) recommends that, when a patient experiences intense affect, the clinician assess the degree of external assistance that might be warranted, ranging from empathic staying-with to behavioral action and direction.

When I believe that something more than traditional psychodynamic discourse is indicated, I may provide on-the-spot instruction in diaphragmatic breathing, which tends to produce relatively immediately reduction of physiological arousal. I also suggest that the patient breathe with me as I model the technique, which not only helps both of us relax but also reminds the patient who is panicking about her internal experience that she is not alone. I believe that this technique nicely embodies both responsiveness and restraint; the patient receives a type of assistance tailored to her state while still employing verbal means rather than attempts to be soothed by way of physical holding and hugging.

After the patient has calmed somewhat from the peak of

emotional intensity, it may be possible to have very fruitful discussions of the affects, cognitions, sensations, memories, and so
forth that arose during the experience. A certain measure of cohesion is required here, however, and attempts to obtain information when a patient is too panicked or disoriented to provide it
will result in frustration for the therapist and escalating arousal
for the patient. The patient may feel that the therapist cares only
to follow her usual agenda, and, if any concerns regarding the
therapist's trustworthiness or ability to help are present, the
patient's experience of feeling unhelped while in extreme distress
will certainly exacerbate those concerns. But if the clinician can
directly assist with amelioration of a disorganized state, the patient
benefits both by having a successful experience of calming herself
and by receiving aid from the therapist in doing so. Powerful new
learning can take place in situations involving aversive states, and
obviously it is of benefit if a patient learns through experience that
needing help and obtaining it can happen in psychotherapy and
in the world: "The potential for profound change is dramatically
enhanced when the patient lives directly through personally significant and emotionally meaningful experiences that provide a
basis for directly repudiating, revising, or creating new internalized patterns (Frank, 1999, pp. 198–199).

CONSIDERING USABILITY

A great need for symptom reduction because of the issues I have
delineated may not correlate with a patient's finding symptom reduction techniques usable. Moreover, patients with little life impairment may welcome them and derive immense benefit. The issue of
usability of such interventions must be considered separately from
that of need. Careful assessment of the likelihood that a patient will
find symptom-focused interventions salient at a particular time may
obviate some mutual frustration in the therapeutic dyad. Several
elements need to be included when considering usability.

Stages of Change

A collection of work that I find extremely valuable in determining usability is that of Prochaska and colleagues (Prochaska,
DiClemente, and Norcross, 1992; Prochaska, Norcross, and

DiClemente, 1994) on stages of change. These authors surveyed hundreds of subjects who had some sort of addictive problem and inquired about their attitudes and intentions regarding it. They also surveyed more than 3000 persons from the general population as well as clinical groups and asked them to identify their major problems, along with any plans for change or specific actions taken. The researchers found that their subjects could be characterized as being in one of several particular stages of change regarding their problem and proposed that the stage of change had implications for therapeutic technique.

The first stage of change is "precontemplation." A person in this stage is unaware of having a problem and may employ such defenses as denial to maintain a sense of being problem-free. Others may be blamed for tensions surrounding the problem, for example, a man may attribute marital difficulties to his nagging wife rather than to his alcohol problem. The individual has no intention of doing anything about the "nonproblem" in the foreseeable future. People in this stage endorse items such as, "As far as I'm concerned, I don't have any problems that need changing," on Prochaska et al.'s (1992) stage of change measure. Prochaska et al. (1992) note that the defining feature of this stage is resistance to acknowledging or modifying a problem.

The next stage of change is "contemplation." In this stage the person has more awareness of the problem and is seriously thinking about making some sort of change in the next six months. People in this stage endorse such items as, "I have a problem and I really think I should work on it," on the stages of change measure. However, ambivalence is the hallmark of this stage. The person in contemplation has more understanding of the significance of the problem than is seen in precontemplation but is torn between the risks and benefits of staying the same versus changing. "I know cigarettes are bad for me, but I'll gain weight if I quit," is a typical statement for a person in contemplation. These people may still feel quite attached to their behavior and are reluctant to face the effort and hardship of changing. Prochaska et al. (1992) found that it is not uncommon for a person to remain in contemplation for a long time, weighing pros and cons without taking any action. They followed 200 persons who were in this stage regarding quitting smoking, and most of them were still "thinking about it" two years after the initial assessment.

The "preparation" stage is next, and this represents a shift from the ambivalence of the previous stage to a decision to make a change within the next month. The person has a sense of commitment to making a change in the near future. She begins planning strategies for changing and often enlists social support. For instance, a smoker may set a "quit date," inform friends and family of the intention to quit, and make plans to confer with her physician regarding use of nicotine replacement. Prochaska et al. (1992) originally termed this stage decision making and reported that people in preparation score high on items measuring both contemplation and action. However, people in this stage continue to feel some degree of ambivalence.

The "action" stage follows preparation, and it is here that concrete behavioral changes occur. Prochaska et al. classify persons as being in this stage if they have been successful in changing the target behavior for a period of one day to six months. The smoker actually quits smoking, the dieter begins following a new eating plan, and the alcoholic attends Alcoholics Anonymous and refrains from drinking. The commitment to change is put into practice on a daily basis. People in this stage report feeling good that they are actually doing something about their problems, not just talking. However, this stage is very challenging owing to the stress of living without some habitually relied on substances or activities. People may experience yearning and craving for the old behavior, and they benefit from a good deal of support from others.

The final stage of change is "maintenance," in which a person attempts to maintain and consolidate the changes already made. Prochaska et al. (1994) underscore that maintenance represents a continuation of change, not a static state. A relapse into previous behaviors is very possible during this stage, particularly when changes are recent. This stage extends from six months after the initial change to an indefinite period. For some people, maintenance will last a lifetime, and ongoing efforts to avoid relapse will be required.

Prochaska et al. (1992) point to several issues that have great relevance for treatment. It is noteworthy that, across large samples of people with problems, only about 10%–15% were in the action stage at any time. Prochaska et al. (1992, 1994) also found that progress through the stages often was not a linear course but something more like a spiral, in which people would cycle back and forth between stages. A major conclusion relevant to our discussion of usability is the idea that the stage of change should inform therapeutic intervention. Offering action-oriented techniques for change to a person who is not convinced that there is a problem will be misattuned. Similarly, a person ready to make a change may be disappointed at the therapist's efforts to explore all the roots of the problem rather than collaborate on action oriented ideas.

Prochaska et al. (1994) suggest that such interventions as education and consciousness raising are most helpful in the earlier stages of change and that action-oriented techniques such as cognitive behavioral interventions are usable only following a commitment to change. They further suggest that it need not be considered a therapeutic failure if a person does not progress to successful maintenance and that helping the person move along a single stage in a particular treatment might be all that is possible. The researchers also found that, when a person progressed from one stage to the next during the first month of treatment, his or her chance of taking action within the next six months doubled.

In my own use of these stages of change ideas, I find it helpful to remember that simply because a person comes to therapy does not imply that she is in the action stage ready to embrace change techniques. But she may be—only careful assessment can help determine this. I pay serious attention to what a patient tells me about her perception of any problems, and I make inquiries concerning wishes and intentions to change, as well as any previous efforts. I also listen very carefully to what a patient tells me he wants from treatment and any requests he makes about how he wants me to help. Finally, I attend closely to what a patient does as well as what he says, including behavior in response to a tentatively offered suggestion of mine.

It is possible that a person will be ready to take action on some issues but not on others. For instance, a patient came to me because she wanted to work on her problems with compulsive eating. She was clearly ready to take action on this issue and quickly was able to make significant changes in her eating patterns. We had also discussed her social drinking and her cigarette smoking. Her drinking had been relatively moderate to begin with and she had no difficulty in following her psychiatrist's advice about limiting it while she was taking medication. Her smoking appeared to be nonnicotine dependent and occasional, primarily in social situations, but it was clear to me that she felt attached to it and that it had meaning related to individuation within her family. This patient recently came in announcing that she wanted to change psychiatrists because her current doctor had spent considerable time "haranguing" her about how she should quit smoking. The patient reported that she had not even had a cigarette for a week or so, but that she couldn't stand the idea that she had to give up everything all at once. She calmed down when I told her that I could really understand why she would react to feeling pushed by someone into yet more changes when she was already doing so much and that we would make sure we concentrated on the changes that she wanted to make at the rate she decided to make them. The patient found my assurances very relieving, and we continued our action-stage work on her eating. She quit smoking a few months later.

High Need, Low Usability

My focus in this book is largely on persons who are at least in the contemplation stage, and much of it is more relevant to people with a greater commitment to change. However, I wish to make a few points about treatment for those in the early stages of change. In addition to more standard psychotherapy for those in precontemplation, I try to take advantage of opportunities to provide education about the symptom. For example, with an anorexic patient who professes great contentment with her adaptation but shivers in my well-heated office, I will point out that her inability to get warm is caused by insufficient body fat. When a patient who drinks heavily opines that he can't have an alcohol problem if he can drink everyone else under the table, I will comment that high tolerance for alcohol, although seen as desirable in our culture, is actually a risk factor for alcoholism. Prochaska et al. (1992) point out that precontemplators typically are not ready to take in a great deal of information, but that observations that gently raise their level of consciousness may gradually take effect.

An approach that has particular benefit with people in contemplation is Miller and Rollnick's (1991) work on motivational interviewing. This approach is oriented toward helping people resolve their ambivalence and increase their motivation to make positive changes. Miller and Rollnick contrast their approach with another strategy that has tended to dominate much addictions treatment—the "confrontation of denial" approach. They note that, in a confrontation approach, there is a heavy emphasis on acceptance of a diagnosis, the therapist presents perceived evidence of problems in an attempt to persuade the patient to accept the diagnosis, and resistance is met with argument and correction. A motivational interviewing approach deemphasizes labels, centers on personal choice and responsibility for behavior, and responds to resistance with reflection. Instead of the therapist's emphasizing the need for change, Miller and Rollnick note the benefits of helping the patient recognize the discrepancy between his own goals and values and his current behavior. One important role of the therapist is eliciting from the patient self-motivational statements on themes of recognizing a problem, expressing concern about the problem, and intending to make a change. For example, they recommend asking such questions as, "What things make you think that this is a problem?" "What worries you about your drug use?" and "What are the reasons you see for making a change?" (p. 82). The use of such open-ended questions heightens the patient's own awareness and intention to change in a collaborative rather than confrontive interchange. It is also helpful to ask patients to discuss the positive as well as the problematic aspects of their current behavior, so that what patients like about their drug use or drinking, for instance, can be included as both sides of their ambivalence are discussed.

A relatively recent approach to certain problems—"harm reduction" (e.g., Marlatt, 1998)—is also relevant here. This viewpoint recognizes that not all people are ready to take action on their problems, desirable as that may be, and pragmatically and realistically focuses on the possibility of changing some of the most destructive aspects of the behavior. A needle exchange program for IV drug users represents a harm reduction approach; although it would be preferable for heroin addicts to stop using, at least they can be protected from HIV infection. Condom distribution in high schools is another example. Harm reduction is controversial, in part because many have strong negative attitudes about certain behaviors and also because of concerns that reducing the risk of consequences from the behavior might enable it to continue more easily. If, however, we appreciate that although we can assist patients in progressing along the stages of change they will do so at their own pace rather than at ours, we may feel comfortable using harm reduction with someone in an attempt to minimize the damage done by symptomatic involvement.

For instance, I treated a woman who had been contemplating doing something about her alcohol dependence for a number of years when she entered treatment. She let me know in the first session that, although she thought she had a problem, she was coming to therapy because of other issues and did not want alcohol to be the focus. After a careful assessment, I let her know I would be happy to address these other issues and deal with the alcohol gradually, but that I was very concerned about her driving drunk and asked if she would be willing to make a commitment to stop that. She was not willing then, but as we began discussing her feelings about it, she revealed much previously undisclosed material and relatively quickly moved into preparation and then into successful action. However, even if she had not taken a more action-oriented approach to the alcohol problem in general, I needed to see if that aspect of her behavior that could have fatal consequences for her and others could be contained. If this priority could be accomplished, I felt I was in a better position to assist my patient in making other changes at her pace rather than urgently demanding that she do so because of my own anxiety.

Another example of harm reduction has to do with the suggestions that I make to eating-disordered patients that are designed to minimize some of the health risks of their behavior. In the 1980s my colleagues and I (e.g., Johnson and Connors, 1987), aware that one of the irreversible effects of self-induced vomiting is serious dental erosion, began advising patients to rinse their mouths with water and a little baking soda to neutralize gastric acid after a purge. We also suggested that patients make an effort to include some high-potassium foods such as bananas in their diet to reduce the risk of potentially fatal electrolyte imbalances. If patients reported inducing vomiting by using Ipecac, we informed them that this substance can be cardiotoxic and that it is essential to refrain from purging in this fashion. My colleagues and I developed these suggestions prior to any guidance from the literature on harm reduction; we simply appreciated that, although certain behaviors may be slow to change, making attempts to protect a patient's well-being is worthwhile whether or not much change occurs.

COUNTERTRANSFERENCE

Feeling Moved in the Countertransference

Let us turn now to issues of countertransference pertaining to the decision to offer active techniques. One important element in a therapist's experience of this possibility is the sense of comfort and permission to proceed (or lack thereof) related to allegiance to theoretical perspectives, training, and identification with personal analysts and teachers. In previous chapters, in the hope of allaying some concerns about symptom-focused work, I discussed aspects of contemporary developments in psychoanalytic thought that endorse an active approach. Even if a clinician decided that such a move could be justified clinically and theoretically, however, lingering doubts and lack of familiarity with the procedures could result in a sense of unease. An idea posed by Renik (1995) is relevant here: "I think the great majority of successful clinical analyses require that, at certain points, the analyst, like the patient, accept the necessity to depart from his or her own preferred ways of proceeding and to bear a measure of discomfort" (p. 488). Analytic clinicians are accustomed to dealing with novel issues in the treatment interaction and to making interventions, such as self-disclosure, that may be experienced as risky and unpredictable. Deciding to experiment with a symptom-focused technique might seem similar.

If the therapist's theory of technique and comfort level do not present insuperable barriers to the use of active techniques, a possibility of another sort of countertransference experience arises. One that I sometimes have is that of listening carefully to a patient and feeling a sense of engagement, understanding, and resonance with the thoughts and affects that are being expressed. I may be aware of the patient's deep distress or frustrated attempts at progressing with some issue, and I find myself feeling that my patient needs something *more*—that he or she is dealing with some sort of skill deficit, insufficiency in self-regulation, self-defeating repetition, or block that might benefit from the addition of a new element. As I continue to focus on the patient's experiences, I am also aware that I am repeatedly having some wish or internal push to offer something different at this moment. I should specify what this countertransference experience is *not:* I do not feel anxiety, a need to rescue the patient, or a sense of coercion (later I discuss a situation in which such elements were present). Rather, I feel a sense of calm and a wish to be of help, along with a recurrent idea that an active technique might assist my patient in organizing at a higher level.

I believe that this sort of countertransference experience results from my empathic immersion in my patient's world and my resonance with her, including my responsivity on the implicit nonverbal level discussed by Beebe (e.g., 2004). Beebe cites research indicating that the perception of emotion in the dyadic partner creates a resonant emotional state in the perceiver, and that this is true for adults as well as for infants. Beebe writes, "Critical aspects of therapeutic action occur in this implicit mode, may never be verbalized, and yet they powerfully organize the analysis" (p. 49). Beebe goes on to say that all verbal forms of intersubjectivity continue to rely on prelinguistic or nonverbal modes, and she emphasizes the importance of experience conveyed through vocal rhythm, tone, gesture, and facial expression. I have a sense that my experience represents a complex "tuning in" to my patient's state as it is communicated to me on multiple levels.

Harmony of Difference and Sameness

There are certain moments in the therapeutic exchange when the patient indicates an openness or a need for certain elements of the analyst's subjectivity, of how his or her separate mind works (Pizer, 2003). It is apparent that one of the ways my mind works has to do with thinking about how helpful symptom-focused techniques can be in alleviating distress and facilitating progressive development, and I want to impart such help to my patient, or at least make an offer that my patient can consider. It may be useful to reflect on some additional points regarding correspondence between the subjective worlds of patient and therapist and in what ways offering active techniques might represent aspects of both similarity with the patient's state and a potentially useful difference.

Self psychologists and intersubjectivists are convinced of the importance of derailed developmental strivings that become reactivated in a context of empathic inquiry. The emphasis on empathy has sometimes been misconstrued as mandating a therapeutic style that precludes the presentation of a point of view different from that of the patient. Several of my students have remarked that their impression of self psychology is that the therapist has to be "nice" all the time and just agree with the patient. An oft-cited example in which Kohut (1984) did not eschew confrontation is of a patient who was bragging about his reckless driving on his way to the session. Kohut, believing that it was essential to curtail the patient's dangerous acting out, informed the patient that he was "a complete idiot" (pp. 74–75). Bacal (1998) offers the example of a very depressed patient who was speaking of her misery while he conveyed empathic understanding. The patient grew quieter and eventually was able to articulate that Bacal's response did not feel right: "I think I need someone to be up there a bit more, while I am down here." (p. 293). Bacal notes that in many instances the optimally responsive therapeutic action will be at variance with the patient's stated perspective.

A valuable point has been added to all this by Fosshage (1997). He observes that much of the time the analyst will be listening from this empathic mode of perception, which Fosshage terms the subject-centered listening perspective. But he also suggests the utility of shifting at times into what he calls the other-centered listening perspective, which he notes is frequently seen in object relations and interpersonal approaches. The therapist can experience the patient from the vantage point of another person, including the therapist's own self or a significant other in the patient's life. The other-centered information enables greater understanding of the ways in which a patient's effect on others contributes to his relational experiences. By oscillating between these perspectives, it is possible to obtain and share a more comprehensive view of the subjective world and the interactional style of the patient.

Intersubjectivist theorists (e.g., Stolorow and Atwood, 1992) have identified two basic situations that they believe occur repeatedly as the different psychological worlds of patient and therapist interact. The first they term an intersubjective conjunction, in which the patient's organizing principles closely resemble those of the therapist in some aspects. In contrast, an intersubjective disjunction arises when the therapist interprets patient material in a way that considerably alters its meaning for the patient because the therapist's internal world diverges from that of the patient. These situations inevitably recur as two people relate to each other, and the therapist's ability to self reflect constitutes the determining factor in whether such intersubjective phenomena will hinder or facilitate the treatment. The therapist who is conscious of the ways in which her internal organization is influencing her interpretation of patient material can use this knowledge to deepen her understanding. Potentially serious impasses in treatment may result from the absence of such reflective self-awareness in the case of an intersubjective disjunction. Unrecognized similarity between the organizing principles of patient and therapist may lead to the therapist's acceptance of the patient's views as reflecting objective reality rather than being meaningful psychological material meriting investigation in an intersubjective conjunction.

Beebe et al. (2003b) draw on the work of several infant researchers to highlight the importance of matching, correspondences, and similarity as a fundamental aspect of preverbal communication. The work of Beebe and colleagues on self- and interactive regulation in dyadic systems suggests that a midrange or balance model is optimal for communication. In this range self-regulation is present but not preoccupying, and it is possible to interact flexibly, with some matching of states but some difference as well. Beebe et al. offer the example of working with an infant in a subdued state; instead of matching this more extreme state completely, the adult provided a partial match of the infant's experience and waited for the response. These authors state, "It is the process of moving back and forth between similarity and difference that fine tunes the alignment" (p. 821). I am reminded of a Zen text written by Shitou Xiqian (2004) in the eighth century. It includes these lines: "In the light there is darkness, but don't take it as darkness. In the dark there is light, but don't see it as light. Light and dark oppose one another like the front and back foot in walking." This ancient text underscores the value of separate or different elements while at the same time decrying viewing them as unrelated and absolutely discrete.

What I take from these diverse sources is the importance of empathic immersion in my patient's states, but at a level that enables me to retain my own self-regulation. Kohut (1984), Bacal (1998), and Fosshage (1997) espouse the desirability of taking a perspective that includes but is not limited to that of the patient. This recommendation parallels some findings from psychotherapy outcome research that patient change in certain beliefs was most associated with the therapist's presentation of a moderately discrepant point of view rather than one that was identical or extremely different (Whiston and Sexton, 1993). Stolorow and Atwood (1992) point out that lack of reflection on the part of the therapist leads to difficulties whether patient and therapist organizing principles are similar or different. I think that the introduction of symptom-focused techniques can represent an optimal blend of sameness—matching of states, profound empathy for the patient's experiences and perspective—and difference, the therapist's interjecting a new element into the dialogue using her separate perspective, based on the information gathered from being in tune with the patient. Careful reflection by the clinician on the wish to offer an active technique, the ensuing discussion with the patient, and subsequent elements in the interaction and in the patient's behavior is essential.

Interactional Pressure to Rescue

Thus far I have been describing a countertransference experience of wishing to be of help by offering an active technique when the therapist feels calm, balanced, and freely able to choose among various possible interventions. Let us contrast this situation with one in which the therapist experiences a great deal of pressure in an interaction with a distressed patient conveying desperation and demand. For example, my very traumatized patient, Sandy, whom I mentioned in chapter two, profoundly resented having to take responsibility for a life impaired by abuse that she did not cause. She longed for compensation for the abuse and deprivation of childhood in the form of being taken care of in adulthood and found it extremely difficult to tolerate the fact that she was never going to have the opportunity to start over as a child with a better mother. Although I believe that I was extremely responsive to her, the collision between her passionate desire for concrete care from me at all hours of the day or night and the limitations of a therapy relationship at times resulted in her feeling frustrated and angry at me. Sandy was also debilitated by a plethora of symptoms and in a panicky tone might say to me, "You have to do something more to help me!"

Although I used a variety of symptom-focused interventions with Sandy in addition to the relaxation tape, offering such a technique did not seem like the best response when I was confronted with such pressure. Examining my reaction to this, I found Mitchell's (1993) ideas about dealing with patients' wishes to be pertinent. Mitchell observed that decisions about whether or not to meet a patient's wish are made on an intuitive level in the countertransference and that the countertransference response can help to determine the difference between responding to genuine helplessness and need as opposed to something less genuine intended to elicit rescue. He noted that the countertransference response is codetermined by the personal qualities of the clinician as well as by the nature of the patient's wishes. Some patients' desires are experienced by the therapist as genuine and fresh and full of possibilities, so that the clinician *wants* to respond, whereas other wishes seem coercive. He emphasized the importance of the clinician's genuine attitude of openness about the potential legitimacy of patients' wishes, and indicated that the process of negotiation is more important than the actual frustration or gratification.

Mitchell's valuable contribution enables our use of a relational context to explore the issue of patients' communicating that they want us to do more for them. Because we are viewing patient needs through our own subjectivity, our countertransference responses may have more to do with us than with our patients. Our responses may reflect longstanding characterological trends to resist or capitulate to others' demands on the basis of our own family experiences, gender socialization, and so forth, in addition to the guidance provided by a theoretical orientation. Exploring my responses to Sandy, I considered that my own interpersonal style is not a withholding one and that I am prone to err on the side of overindulgence (the behavior of my Golden Retriever might be cited as evidence). Yet my response to Sandy's plea that I do more for her at times was to feel that I could not, should not, and actually did not want to, in the moment, which I took to mean that some themes were becoming activated in our relationship that required a response different from that of offering symptom-reduction techniques.

I was aware that part of Sandy's experience of me as unhelpful was related to her rage about mistreatment earlier in life. Sandy's resentment about having to take responsibility for repairing a life damaged by abusive caregivers was communicated to me in part through urgent messages that it was my job to fix it, rather than hers. And, although I did not want to reject entirely the notion that I did have a job here and thus replicate her adamant refusal to accept responsibility, I wanted to communicate also that ours was a collaborative effort. I wished to help her understand that her experience of angry desperation with me related not only to her current suffering but also to past abuse and insufficient protection from her parents. So I might respond to one of her entreaties with something like this: "It's really hard to tolerate how you're feeling, and you wish so much that I could just fix it and somehow take the pain away. And as much as I'd like to, I can't do that—but let's keep talking about what might help you right now." Or I might ask her what she would like to have me do, or simply let her know I understood something about how tormented she was feeling. I would then ask how these responses were affecting her feelings about me and her sense of what was happening in our relationship. If I felt that she was in a state in which it was possible to have a bit more perspective on her experience of wanting me to rescue her, I might venture a genetic interpretation concerning her anger at past figures and her profound wish that I make up for their abuse and neglect. In all these interventions I attempted to express empathy for her suffering and her wishes that I help, while also conveying that there were realistic limits on what I could provide and that she needed to use her own resources to get better. I found that offering Sandy symptom-reduction ideas seemed natural at other points in our interactions that were not imbued with heightened demand that I rescue her.

TRANSFERENCE AND COUNTERTRANSFERENCE

The stages of change model, useful as it is, centers on a patient's motivation to change. Although well-chosen therapeutic interventions may affect the patient's motivation level, the stages of change concept is oriented toward the patient rather than taking a more intersubjective or systemic approach. But to assess the usability of symptom-focused interventions, it is important not only that the patient have some readiness to change but also that this motivation is present in the therapeutic relationship. That is, is my patient ready and willing to change *with me*? The patient may be in the preparation or action stage regarding certain issues without viewing the therapy relationship as the venue in which to seek assistance. For example, several of my patients have quit smoking (for varying lengths of time) without advance discussion in therapy. They may casually mention at the end of a session that it has now been two weeks since they had a cigarette, or that they have noticed more irritability since quitting the previous month. The majority of smokers who quit do it on their own, and it is not surprising that some patients use their therapy time for concerns that they consider less amenable to personal effort alone. If patients report difficulty quitting or a quick relapse, I can then offer to collaborate with them on this effort if desired.

Patients who are able to make some changes on their own or to use such other resources as smoking cessation courses, self-help groups, or weight management programs might not require therapist assistance for certain problems. I may ask how things are going or inquire if there is anything that we can do together that the patient feels would be helpful with the issue. Otherwise, I would probably do little more than offer support and assess the impact of such changes on the patient's overall life. If I feel that the patient's decision was impulsive and not well thought out, and that there might be significance to my not having been consulted beforehand, I might wonder aloud why the patient decided to go through such a stressful change without telling me. Patients with more dismissive attachment styles may be unaware of many possibilities for help from others, and with these patients I may say very directly that, although I appreciate their resourcefulness, this is actually the kind of thing that I have a lot of training in and that I might have some ideas that would make changing a bit easier if they are ever interested.

A more problematic situation is one in which the patient truly does need the therapist's help but is unable to accept it. At times this reluctance might be grounded in longstanding organizing principles of the patient. For example, a patient may resist any hint of a suggestion from a perceived authority figure because growing up with a dominating father resulted in his feeling his autonomy was usurped if he complied with another's idea. Another patient may find it difficult to let the clinician know that there *is* a problem because vulnerability is experienced as intolerable. Others may have issues of intense competitiveness or feel such shame at not knowing something that the therapist knows that accepting help is reprehended. As Mitchell (1988) aptly stated, "We are . . . active creators and loyal perpetuators of conflicted interactional patterns in a relational world which, if not secure, is at least known" (p. 172). In such situations it is unlikely that the patient will find symptom-focused interventions in treatment usable, at least for some time.

Thelan (2005), discussing complex systems, writes, "The job of a skilled therapist is to detect where the system is open to change, to provide the appropriate new input to destabilize the old pattern, and to facilitate the person's seeking of new solutions" (p. 280). In this chapter I describe certain situations in which an offer of an active technique might well be the needed input to shift an old pattern and foster a progressive new one; however, experiences familiar to psychoanalytic clinicians, such as insight and provision of a different relational experience might be viewed as providing new inputs into previously closed systems (Seligman, 2005). When patients have entrenched organizing principles that hinder their ability to use the therapeutic relationship and they cannot tolerate suggestions, the standard techniques of psychodynamic psychotherapy, including a focus on defenses and various aspects of the transference and countertransference, are indicated. Possibly active techniques could be employed at a significantly later point, but successful resolution of the characterological issues may be such that nothing further would be needed.

In other cases, techniques of symptom management may be temporarily unusable, not because the patient's organizing principles are so fixed, but, rather, because of some intersubjective situation in the treatment relationship. There may have been an insufficiently repaired empathic break, for example, or a patient may be worried that the clinician's recent absence means that she is seriously ill, or therapist and patient may be dealing with the patient's dilatory payment schedule. I must emphasize very strongly that in situations involving transference and countertransference dynamics of tension, anger, confusion, hurt, and the like, such affects must be fully processed before a new element in the treatment is introduced. Frank (1992) wisely cautions against the use of active techniques on the basis of an inadequately understood countertransference reaction. He recommends that the therapist evaluate the idea of introducing active techniques for its possible countertransference meaning before deciding how to proceed.

But what if a treatment impasse involves symptomatic problems? Refraining from the use of symptom-focused techniques in a situation of intersubjective tension or impasse is a general rule to which I would make one possible exception: when the impasse itself results from a patient's request that the therapist provide such assistance and the therapist demurs. If the state of the relationship is such that the patient feels mild to moderate frustration surrounding this issue but generally finds treatment helpful, some discussion of the clinician's stance and its impact is in order. I believe, however, that optimal responsiveness in this situation requires an attempt at directly addressing the patient's need without prolonged delay. If the patient is extremely angry or conveying urgency and desperation, careful exploration is warranted. Possibly the symptom itself is so distressing that the patient is attempting to communicate the need for effective help *now*. However, urgency and anger about what the therapist is not providing might result from diverse causes, as in the case of Sandy, and dealing with the interactional pressure through discussion of the transference and countertransference must precede any action regarding symptoms.

One potentially problematic situation is that in which a clinician consistently refuses to accede to any patient wishes because the clinician's organizing principles may have withholding, distancing, or sadistic elements that are buttressed by adherence to stringent notions of abstinence. It is entirely possible that much anger might be provoked in a treatment overly dominated by abstinence; analytic treatments have often erred in the direction of therapist underactivity and underinvolvement as experienced by the patient (Lindon, 1994). The iatrogenic effects of a treatment relationship that is not felt to be sufficiently active and helpful may be considerable. In such situations, it is difficult to ascertain what organizing principles the patient may be bringing to the relationship, as the deleterious impact of nonresponsiveness is the supraordinate factor in the treatment.

A COLLABORATIVE PROCESS

Renik (1995) has recommended not only that we discard the notion of analytic anonymity, but also that we actually contradict it by making sure that our methods and purposes are clearly and explicitly presented to the patient: "An analyst should aim for comprehensibility, not inscrutability" (p. 482). Renik suggests that we make our thinking available to the patient concerning our activities. I share Renik's ideas about the desirability of such transparency, and I propose that discussion of symptom-focused techniques be conducted in a spirit of collaboration with the patient and a willingness to share one's ideas about their use at this particular time.

The decision to offer a symptom-focused technique should be guided by the clinician's sense that there is both some need for this type of intervention and that the patient has at least a modicum of ability to use it. Often the situation may not be so clear. In the absence of a strong contraindication for offering active techniques, such as a patient whose stage of change is precontemplation or a disruption in the treatment relationship requiring immediate processing, the clinician may decide to proceed on the basis of a countertransference intuition that such a move might be helpful.

I recommend that a technique be offered with a degree of tentativeness as well as openness to the patient's reaction. I might begin with a statement like, "There's something that we could do together that might help you with this—it involves. . . ." Next I give a very brief description of the technique, for example, "learning how to talk to yourself in a different way" or "learning how to relax more deeply." Then I inquire, "How does that sound? Do you think you might be interested in trying it?" If I am especially uncertain whether the timing is right, I might express my ambivalence by saying, for instance, "I have an idea about a technique that might help you with this, but I'm not sure if that would feel like the best thing to you right now or if you'd rather tell me more about what you've been going through."

Careful observation of the patient's verbal and nonverbal behavior following such an offer can reveal much, but in my experience it is common for patients to accede readily, sometimes expressing relief that there is something they can *do*. Patient and therapist may then begin implementing the technique in an exploratory fashion and processing the experience (see chapter four). Occasionally a patient will decline, perhaps saying that she does not feel ready or that a technique such as self-monitoring seems too embarrassing. All such responses may be very usefully explored. Once I believe that we have an understanding concerning the patient's feelings about using a symptom-focused technique, I may suggest that the patient keep this idea in the back of her mind and we can see if at some later point she might be interested—that is, provided I still think that the technique could be beneficial. Such a dialogue with the patient may, in fact, convince me that a particular idea is not a good fit in this specific situation, in which case I will tell the patient that I really see her point, and we will keep working to find the best ways to be helpful to her.

So far I have discussed attending to what patients say when I introduce the idea of using a symptom-focused technique. However, monitoring what patients do following this suggestion is of at least equal importance. Some patients will arrive at the next session beaming as they describe their use of a technique between sessions, or they may pull out their new self-monitoring journal to share with me. Other patients fail to mention anything about the earlier discussion, or they report that they totally forgot what they had planned to do between sessions. Patients will bring their own unique organizing principles to this work as they do to all other interactions, so that reactions may range from gratitude and relief to fears of disappointing the therapist to resistance against perceived demands. All should be discussed fully, and on this basis therapist and patient together can decide the appropriate place, if any, of symptom-focused work in the current treatment.

The issue of therapist investment in patients' use of active techniques is a challenging one. Most clinicians feel a deep commitment to their patients' well-being and experience gratification at their improvement. When we proffer symptom-focused techniques, we may have higher expectations than we otherwise would concerning patients' behavior between sessions, and we might well experience some frustration, impatience, anger, or disappointment at patients who fail to use (or remember!) our ideas. Our narcissism can be punctured, as it can in other situations in which we are invested in offering something to a patient that represents our skill, attunement, and creativity. Patients can ignore a symptom-focused intervention just as they can disregard an interpretation that we consider particularly incisive, and we just have to deal with this. It may be less self-enhancing, but ideally we will find it tolerable and be able to some extent to proceed in a balanced way. We may, for instance, try to ascertain why something was not usable at this time in the way we expected and avoid the extremes of perseverating on our idea while the patient feels badgered, or silently distancing and vowing to eschew such rejected attempts in the future.

It is important that we not become overinvested in the outcome or assume too great a degree of responsibility or control. Doing so may be difficult, especially if the symptom is dangerous or if it provokes in the therapist a powerful countertransference reaction owing to personal issues. For example, a therapist with an alcoholic father may feel impelled to become overcontrolling with an alcoholic patient. The traditional analytic values of respect for a patient's autonomy and concern that appropriate boundaries be upheld can be very beneficial in such situations. Additional personal treatment or consultation may be needed if a clinician becomes overly affected by a patient's choices regarding symptomatic behavior.

I have found it helpful to cultivate an attitude in which I have no particular expectations concerning my patients' progress or what aspects of our work together they will find helpful. I take pleasure in their growth and their successes, but, when something does not work well, I try to remind myself that many factors are operating in a multidetermined situation that I do not control. One of my long-term patients frequently describes interchanges with others or incidents to which she responds with a verbal or interior comment, "OK—fine—whatever!" Just as I know that my voice has become part of her over time, I have internalized this aspect of her, and I find myself thinking these words sometimes when patients tell me that my idea did not work, they forgot about my suggestion, their symptoms have worsened, and so on. OK—fine—whatever!—let's keep working. This is not to say that I think we should be dismissive of such experiences or regard the interactional implications as unimportant; it is our investment in controlling events that may require greater detachment.

Clinicians who are concerned about erring in a decision to use active techniques may consider that all therapeutic exchanges occur within a context of particular transference–countertransference configurations. It is ineluctable that the use of active techniques, as well as failure to use such measures, furthers particular transference and countertransference experiences. Because these techniques can be so beneficial, my preference is to err in the direction of offering them, and allow the patient to consent or not. Provided that conditions of need and potential usability are

present, and if the therapist, on reflection, feels moved to offer
an active technique, then I think it is more salutary for the
patient's well being and the therapeutic alliance if a patient is
respectfully presented with this treatment option than if the clinician preempts such choice.

CHAPTER FOUR

Cognitive
Interventions

COGNITIVE INTERVENTIONS TARGET COGNITIVE PROCESSES specifically as an area for therapeutic change. In actual practice, cognitive interventions are frequently combined with behavioral techniques, and the interrelationships between internal processes and overt behavior are emphasized. For the purposes of clarity and organization, I am separating interventions that may be combined in cognitive behavioral therapy into cognitive and behavioral components and discuss behavioral interventions in the next chapter. Cognitive treatment has become very popular since its inception, and its growth is reflected in a burgeoning collection of books and journals. As is true throughout this book, I am extracting selected elements that I find most compatible with an integrative dynamic approach.

THE COGNITIVE MODEL

Cognitive therapy, particularly that pioneered by Beck and colleagues (Beck, 1976; Beck et al., 1979; Beck and Emery, 1985) is an extremely valuable addition to psychotherapeutic technique. A psychoanalytically trained clinician, Beck originally sought to confirm certain psychoanalytic formulations of depression by conducting empirical studies. However, he concluded that his data did not in fact support such conceptualizations and experienced what he termed an "agonizing reappraisal" of his psychoanalytic belief system. Beck also observed that in many situations psychoanalysis produced little improvement, and he believed that it did not live up to its earlier promise as a treatment approach. He developed cognitive therapy in an attempt to find a brief and effective therapeutic method that addressed patients' focal pathology as he reconceptualized it. Although Beck ultimately rejected most psychoanalytic theory, his sophisticated formulations and his appreciation of the impact of earlier events on adult personality render much of his work compatible with an integrative psychoanalytic approach.

Cognitive therapy "is based on an underlying theoretical rationale that a person's affect and behavior are largely determined by the way in which he structures the world" (Beck et al., 1979, p. 3). In the words of Shakespeare's (1600–1601) Hamlet, "There is nothing either good or bad but thinking makes it so" (p. 78). In the cognitive model, people are seen as actively processing perceptions and experiences in general. Beck attends primarily to cognitions, which he defines as thoughts and visual images in a person's stream of consciousness or phenomenal field. These cognitions evolve from previous experiences and represent a blend of internal and external phenomena. Cognitive therapy is based on Beck's observation that changes in the content of a person's underlying cognitive structures have effect on that person's affective states and behavior as well. A key element in the cognitive model is the principle that persons form relatively stable and consistent cognitive structures or schemata. In any particular circumstance a person confronts, a schema relevant to the circumstance is activated, and this schema forms the basis for the person's organization of subsequent data. A schema may be inactive for long periods of time but may become revivified by the stimulus of particular environmental circumstances. Schemas may be very narrow in range or more complex (Beck and Emery, 1985). Complex schemata may be further broken down into rules, beliefs, and assumptions that then lead to conclusions and self-instructions when they are activated in a particular situation. Beck and Emery give the example of assumptions made by anxious patients concerning the danger-ousness of strangers. Such a patient, if faced with the problem of approaching a stranger to ask directions, will assume hostility on the part of the stranger, conclude that it is unsafe to approach, and will instruct himself to keep his mouth shut.

Another important aspect of the cognitive model is its empha-sis on faulty or distorted information processing. In such patho-logical conditions as depression or anxiety disorder, dysfunctional and idiosyncratic schemas become supraordinate, dominating the patient's cognitive processes in such a way that interpretations of various situations become quite distorted. Beck et al. (1979) iden-tified a number of systematic errors in the thinking of depressed patients, who maintained a belief in the validity of their negative views despite the existence of evidence to the contrary. Among these errors were such phenomena as personalization, a proneness to relate external incidents to oneself in the absence of any evi-dence that they actually pertain; overgeneralization, drawing a conclusion on the basis of one or a few isolated incidents that is then applied generally; magnification and minimization, the eval-uation of situations with gross misjudgment of their significance; and dichotomous thinking, the tendency to view events in terms of opposite categories with no options in between. Beck and Emery (1985) also identified catastrophizing, the anticipation of disas-trous outcomes, as characteristic of anxious patients in addition to some of the previously mentioned cognitive distortions.

Therapeutic techniques in cognitive therapy are oriented around helping patients to identify, assess, and correct distorted cognitions and the dysfunctional schemas underlying them. The cognitive therapist instructs the patient to monitor his cognitions and to recognize connections between those cognitions and vari-ous affects and behaviors. The patient is then taught to scrutinize the observed cognitions and consider whether or not they are valid and logical and what effect holding such views has on the patient's overall well-being. Beck et al. (1979) suggest asking such ques-tions as, What is the evidence for this belief? Are there alternative explanations? What is the worst that could happen here? The cog-nitive model endorses empirical investigation of a patient's cogni-tions, including the formulation of hypotheses based on beliefs about the self and the world that are then tested. Gradually a patient learns to substitute more reality-oriented cognitions for the irrational ones and ultimately becomes able to recognize and change the dysfunctional beliefs that lead to cognitive distortions (Beck et al., 1979).

In practice, cognitive therapy is brief, time limited, structured, and directive. The Socratic method is employed, and patients are taught to consider beliefs as hypotheses. Patient and therapist develop an agenda for each session and remain problem focused. Patients complete homework assignments between sessions (Beck and Emery, 1985). Content has to do with issues in the present, little attention being paid to past events except as they clarify present observations. Investigation of a patient's thinking and feeling in the session and between sessions is primary. No interpretations are made of unconscious processes; the cognitions attended to are those which a patient is aware of as he or she observes them (Beck et al., 1979).

PSYCHOANALYTIC AND COGNITIVE THEORY

Psychoanalytic clinicians reading this summary may have found themselves reacting with distaste and alienation as the description progressed. The previous paragraph in particular delineates some very clear differences between cognitive treatment and psychoanalytic psychotherapy. Cognitive and behavioral therapists implicitly assume discontinuity in development with an exclusive focus on the present, and obviously this conflicts with the centrality of developmental issues for analytic clinicians (Thelan, 2005). Some selected ideas and techniques of cognitive therapy, however, may be profitably employed in a dynamic treatment. This is so in part because principal components of the models' underlying assumptions are not dissimilar, although many of the ways in which treatment is typically conducted differ. I believe that the compatibility of salient concepts, together with a synthesis of some methods of both perspectives, offers the possibility of a treatment that is deep, effective, and efficient, although not necessarily brief.

In my view, the primary elements of the cognitive perspective are similar to relational psychoanalytic concepts about the construction of mental models based on a person's experiences (Connors, 2001a). Stolorow et al.'s (1987) concept of organizing principles, Bowlby's (1969) internal working models of self and other, and self and object representations posited in various object relations perspectives all connote ways in which people develop internal configurations that they carry forward and apply to new experiences, just as Beck (1976) suggested in theorizing that "schemas" determine responses to various situations. Beck et al.'s (1979) postulation that a person's cognitions represent an amalgam of internal and external factors is entirely in keeping with Stolorow and Atwood's (1992) assertion that "one's personal reality is always codetermined by features of the surround and the unique meanings into which these are assimilated" (p. 21). Beck et al.'s (1979) conceptualization of ways in which various schemas become activated under certain environmental conditions parallels Stolorow and Atwood's (1992) idea that invariant organizing principles will shape experience only when a situation that lends itself to such a process occurs, so that the organization of experience is codetermined by preexisting principles and a particular context that evokes one or another principle over others.

Specific attention to treatment of cognitions or beliefs is not unknown in psychoanalytic writings. Gedo (1988) discusses a case in which a patient had acquired some rather bizarre beliefs as a result of identification with disturbed caregivers. Gedo proposes that the appropriate role of the analyst here is to point out (tactfully) that the patient is engaging in faulty thinking. Weiss (1993) describes the task of psychotherapy as a collaboration with the patient to disconfirm the patient's pathogenic beliefs. According to Weiss, patients are motivated to change their problematic beliefs because they result in shame, guilt, and limitations in functioning. Patients will unconsciously test their pathogenic beliefs with the analyst by turning passive into active—identifying with a parent and doing to the analyst what the parent did; or transferring—enacting with the analyst the behaviors that the patient unconsciously believed resulted in traumatic parental reaction: "The present theory assumes that the patient seeks corrective emotional experiences through his testing, and that the therapist should provide the patient with the experiences he seeks" (p. 23). Weiss's focus on the significance of the treatment relationship, as well as the importance of pathogenic beliefs, provides a model for the integration of cognitive and dynamic thinking.

The concentration on conscious cognitions in cognitive therapy need not be viewed as conflicting with relational psychoanalytic theory; however, cognitive therapy's emphasis on cognition as the specific point of intervention represents a type of technique not typically seen in psychoanalytic psychotherapy. Certainly cognitions comprise much of the basic data in any treatment in which some degree of free association is used, but cognitions in psychoanalytic treatment might be regarded more as links in complex chains of associations than as entities in themselves. I suggest that cognitive therapy's focus on cognitions in the present that are to be observed, assessed, and ultimately changed represents a unique strength of this perspective as well as a significant limitation if technique does not extend beyond this emphasis.

I value this method because in my experience it is very empowering for patients to believe that they can exercise some conscious control over their thoughts and that such control can result in their feeling better and acting differently. I have had many patients respond to various interventions, such as genetic interpretations, by commenting that yes, this seems right, "and now what can I *do* about it?" Of course, patients can be encouraged to remain in treatment and work to resolve issues over time, and so forth, but I find that patients are much more satisfied if instead I propose that we do some work together on how they are talking to themselves and that there definitely is something they can do to facilitate change. In a cognitive therapy perspective cognitions are seen as mutable. If a patient decides that certain cognitions are incorrect and that holding them is having a deleterious impact on her life, the answer, from a cognitive therapy perspective, is to substitute more adaptive cognitions. Psychoanalytic clinicians might have concerns about the possibility of suppressing affects or defensively covering over important although painful material. From a cognitive perspective, however, affects are seen as consequences of particular cognitions, so that, if the cognitions change, the affects will alter as well—and authentically rather than defensively. (I believe that both positions have merit; I would refrain from suggesting cognitive interventions if I feared they might be incorporated into a self-suppressing stance for a particular patient.)

Cognitive Distortion

The notion that peoples' cognitions often are distortions of reality is an interesting one in our postmodern world. The idea that patients' views might be erroneous in some important ways has a long history in psychoanalytic thought. Sullivan (1953) used the term parataxic distortion to suggest that a current relationship could be "warped" by attitudes and expectations formed in earlier relationships (Beck at al., 1979, cite Sullivan as influential in the development of cognitive therapy). Historically the psychoanalyst has been viewed as the dispassionate, objective, and expert interpreter of the patient's associations. In recent years this epistemological stance has been regarded as untenable by relational theorists, who stress the subjectivity of the clinician (e.g., Stolorow et al., 1987; Renik, 1995). Such theorists have been particularly cautionary concerning the ability of clinicians to determine what is objectively true and what is a distortion of truth in the area of the transference; Stolorow et al. (1987) noted that therapists often regard a patient as distorting when the patient's views contradict perceptions of the therapist that are important to his own self-esteem. Relational theorists seem to recoil at the notion of distortion because they perceive it as an unjustifiable and potentially self-serving privileging of the clinician's knowledge above that of the patient. Gill (1982), critiquing the idea of distortion, protested that it suggested that a patient was creating his experience out of nothing rather than from something plausible. He proposed that a more accurate conceptualization "is that the real situation is subject to interpretations other than the ones the patient has reached" (p. 118). Although Gill was arguing against the notion that the patient is distorting reality, his suggestion that there may be alternative perspectives on a situation mirrors one of the primary questioning methods used in cognitive therapy.

For Frank (1993), cognitive therapy techniques aimed at "correcting" cognitive errors are incompatible with a psychoanalytic approach because it is difficult to reconcile such correction with a view that the patient's interpretation of reality is valid. Neither patient nor therapist has privileged access to truth, and it must always be remembered that experience is cocreated by the continuing influence of internalized past experiences and the present context, which, of course, must include the behavior of the therapist. Yet it seems self-evident that people possess their characteristic organizing styles. In Beck et al.'s (1979) terms, some of these styles at times become more primitive, absolute, and global (e.g., responding to a poor grade with "I'm a total failure who should just give up" compared with "I guess I partied too much this semester"), and the notion that these cognitions are erroneous or distorted seems an efficient way to convey that reasonably plausible ways of construing events are interfered with by repetitive mental templates. Bacal's (1998) statement that often the optimally responsive therapeutic action will be at variance with the patient's stated perspective suggests that articulating the nature of such problematic cognitions may be helpful and empathic.

Cognitive therapy techniques aimed at remediating faulty information processing can be implemented in a fashion that is respectful of the patient's subjectivity by underscoring the genesis of problematic perspectives on self and others in early interactions with caregivers (Connors, 2001a). In contrast to the nearly exclusive focus on the present time in cognitive therapy, I propose that the clinician devote much attention to the formation of various schemas as they gradually arose in the earlier history of the patient. Most psychoanalytic clinicians conduct detailed explorations of various historical events and interactional patterns, with some emphasis on enabling patients to express disavowed affects. I add a particular focus on conclusions that a patient reached about self and others on the basis of such experiences, with interpretative attention to what the patient *learned*. I like to refer specifically to concepts of learning in such discussions because doing so underscores the validity and plausibility of the conclusions that the patient reached about the self and the world on the basis of life in a particular family. I concentrate on the adaptive context, and I emphasize that in such a milieu it was eminently sensible to conclude, for instance, that one's emotional needs could be met only covertly, or that one must take complete responsibility for others' emotional well-being, or that only perfect performance is acceptable. Honoring the patient's attempt to construct such rules for living out of his experiences can help lessen the patient's worries about having irremediable defects or "being crazy." I also point out, however, that the conclusions reached on the basis of life in a specific environment, however adaptive then and there, may not completely apply in other settings. Patients have varying degrees of perspective on the lack of generalizability of their schemas, and this is an area that invites much integration of psychodynamic and cognitive work.

Self and Other

The cognitions that patients report frequently illuminate something about their relationships with self and with others, and often these relationships must be understood on a deeper level before cognitive interventions will prove enduringly effective. Stern (2002a, b) has elucidated the self's relation to itself in a manner I find most incisive. Stern refers to the work of Bollas (1987), who suggested that the relationship between the ego and the true self is an internal object relationship in which the ego treats the self in a manner very similar to ways in which the caregivers responded to the child. Stern proposes that the child brings a "primary subjective experience" to an interaction with the caregiver (the primary subjective experience roughly corresponds to Bollas's [1987] and Winnicott's [1960] concept of the true self). The caregiver responds, and the young child automatically identifies with the caregiver's responses to this primary subjective experience. Stern suggests that the quality of self-experience moment-to-moment will be determined by the relationship between a person's primary subjective experience and what comes to be organized as an intersubjective self. If the caregiver's responses were attuned and sensitive, the identifications become the basis for self-realization and the foundation for a cohesive self. If, however, the child must identify with responses that are traumatizing, her relationship to her own internal reality becomes impaired. In psychopathological conditions, intersubjectively constituted experience consistently overrides, invalidates, or alienates the child from her current primary subjective experience. In addition, because early identifications represent the way in which a young child comes to know herself, the child does not experience them as differentiated from her primary subjective experience. This lack of discrimination leads to the peculiar quality of the identifications being simultaneously of the self and foreign to the self, which Stern notes was identified by Ferenczi when he introduced the concept of identification with the aggressor. Stern suggests that a primary task of the clinician is to assist the patient in delineating primary subjective experience from these negative identifications.

Another issue pertaining to self and other relationships is that of the need for both attachment and individuation (Lyons-Ruth, 1991). I have suggested that, because the attachment system

functions to ensure survival, needs for self-development will probably remain subordinate if survival is experienced as threatened
on some level (Connors, 2000). But what of self needs under circumstances in which security is continuously threatened? Blizard
(2001) has described the relational dilemmas for patients who
were abused by a primary caregiver. Although she was referring
to seriously traumatized dissociative patients, her points may have
relevance to a large clinical group. Blizard states that the abused
child will attempt to ensure safety by placating the abuser, suppressing anger, and rationalizing that the abuse is deserved.
Ultimately the child may adopt a stance in which the injustice of
the situation is denied, the abuser is idealized, and anger, pain,
and memories of abuse are dissociated. However, this attempt to
preserve attachment is unstable because it does not meet the child's
basic needs for self-protection and some measure of rationality
and justice in the interpersonal world. Eventually the dissociated
pain and outrage can no longer be contained, leading to a shift in
which needs for attachment are denied and the child feels powerful (again, similar to Ferenczi's idea about identification with the
aggressor). This position is problematic, however, because overt
displays of rage and power are dangerous in an abusive environment. The child turns anger on the self, and the dilemma remains
unresolved; the child can preserve attachment at the expense of
self-protection or risk abandonment through greater self-assertion.

Both Stern (2002a, b) and Blizard (2001) delineate ways in
which difficult early experiences result in psychic structure that is
not well integrated with regard to self and other. Stern describes
a developmental pathway wherein the caregiver's responses hinder rather than facilitate the development of authentic selfhood
yet become part of the self, and Blizard discusses the more extreme
situation in which an irreconcilable conflict exists between the
basic needs of the self and the need for attachment. Stern points
out that identifying with the other's response to primary subjective experience comes as naturally to the child as breathing.
Moreover, adopting the other's point of view preserves attachment,
including in circumstances much less extreme than those described
by Blizard. Cognitive therapy's emphasis on the Socratic method
and rational disputation of erroneous cognitions must be combined with the insights of psychoanalytic authors such as Stern
and Blizard so that the full import of early identifications with dif-

ficult or frightening caregivers can be appreciated. The eruption of traumatic memories and frightening internal representations may result in fragmented states that are not compatible with rational discourse. Parallel systems of information processing without full integration are operative, as in pathological emotion schemas dominated by subsymbolic processing (Bucci, 1997) and maladaptive schemas representing experiences that cannot be assimilated (Epstein, 1994).

Clinicians may treat many patients whose cognitions reveal an intersubjectively organized experience that subordinates primary subjective experience. This latter sector of self-experience may be more or less successfully dominated by pathogenic identifications and the adoption of a self-punitive stance in which anger is reserved for the self alone. The self is overly critical, harsh, judgmental, and rejecting of itself, while others may be idealized. The patient as a child identified with parental responses indicating that the child was inadequate, disappointing, a failure—perhaps representing the parents' feelings about their own selves that were transmitted down the generations—and internalized these responses. The result is a tormented self-experience of unremitting self-criticism, perhaps with sporadic movement into a more self-oriented stance; at times some patients will assert the primacy of self-object needs or other aspects of primary subjective experience and may express negative rather than idealized views of others. However, intense guilt and anxiety quickly erupt as attachment needs are threatened, and this temporary stance is supplanted by the usual self-denigration.

Techniques of cognitive therapy involving the analysis of faulty logic and the generation of alternative perspectives may be quite effective for patients whose internal worlds are at least partially integrated and flexible. However, patients whose primary subjective experience was not supported by caregivers have internalized self-condemnation as a way of life. For these patients, the exploration of alternative perspectives, such as that perhaps they are not entirely deficient, is extremely threatening to their intersubjective organization. I believe that such a patient will be able to relinquish what Stern (2002a) refers to as "toxic identifications" only through the relationship with the therapist.

In contrast to cognitive therapy, which does not recommend long-term therapy or much dependence on the therapist, an integrative approach will enable some patients to progress because they have found the clinician reliable over time, and in the context of ongoing selfobject responsiveness they come to believe new things about themselves and about others. For instance, I was working with a depressed and anxious patient who was exceptionally harsh with herself and criticized herself mercilessly for being superficial, for not being happy when she had nothing to be unhappy about, for being selfish, and in general for failing to conform perfectly to the extremely rigid rules of living on which her parents insisted. I intervened multiple times per session to tell her that I thought she was being overly harsh, critical, and unfair to herself. After some months she reported, "I do know I'm too hard on myself." Curious about a possible shift in perspective, I inquired, "Oh, you do know this?" and she replied, "Yes, when I'm here with you! And then I lose it." This patient required much more time in therapy before her identification with my view of her became more stable.

The process of this type of change through the relationship may be conceptualized in several ways. The therapist becomes a new attachment figure with whom a greater measure of security is possible. The patient develops an idealizing transference, in which he feels strengthened and enlivened through connection to the powerful therapist. Hoffman (1998) referred to the authority of the psychoanalyst in the patient's life, and suggested that immersion in treatment can constitute a powerful process of social influence that enables alteration of a patient's subjective reality in ways that resemble the primary socialization of childhood. The identification process continues to be central, and, as the clinician responds to aspects of the patient's primary subjective experience, the patient identifies with this new intersubjective experience (Stern, 2002a, b). Stern holds that the patient's dissociated subjective states enter into a new relationship with the clinician, and as the patient identifies with this new recognition she forms her own novel relationship with these aspects of the self. Common to these conceptualizations is that the patient has some sort of new experience with the therapist that permits different possibilities. The old relational dichotomy of attending to self-needs versus seeking attachment is at least somewhat attenuated in a context that welcomes both. The relevance and possible efficacy of cognitive techniques must be considered in relation to these larger issues.

APPLICATION OF THE TECHNIQUES

I am suggesting that cognitive therapy techniques be employed in an overall treatment structure that diverges considerably from that prescribed in cognitive therapy manuals. Although cognitive therapy as commonly practiced is relatively brief, its techniques may be employed in a treatment of any length. I not infrequently use some cognitive techniques with patients whom I have treated for several years or longer. Moreover, rather than focus exclusively on the here-and-now, patient and therapist may weave back and forth between current issues and their earlier determinants. More or less session time may be allocated to historical events or to present problems on the basis of a number of factors, including the nature of the symptomatic concerns and how pressing they are, the level of exploration and resolution of past events, and, of course, the patient's wishes. Some discussion of structured tasks (such as any records the patient is keeping of cognitions) is interspersed with a more expressive and nondirective stance.

One possible general approach is to begin with an analysis of recent cognitions in problem areas, to spend time in midsession linking such cognitions to genetic determinants, and to conclude the session with some ideas about applying the new insights to the current problem. For example, Ron, a patient in a new relationship, came in reporting that he had had a very difficult few days of feeling distraught because his new boyfriend had not yet suggested their next date. Ron worried that the new man did not really like him, thought that their relationship was over, and despaired that he would never find anyone who was truly interested in him for a sustained period. We explored these cognitions and the fact that there was a good deal of evidence to suggest that the boyfriend liked my patient quite a bit but that he was extremely busy with a demanding job. We then moved into a longer discussion of Ron's family relationships. His father had died of cancer when Ron was 11, and his mother had been preoccupied with her husband's care throughout his long illness and absorbed in her grief after his death. We articulated ways in which these painful experiences of loss and emotional unavailability had led to Ron's fears that no one would love him over time. In the last 10 minutes or so of the session, we returned to the present situation, and he reported much greater awareness that his perception of his boyfriend's attitudes toward him had been colored by his earlier experiences. We constructed a few soothing self-statements for him to remember if his anxiety rose again, such as, "Fred must really like me, because otherwise he wouldn't want me to meet his family and friends" and, "There is every reason to believe that Fred is interested in me, and he's probably just having a really busy week at work." This patient's past experiences of loss and failures of mirroring required long-term therapy for more complete resolution, but the way they were triggered in the current relationship was contained to some extent by a concentration on the concrete evidence that the relationship would continue. Ron reported feeling much better at the end of the session.

A primary goal of cognitive therapy is to help patients realize that particular thoughts have consequences for mood states and behaviors. Patients observe the thoughts they are having in certain situations, and therapist and patient analyze the links between various cognitions and subsequent mood states and behaviors. I might introduce this idea with a statement such as, "You know, the way that we talk to ourselves can have a lot of impact on us—why don't we take a look at what you were saying to yourself in that situation and how it was affecting you." For instance, a patient with bulimia reported that she had decided not to attend a friend's party, and that after she had made this decision her depression and binge eating had worsened. When we discussed what had been going through her mind prior to the party, the patient reported a stream of negative cognitions related to thinking that she was fat as she tried on clothes for the party, for example, "My butt looks huge in this dress. . . . I look disgusting in this too, and I'll look like such a fat pig with all my tiny friends . . . now I look like a refrigerator box with a beachball on top . . . forget it, I'm not going!" The patient reported feeling self-hatred, depression, and the wish to hide. She said that she had felt fine before she began to try on clothes for the party and now saw clearly that her self-deprecating thoughts concerning her appearance had triggered negative moods and social withdrawal. Of course, painful situations that activate one's vulnerabilities are not utterly transformed by the cessation of self-critical thoughts; this patient evaluated herself chiefly with reference to her weight, and a situation calling for her to present herself for the perceived scrutiny of others whom she regarded as superior was fraught with intense memories and affects. Such an event would be difficult regardless of the patient's self-statements; her vicious self-attack, however, rendered a challenging situation intolerable. As she tried to shift her internal dialogue in a more realistic direction, her vulnerability to fragmentation under such conditions decreased.

Regarding Beck et al.'s (1979) injunction to refrain from interpretation of unconscious material, obviously psychoanalytic therapists are going to have a different take on this! I see no inherent difficulty in joining interpretations of unconscious material with analyses of more conscious cognitions; psychoanalytic therapists probably do a great deal of such work. Moreover, intersubjective thinking renders the notion of a firm and discrete boundary between conscious and unconscious improbable; this boundary is fluid and always reflects a particular intersubjective context (Stolorow and Atwood, 1992). A therapeutic relationship in which the clinician is sensitive, attuned, and understanding may enable the boundary between material to which the patient has access and that which is unavailable to shift such that previously unconscious contents emerge into consciousness. Techniques of cognitive therapy may be introduced without concern about any demarcation between conscious and unconscious material.

Stolorow and Atwood have emphasized the importance of the prereflective unconscious, or the organizing principles that unconsciously shape a person's experiences. They regard psychoanalysis as a method for illuminating these unconscious organizing principles by exploring the ways in which the patient organizes her experience of the analytic relationship in terms of patterns that she carries forward. An exploration of how the patient is organizing her experience of the treatment is certainly one means of illuminating her schemas. I find that many times these organizing principles, even if unconscious initially, may be brought to awareness through concerted effort by the patient and the provision of an interpersonal milieu experienced as relatively safe. For instance, one patient began talking about unhappy she was and quickly silenced herself. When I noted this sudden silence and asked what had happened, she said that she had begun to worry that I must be thinking how petty her problems were and feeling disgusted that she was "wallowing" in them. I responded by clarifying that I was having a very different reaction from the one she anticipated and told her of my concern for her suffering and interest in hearing more about it. When I asked for her ideas about what might make her worry in this way, we began to identify some schemas based on experiences of having parents react negatively to any expressions of emotional pain and convey that such things were not worth discussing. Although the patient had been unaware that she had organized her experience in this way, these schemas were quite accessible once she felt more assured that in the current situation they were incorrect.

With regard to specific technique, I employ the cognitive therapy technique of having the patient observe and sometimes record cognitions. It is particularly useful to obtain information about cognitions preceding a symptomatic episode or a strong affective state, and in session I will ask such questions as, "What was going through your head during that time?" or, "What were you saying to yourself before you did that?" Obtaining further information about verbal self-statements and any visual images during and subsequent to the symptomatic or affective situation is also important. When the cognitions are articulated in as much detail as possible, the clinician may elect to explore their genetic determinants for some time and ultimately assist the patient in getting more perspective on the context-specific learning that took place. For example, with the patient who worried that I was disgusted by her distress about her "petty problems," I responded, "I can see how you might come to the conclusion that everyone would react in this way, since both of your parents did. But you might want to consider that your parents were more uncomfortable with upsetting emotions and open communication than a lot of people are, for reasons we've discussed, and that not everyone is going to respond as they did—for instance, I'm not." We had had some discussions earlier about aspects of her parents' own history and cultural background that rendered them particularly dismissive, and the patient was able to make very good use of the idea that perhaps all she had learned in her particular family was not accurately applied to the rest of the world.

Beck and Emery (1985) have proposed many ideas, involving a more present-day focus, to help a patient to gain perspective. Asking questions is their primary method for correcting thinking errors, and most of the questions of a cognitive therapist fall into three general categories: those assessing evidence related to a particular conclusion, those attempting to expand limited perspectives, and those related to a patient's worst expectations. In the first category are such questions as, What's the evidence for or against this idea? Are you confusing a habit with a fact? Are you thinking in all-or-nothing terms? Are your judgments based on feelings rather than facts? Are you overfocusing on irrelevant factors or taking examples out of context? A technique for analyzing faulty logic is to construct a three-column record. In the first column, the patient records some data, followed by her interpretation in the second column. For the third column, the patient describes an observer's perspective on the situation, which might reveal that the patient was drawing unwarranted conclusions from a situation such as a stranger's glance or a friend's remark.

In the second questioning category, the major technique for enlarging perspective is having the patient articulate a particular cognition and then attempt to generate alternative explanations by asking if there is another way to look at it. Often this generative thinking requires that the therapist help the patient to decenter from an overly personalized view of a situation or reattribute the degree of responsibility for a particular outcome. One method I use is to suggest possible alternative ways to construe events on the basis of psychological explanations involving others' motives. It is not uncommon for patients to interpret situations in an overly negative and self-focused fashion; they infer that others dislike, reject, and disapprove of them. If a patient is unable to generate any less personalized explanations, for example, regarding a boss who snapped at her, I might say something like, "Is it possible that he was anxious about this project deadline and he took it out on you?" Psychoanalytic therapists are in a particularly good position to raise questions involving complex human motivations when patients are interpreting events in negative and simplistic ways.

The third major area of questioning has to do with patients' tendency to anticipate catastrophic outcomes. The clinician asks the patient what is the worst that can happen. Beck et al. (1979) suggest that the therapist try to help the patient broaden the range of information on which the patient is basing his prediction and to realize that many dire forecasts in the past did not come true. Another therapeutic task is to collaborate with the patient on developing coping strategies for the worst possible outcome. One of my patients spontaneously took herself through this process and related to me that she had asked herself what was the worst that could happen if she stood up to her friends more and what she would do if it occurred. The worst thing she could come up with was that all her friends would leave her, and, if that happened, she could make new friends because of her newly assertive personality, which would be just fine. The patient described feeling much more free to take risks with her friends after realizing that she would be able to cope with the worst outcome she could imagine.

Once cognitions have been identified, linked both to genetic determinants and to subsequent moods and behaviors, and assessed for their veracity, balance, logic, and helpfulness, the patient is ready for the final stage of cognitive work—actually changing the thoughts. This process is sometimes referred to as cognitive restructuring. To begin the process of generating alternative cognitions, I might ask the patient what she could say to herself in this particular situation that would be more accurate and less harsh. Frequently this task will involve helping the patient shift from views of the self that are extreme and characterized by dichotomous thinking and perfectionism to a stance that is more balanced and moderate. For instance, "I really look fine," supplants "I'm a fat pig." Patients often find this exercise immensely challenging, even if they have been able to achieve a fair degree of perspective on the extreme nature and inaccuracy of their thoughts. It is here that the authority of the clinician to which I referred earlier is especially effective. If patients are unable to explore reasonable alternative thoughts with any sense of conviction, I might suggest statements that underscore the idea that the patient is a worthwhile human being with valuable qualities who has something important to offer others in relationships. Patients can take from my comments a sense of permission to think better of themselves, and, because it is on my authority, daring to do this seems more possible. Patients not infrequently report that they were able to remember what I had said and that reminding themselves of my words helped them to combat some of the relentlessness of the internal critic.

I also make clear to patients that they might not be able to believe the alternative self-statements at first. I convey that in some ways this is to be expected and that it really does not matter— what matters is practicing the alternative thought so that the strength of the old habit decreases while the new one increases. This caution seems to help patients to persist in working with alternative cognitions rather than feeling hopeless if the technique is not immediately transformative. I stress to patients that it is not easy to think different thoughts, but that they can choose to do it. I like to use an example described by Beck and Emery (1985) that habitual thoughts form something like a Grand Canyon in the mind. It takes much work for alternative thoughts to carve their own groove when a certain channel is so well worn, but with effort it can be done. I tell my patients that every time they choose to control their thoughts and substitute alternatives for problematic ones they are adding to the strength of the new path.

A related area of cognitive restructuring is sometimes referred to as self-instructional training or cognitive coping skills training (e.g., Spiegler and Guevremont, 1993). This technique can be employed in situations in which the patient identifies certain behaviors that would be desirable, for example, performing at one's best level on an exam or while giving a speech, remaining calm in a feared situation such as taking an airplane trip or controlling anger in a provoking situation. The therapist helps the patient identify the self-instructions that would be most helpful in facilitating the desired behavior by asking such questions as, What tends to be the hardest thing for you in that situation? What might you say to yourself that could help you with that? For instance, a test-anxious patient could rehearse some test-taking strategies in conjunction with relaxation procedures (described in the next chapter), such as instructing herself to take a few deep breaths while the test is being distributed, reminding herself to read the directions carefully, and telling herself to focus. It is helpful if the patient rehearses the self-statements thoroughly, perhaps visualizing herself in the difficult situation, so that they will be more accessible under stressful conditions.

Patients may be reminded of the notion of making "affirmations," which has been touted in a variety of self-help materials and also satirized in such presentations as the Stuart Smalley character on the *Saturday Night Live* show ("I'm good enough, I'm smart enough, and, doggone it, people like me!"). If patients have a positive association to the idea of affirmations, they may feel very comfortable with affirming the more positive aspects of themselves as they work with their thoughts. Some patients, whose exposure to various presentations of affirmations has resulted in their finding such ideas distasteful, may be told that in cognitive restructuring the new cognitions are logical and realistic rather than full of hyperbole (or whatever it might be that evoked a negative reaction). Moreover, we are always affirming things about ourselves, but cognitive work provides an opportunity to scrutinize such self-statements and alter them if we wish.

Selective Application of Cognitive Interventions

A psychoanalytic clinician employing an integrative approach is well positioned to employ cognitive interventions selectively by considering such factors as the patient's attachment style, trauma history, and characteristic defenses. One must consider which patients may find cognitive interventions helpful early in treatment and those for whom this technique is contraindicated. I find that cognitive work is particularly compatible early in treatment for those with a dismissive attachment style. Those patients who have been oriented away from dangerous affects and longings may initially feel more secure with a therapist who offers some clarity of focus and a less ambiguous task than free associating. For instance, one patient described his distaste for discussions of emotion in his marriage ("that touchy-feely crap!") and said that emotions just seemed "esoteric" to him. He expressed relief when I suggested a focus on thinking and proposed some structured tasks involving recording cognitions. He noted that he liked the fact that these tasks gave him something "concrete" to do in therapy, which made him feel a sense of accomplishment. Ideally the lack of trust of self and other that characterizes dismissive attachment will be mitigated over time, so that such patients can become more comfortable with a less structured treatment and more emotional expression. However, their initial comfort level and willingness to tolerate treatment may be enhanced by careful use of cognitive interventions.

Patients with a more preoccupied or disorganized style who enter therapy in great distress do not seem to find such techniques highly usable in earlier stages of treatment. These patients may feel much internal pressure to relate their stories and be assured of the therapist's understanding. Until they experience greater cohesion in the context of increasing security in the treatment relationship, such patients may have difficulty processing on a cognitive level and may easily misunderstand or be alienated by attempts to help them to examine their thinking. Standard techniques of relationally oriented dynamic treatment are most appropriate for these patients until much of their distress abates in a milieu of selfobject responsiveness. Some of these patients may benefit greatly from cognitive interventions later in the therapy process, when the relationship is more consolidated. The integrative clinician who is familiar with cognitive therapy can decide which interventions might constitute optimal responsiveness at any particular point in treatment.

CHAPTER FIVE

Behavioral
Techniques

THE BEHAVIORAL LITERATURE IS VOLUMINOUS, and selecting symptom-focused interventions that are compatible with a psychoanalytic psychotherapy is challenging. Some behavioral techniques, such as systematic desensitization, are quite time consuming to implement. My focus here is on effective interventions that can easily be integrated into a psychoanalytic treatment. In choosing them, I used the following criteria: employing the technique should not require sustained blocks of session time; discussion and use of the technique can easily be interspersed with dialogue on other topics, including insight-oriented material prompted by the technique; and use of the technique should not be so discrepant with the usual roles of the therapist and the patient that it generates significant confusion or discomfort.

The techniques of self-monitoring and the various relaxation methods that I discuss here can be used alone, in conjunction with the cognitive methods discussed in the previous chapter, or as part of a more multidimensional program encompassing some of the self-management ideas discussed later in this chapter. Much of the material in this chapter may seem foreign, superficial, or alienating to psychoanalytically trained clinicians. My intent is to describe the techniques in sufficient detail so that you can begin to use them. Later chapters contain detailed case material illustrating ways in which these techniques can be incorporated into psycho-dynamic psychotherapy and further the goals of such treatment.

SELF-MONITORING

Self-monitoring consists of keeping records of various behavioral events so as to understand them more clearly and ultimately for-mulate interventions based on the information obtained. Self-mon-itoring data are highly useful in illuminating three aspects of behavior: its antecedents, dimensions of the behavior itself, and the consequences that follow. I am especially likely to recommend self-monitoring when patients wish to increase or to decrease par-ticular behaviors. For example, patients may wish to quit smok-ing, cut down on alcohol use, or reduce compulsive eating, and they may desire to increase such lower frequency behaviors as exercising or studying. Patients who report distressing sympto-matic events, such as panic attacks or rageful episodes, also may benefit from self-monitoring. Records can serve as chronicles of shifting mood states as well as behavioral events.

Using the format of their choice, patients would record infor-mation on a regular basis. Many patients prefer to use a small notebook or their daily organizer, whereas others employ the lat-est information technology to create detailed charts, graphics, and reminders on their hand-held devices and laptop computers. The level of detail recorded will vary depending on the nature of the situation and what is already understood about it. It is useful to obtain sufficient detail so that elements of the situation become clarified, but recording should not be unduly burdensome for the patient or it will not be sustained. It may be helpful to suggest for-matting ideas that eliminate some tedium, such as the use of columns with identical headings that need not be specified repeat-edly. Commonly patients begin self-monitoring energetically and record much detail, after which they shift into a more abbreviated but still useful method.

Principles of learning theory converge with psychoanalytic ideas of behavior as meaningful and related to various causes, whether conscious or unconscious. The idea of attending to antede-cent events when attempting to understand behavior is very familiar to psychoanalytic clinicians tracking complex processes in the therapeutic relationship as well as in the patient's life outside treatment. Self-monitoring simply provides an immediate rather than a retrospective view of what preceded certain experiences. Self-monitoring for a particular patient might include recording information concerning some external and internal events that might have acted as triggers for the symptomatic episode. For instance, a patient recording bulimic episodes would describe what was occurring just prior to a binge. Ideally this notation would include any relevant external events such as interpersonal interactions, her mood state, any cognitions of which she was aware, and her level of hunger. A patient who is in the preparation stage to quit smoking may find it helpful to record circumstances in which he smokes and note the situations that prompt the most intense wishes for a cigarette.

Another important aspect of self-monitoring is the information it provides on the behavior itself. Patients are asked to record every episode of the behavior so that the frequency of its occurrence can be understood. Such dimensions of the behavior as duration of the episode and what specifically was drunk, used, consumed and so on, may also be salient. Or patients may be asked to rate the intensity of the episode, frequently on a 10-point scale from least to most intense. This aspect of the task is often particularly easy for patients because the idea of recording various behaviors in order to set goals and assess progress is standard practice in numerous areas, including many weight-control programs and ideas offered by financial and organizational experts.

It may also be useful for patients to record some information concerning the consequences of the behavior on their internal states and any interpersonal sequelae, if relevant. A patient who has engaged in some addictive behavior may report that his mood changed in a positive direction, that welcome numbness had occurred, or that no relief was obtained because the guilt was too great. Any shifts in interpersonal interactions as a result of the behavior are salient. For example, it may become apparent that significant others are supporting unhealthy behaviors and that interpersonal consequences may ensue if change occurs. As Freud (1917c) stated, "No one who has any experience of the rifts which so often divide a family will, if he is an analyst, be surprised to find that the patient's closest relatives sometimes betray less interest in his recovery than in his remaining as he is" (p. 459). Additionally, other symptomatic behaviors may be employed as a consequence of the initial behavior. A patient who binged may abuse laxatives following the binge episode, or a patient who got drunk may then use cocaine and have unsafe sex.

I usually introduce the topic quite simply by saying something like, "It would really help us to treat your problem if we had a better idea of what kinds of things were triggers for you—what would you think about keeping a record of how often you end up doing X and what's happening just before it?" I try to provide a rationale that the patient can understand and that will have clear value to her treatment. I also might talk about how use of this method increases awareness and sometimes has a positive effect all by itself. If a patient in an early stage of change is not sure if his behavior actually constitutes a problem, I can propose self-monitoring as a way to have all the relevant information that will help him decide whether or not changes are warranted. Finally, I might comment that self-monitoring is a great way to observe his progress in actually making changes.

This technique is invaluable for expanding patients' awareness of their behavior, including behavior that may be denied or disavowed to some extent. Patients will often report that the act of recording really clarified the true level of their involvement in certain behaviors, as in, "Wow! I really had no idea how much I was truly eating—no wonder I gained all this weight!" or, "I thought I was getting high a couple of times a month, but I see it's really several times a week." Self-monitoring interferes with the tendency to minimize negative behavior and inflate positive behavior in one's own mind, for it requires attention to current actual behavior rather than hazy and defensive recollections. Patients in the contemplation stage of change who become engaged in using self-monitoring to evaluate whether or not any changes are really needed may move to the preparation stage because they find the results compelling.

Patients may also find that a conscientious effort to explore the antecedents of certain behaviors is quite fruitful. People often experience symptomatic behavior as mysterious and senseless ("I don't know why I did that; it just happened") and are often surprised and relieved to see that their behavior can be understood in a context of internal and external events. Discovering links between certain affect states or interpersonal events and symptomatic behaviors deepens insight into a patient's self-regulatory strategies. This discovery may evolve into helpful discussions of interactions within one's family and current significant relationships, in addition to suggesting ideas for individualized change strategies. Moreover, patients experience a greater sense of efficacy, mastery, and control when they can regard their behavior as meaningful and motivated by reasonable wishes, such as the desire to relieve painful feelings.

Self-monitoring alone often results in some positive changes in problematic behaviors, perhaps because it heightens awareness and interjects greater consciousness into habitual behaviors. I have had patients tell me that they deliberately curtailed some of the behavior in question because they found it so distasteful to have to record yet another episode (of course, at this point many patients will dispense with the self-monitoring rather than the target behavior!). This concern relates to some of the most difficult issues patients experience when using this technique. Patients have to find the time, privacy, and means on a very regular basis to record their behavior, and some feel that the "hassle" of doing so is considerable. But even more troublesome is that self-monitoring involves letting two people know about aspects of life that may be kept quite private: oneself and the therapist. Patients do not have to be in the action stage of change to self-monitor, but many people at earlier stages may not be ready to acknowledge the nature of their involvement in particular behaviors to themselves because the data will suggest that a change is needed.

Typically, self-monitoring records are shared with the therapist, and the prospect of this technique can generate many feelings for a patient contemplating disclosure of information that seems very intimate, embarrassing, and shameful. When I first propose the technique, I often ask patients, "How do you think it would be for you to let me see those records and have us talk about them together?" Patients will frequently respond that they anticipate some embarrassment, but they believe that it will be tolerable and that they expect such frankness to help. These patients usually find the technique quite usable. Others will find the prospect of such vulnerability too aversive. Some will be able to say, "Forget it!" or, "I'm not ready for this." Still other patients may accede verbally but resist the task. When asked, they say they "forgot" to keep records or to bring them to session. Generally in such a case I recommend detailed inquiry rather than any attempt to persuade the patient to comply. Exploring this avoidance may promote greater awareness and discussion of a patient's fears of exposure, rejection, and shame in the therapeutic relationship. Of course, psychotherapy in general affords numerous occasions for such vulnerability, but many patients are adroit at titrating potential humiliation with topic shifts, evasiveness, humor, storytelling, and so forth. Such maneuvers may not be immediately obvious in the therapeutic interaction and may continue for some time. It is not uncommon for patients to mention a troublesome problem in the first session and barely allude to it again; they fill session time with other material because the potential for humiliation feels so great. Although such interpersonal anxieties would become apparent in various ways over the course of treatment, processing the experience of self-monitoring can provide a usefully direct route to such issues in the transference.

Kohut (1971) identified the "vertical split," a defensive structure that functions to keep shameful or contradictory aspects of self less accessible to awareness. Goldberg (1999), elaborating on this concept, describes those suffering from a vertical split as "being of two minds," and discusses the vertical split as a defensive division of the self into "opposing but parallel psychic configurations" (p. 83). Failure to integrate disavowed material persists because the person regards it as unbearably threatening or painful. Kohut (1971) proposed that analytic work should aim at bringing the central sector of the personality to acknowledge the psychic reality of the split off contents. For Goldberg (1999) the relationship with the therapist is vital in this regard: "the therapist becomes the vehicle of integration to the extent that he or she can observe and tolerate the content of the disavowed material" (p. 126). These disavowed aspects of self, however, are available to consciousness should the person wish to confront them, and I suggest that offering patients an opportunity to monitor their own behavior in the context of an accepting relationship can help to repair such defensive splits.

RELAXATION METHODS

The use of relaxation methods has a long history in medicine, psychiatry, and clinical psychology (see Goldfried and Davison, 1994).

Much of the work within the behavioral tradition has focused on the principle of counterconditioning, that is, the use of learning procedures to substitute one type of response for another. Wolpe (1958) introduced the term "reciprocal inhibition" to suggest that one response potentially could inhibit another response. Relaxation techniques are employed to replace tension and anxiety with relaxation. In the last few decades some focus on the Eastern traditions of meditation and yoga has greatly added to the interest in relaxation methods among professionals and the public. For example, Benson (1975) found that meditation produces significant physiological changes, which he termed the relaxation response, as he considered it to be the opposite of hyperarousal. Kabat-Zinn's (1990) stress-reduction program draws on Buddhist traditions and promulgates such practices as deep breathing. Linehan's (1993) dialectical behavior therapy for treating borderline personality disorder employs mindfulness skills as a core aspect of the program. Many patients come to treatment already having had some exposure to various relaxation techniques, ranging from Lamaze natural childbirth training to progressive relaxation instruction on tape, and find the concept of learning to relax familiar and plausible.

Diaphragmatic Breathing

I use this technique very often with patients because it can be extremely powerful and requires little investment of time or energy. Kabat-Zinn (1990) reported that when hundreds of patients who had undergone his stress reduction program were later surveyed on the benefits they derived from the program, the majority responded that the breathing training had been the most helpful element. Deep breathing is incompatible with anxiety, and people often notice a reduction in their tension level immediately. In addition to the beneficial physiological effects, patients also like the sense of control they derive from knowing that there is something they can do to help themselves quickly when they are anxious. I use this technique with patients who describe anxiety-related problems, including social anxiety, panic attacks, anxious ruminative thoughts, and insomnia. As I mentioned earlier, I also employ it if a patient is perceptibly quite anxious in session.

The technique simply involves teaching a patient to breathe

slowly and deeply from the abdomen. On inhalation, the patient should feel the abdomen move outward as the diaphragm pulls the air into the lungs while the shoulders remain motionless (Poppen, 1988). Tense people commonly breathe rapidly and shallowly from the upper chest, indicated by upward movement of the shoulders during inhalation. Kabat-Zinn (1990) recommends placing one's hand over the belly and observing the rise and fall as one breathes; if it is visible then diaphragmatic breathing is occurring. Typically in diaphragmatic breathing each inhalation lasts from three to five seconds and is followed by an exhalation of similar length, all breathing being done through the nose. Patients should be directed to focus their attention on the bodily sensations they experience upon inhalation and exhalation, so that their attention shifts away from anxiety-provoking stimuli at the same time that they decrease physiological arousal through the breathing.

I might introduce the technique by saying, "There is something very effective that you can do right in the moment when you are anxious that involves breathing in a particular way—would you like to know about this (or try it)?" I will typically demonstrate deep breathing for the patient, and then ask if she will try it with me. The abdominal area is one about which many patients (particularly females) feel self-conscious because of weight concerns, so it seems to help if I emphasize that this part of the body is supposed to expand during deep breathing. I might ask patients to count to four or so as they breathe in, hold for a second or two, then slowly breathe out, counting if they wish, and focusing on the movement of air throughout the body. Following Benson (1975), I encourage people to experiment with the technique by varying whether they count or not, or trying to focus on a word like "calm" or "peace" during a breath if they wish. I recommend that patients practice this deep breathing frequently for a few minutes at a time during nonanxious periods, so that they have confidence in being able to use it when arousal is high.

Many patients find this technique very usable and, when describing various difficult events in session, may refer to "doing the breathing" in an attempt to cope with the stress. There are few contraindications for use of this technique. Careful thought is warranted with patients who report breathing difficulties with a physiological component such as asthma, or psychological concerns about breathing such as a history of hyperventilation or anxiety concerning forgetting to breathe and dying. Kabat-Zinn (1990) reports excellent success with some of these issues in a more intensive program; in an outpatient psychotherapy I recommend collaboration with the patient and detailed discussion of any use of deep breathing and its impact.

Progressive Relaxation

Progressive relaxation training has its root in the fact that muscular tension is one physiological component of anxiety, and muscle relaxation reduces anxiety. Relaxation training involves sequential relaxation of various muscle groups until the whole body is deeply relaxed. There are two major types of relaxation exercises. One involves first tensing and then relaxing various muscle groups so that a person can compare the difference in sensations and strive to recreate a relaxed feeling. The second type is suitable for people who already have a good sense of what relaxation feels like; the approach for them consists of progressive relaxation only. Patients typically find the latter more enjoyable and have greater motivation to practice it, so I tend to rely on this version. If it is not clear that a patient really knows what deep relaxation, as opposed to tension, feels like, she can be asked to tense one muscle group in session, perhaps clench the fist, hold it for a few seconds, and then relax. Or the therapist can conduct a session in the office that involves both tensing and letting go, but thereafter the patient practices relaxation alone.

I am especially likely to use this technique with patients who have high general levels of anxiety, especially if they complain of muscle tension or are visibly tense and tight, and with people who have sleep disorders because of overarousal. This technique is more time consuming for patients than is deep breathing, so some motivation is required, but once patients begin using the technique they often find it helpful and pleasurable. I might introduce it like this: "I can really see that one way your anxiety affects you is that your muscles are tense and tight. Learning how to relax those muscles deeply can be very helpful when someone is anxious. It would take a little time and practice, but it might really be worth your while to learn how to relax more. Would you be interested in having us pursue this a little?" If the patient accedes, I will explain about learning to tell the difference between tension and relaxation and practicing relaxing all the muscles of the body. I then suggest that, if the patient is interested, we can conduct a relaxation exercise in an upcoming session and tape it for use at home.

Scheduling the exercise for a predetermined future point allows time for more discussion and an opportunity for the patient to raise any concerns. Sometimes patients are worried about somehow losing control and being overly vulnerable. Other patients feel self-conscious about how they might look in a deeply relaxed state. As with self-monitoring, the exploration of patients' concerns about engaging in certain interactions with the therapist affords valuable opportunities to illuminate various organizing principles. What does the patient fear may happen if she permits herself to be relaxed and vulnerable, relinquishing some of her ordinary sense of control? What judgments does she worry the therapist will make if she lets herself be unguarded about her appearance and manner? The clinician should investigate the patient's experience of these concerns in detail. From such exploration may arise material relating to earlier experiences with parents and other caregivers who may have taken advantage of the patient's vulnerability, criticized her appearance, advised and modeled constant vigilance in interpersonal interactions, and so forth. Depending on the nature of the concerns and their gravity, the patient and the therapist may elect to continue discussion and at least temporarily dispense with use of the technique.

If the patient's worries are not severe, however, and if she has built up a certain level of trust in the clinician over sufficient time, she may wish to try relaxation in the session. Such an interaction has the potential to be something of an antidote or corrective to earlier traumatic experiences as the patient's anxieties about further trauma are disconfirmed (e.g., Weiss, 1993). Often patients find it reassuring to be told that, in fact, they are in complete control of their level of relaxation and are free to stop the exercise at any point and that I will absolutely respect their wishes. If a patient is worried about how I might judge her appearance when she is relaxed, I provide verbal assurance that, although her appearance might have been the focus of others in her life, it is not mine, and I will be concentrating on how to help her relax. I might also ask if she would feel more comfortable proceeding if I turned my chair at an angle and looked away from her. Discussion of concerns, reassurance, and demonstration of flexibility about modification or elimination of the technique may help to build greater trust in the therapist and modify certain organizing principles, whether or not relaxation is ever conducted.

If the patient wishes to proceed with the scheduled exercise, she should make herself comfortable lying back in a reclining chair or couch, and office lights and noises should be adjusted to facilitate relaxation. Here is an example of a relaxation exercise I like to use (from Goldfried and Davison, 1994).

You are lying comfortably with your eyes closed, all parts of your body supported so that there is no need to tense any muscles. Just let go as best you can. (*3-second pause*) Focus in on the feelings in your right hand and let go of whatever tensions might be there. (*3-second pause*) Just relax. (*3-second pause*) Relax all those muscles to the best of your ability. (*3-second pause*) Relax the muscles of the right forearm; just let go further and further. (*3-second pause*) Just let go of those muscles more and more, deeper and deeper. Relax. (*3-second pause*) Now relax the muscles of the upper right arm, just relax those muscles as best you're able. Continuing to let go further and further your entire right arm, forearm, and hand right down to the fingertips, just relax and let go. (*3-second pause*) Relax. While you continue to let go of your right arm and hand, turn your attention to your left hand and relax your left hand to the best of your ability. (*3-second pause*) Just let go further and further. Let go of the muscles in the left forearm; just relax. Further and further relaxed. (*3-second pause*) Just feel the relaxation coming now into the upper left arm, those muscles also beginning to relax further and further, more and more. (*3-second pause*) Just relaxing, further and further, more and more relaxed. (*3-second pause*) Relax now both your left and right shoulders and feel the soft heaviness, the calm relaxation coming more and more into both your left and right arms, hands, fingertips. (*3-second pause*) Just let go of those muscles further and further. (*3-second pause*)

Now we turn our attention to the muscles in the face. Smooth out your forehead; just relax those muscles. (*3-second pause*) As you think of relaxing those muscles, you'll gradually become more and more able to feel the relaxation coming into them. Your eyes lightly and comfortably closed. (*3-second pause*) Relaxation spreading warmly to your cheeks, these muscles looser and looser. (*3-second pause*) Your jaws loosely relaxed, more and more, further and further. (*3-second pause*) Feel the relaxation moving calmly into your neck, and down into your chest, as you relax further and further. (*3-second pause*) As you think of letting go, you somehow are able to let go further, more and more than before. (*3-second pause*) You're breathing slowly and regularly, letting go a little bit more each time you exhale. (*3-second pause*)

Relaxation coming down into your stomach now, more and more relaxed, just letting go further and further. (*3-second pause*) Relax, just relax. Feel the relaxation in your hips and buttocks, as you are resting heavily and comfortably. Further and further relaxed. (*3-second pause*) Relaxation spreading out into your thighs, more and more relaxed. (*3-second pause*) Deeper and deeper. Just continuing to let go further and further, more and more. (*3-second pause*) Relaxation spreading now to the calves of both your left and right legs, further and further relaxed. (*3-second pause*) Relaxation down now into your feet, further and further relaxed. Just continuing to relax, further and further. (*3-second pause*)

To help you relax even more, I am going to count slowly from 1 to 10. As I call out each number, see if you can relax a little bit more than before. Even when it seems impossible to relax any further, there is always that extra bit of calm and relaxation that you can enjoy, just by letting go further and further. (*3-second pause*) 1, relaxing more and more. (*3-second pause*) 2, further and further relaxed. (*3-second pause*) 3, more and more, further and further. (*3-second pause*) 4, more and more relaxed. (3-second pause) 5, relaxing your whole body, getting heavier and looser and more relaxed. (*3-second pause*) 6, deeper and deeper, further and further relaxed. (*3-second pause*) 7, your whole body further and further relaxed, heavier and looser, more and more calm. (*3-second pause*) 8, further and further, more and more relaxed. (*3-second pause*)

9, further and further relaxed. (*3-second pause*) and 10, just continuing relaxing like that. Continuing to relax further and further. (*3-second pause*) Now I'm going to count from 5 to 1, and at the count of 1 you will open your eyes and be alert and wide awake. 5 . . . 4 . . . 3 . . . 2 . . . 1 . . . [pp. 95–97; used by permission].

Depending on the use to which the patient will put relaxation, the ending, which directs the patient to be wide awake as the therapist counts down from 5 to 1, may or may not be appropriate. Patients who wish to use relaxation training for insomnia obviously would derive more benefit from an alternative. Another technique that may be added to relaxation training is guided imagery or visualization, in which a relaxed patient is asked to imagine being in a place that feels safe, peaceful, and relaxing. Using all sensory modalities seems to facilitate relaxation, so a patient who selects a beach scene as her favorite place might be asked to feel the warm sand under her body, smell the tang of the salt air, hear the cries of the seagulls, and so on. This technique is familiar to many patients and requires little explanation. I ask the patient if she would like to conclude her relaxation exercise by going to a favorite relaxing place in her mind and staying there while she falls asleep. If so, I ask for a brief description of the type of place that comes to mind. Beach scenes, gardens, and scenic spots by lakes or mountains are favorites, but the natural environment is not universally preferred; one patient selected Dairy Queen as her relaxing place, and the therapist should be prepared for a patient's individuality in this matter as in all others.

Conducting a relaxation exercise in the office might take 20 or 25 minutes, perhaps a bit more if the patient has particular areas of tension and needs additional time to focus on them. After the exercise has been conducted, there should be a full discussion of the patient's experience, including (but, of course, not limited to) the patient's perception of the efficacy of the technique. If a patient says she was not able to relax at all, she can be told that this is something to learn that requires practice over time for best results. Other patients will say that they did not hear the end of the exercise because they fell asleep. If they are planning to use the tape for sleep purposes, I tell them that here is some good evidence already that this will help them! Patients who are practicing relaxation to help with daily life may wish to sit up in a chair rather than lie down so that they can learn to relax without falling asleep.

Not surprisingly, anxious patients are particularly prone to performance-based worries that they are not doing a technique correctly, are failing, are disappointing the therapist, and the like. Reassurance, encouragement, and modeling a technique again all may be helpful in addition to detailed discussion of the patient's experience and concerns about the therapist's reactions. Occasionally a patient (particularly one with a dismissive attachment style at an early point in treatment) will prefer to use a relaxation tape made by someone other than the therapist because it might feel "too weird" to hear the therapist's voice while going to sleep. If this level of intimacy and dependence is an anathema to a patient, it should be explored to the extent the patient can tolerate such discussion, but I also suggest that the patient purchase a tape of her choice from the large selection currently available.

The efficacy of relaxation methods for many patients enables hope and confidence that their anxiety can diminish and that the therapist can be helpful in this process. The direct calming and soothing provided when the therapist teaches deep breathing and relaxation training may address idealizing, instructional, and attachment needs in a relatively powerful fashion. Learning techniques for self-calming makes possible a fundamental self-regulatory skill that was not available for many patients in their families of origin. Relaxation training is a helpful technique in general, but adding to the potency of this intervention is the impact of the patient's being given a tape of the therapist's soothing voice that he or she may listen to any time some calming is needed. Similar to Donnelly's (1980) suggestion that patients increase their self-calming abilities through imagining being in the therapist's presence ("the positive introject"), offering patients a relaxation tape can aid the internalization of self-soothing by way of a relationship with an idealizable therapist. Patients who are quite vulnerable to severe states of fragmentation (such as Sandy in chapter three) may especially benefit from having a concrete representation of a regulating other during states of tension.

SELF-MANAGEMENT

Self-management procedures, also called self-control procedures, refer to the implementation of strategies designed to decrease certain behaviors and increase others. People may wish to reduce such problematic behaviors as smoking, nail biting, binge eating or overeating, substance use and abuse, overspending, and procrastinating. Or the primary goal may be to increase certain behaviors, such as exercising, managing one's finances, eating nutritious foods, or studying. In practice, increasing or decreasing certain behaviors results in changes in the frequency of other behaviors, and usually it is helpful to focus on both increasing desired behaviors and decreasing targeted behaviors simultaneously. Generally patients have to be in the preparation, action, or maintenance stages of change before the techniques discussed here will be of use to them. However, it can be helpful for patients in the contemplation stage to be aware that a variety of techniques to assist them in making changes do exist should they ever desire to do so.

The sorts of problems that may be amenable to self-management strategies are those which have a short-term impact experienced as positive by the patient despite the long-term negative consequence. In behavioral terms, the reinforcement of the cigarette or the impulsive purchase is more powerful than future outcomes because of its immediacy. The experience may include positive reinforcement, such as enjoyment of certain sensations, that leads to increases in the behavior. It may also involve negative reinforcement, which refers to the removal of something aversive when the behavior occurs, such as the cessation of anxiety when smoking. Self-management strategies help the patient to take control of factors that can make it easier to perform the desired behaviors and more difficult to engage in the problematic activities. Some of the interventions discussed in this section include use of techniques described earlier, particularly self-monitoring and relaxation methods, in conjunction with additional change strategies.

Control of the Environment

Interventions of this type will be familiar to any patient who ever decided to quit smoking and threw away her cigarettes. The old adage "Out of sight, out of mind" sums up the rationale for many of these strategies. In behavioral terms, they are called antecedent manipulations or stimulus control, because they pertain to changing events or stimuli that are antecedent to the behaviors a person wishes to change. Many strategies in this category present cues for the desired behavior and remove cues for the undesired behavior so that the environment will be more conducive to behavior change. For example, a person wishing to quit smoking might rid his house of all smoking materials so that cigarettes and ashtrays are not cueing smoking behavior. If certain situations outside the house are strongly associated with smoking, such as drinking in a bar, it is advisable for the patient to avoid such situations until smoking cessation is more established. Social contacts with nonsmoking friends, such as dining in the nonsmoking section of a restaurant, help cue nonsmoking behavior. Alternative behaviors could be prompted by the availability of some sources of oral gratification; for example, the person might chew gum, nibble carrot sticks, sip drinks through straws, or suck on a cinnamon stick. The alternative behavior of deep breathing could be cued by posting notes to oneself in strategic former smoking locations reminding oneself to breathe.

Many patients seek help in improving their eating habits, which may include the wish to cease binge eating or overeating, to lose weight, or simply to improve consumption of healthful foods. Ridding the house of foods that are typically overeaten will remove cues for overindulgence. It is common for people to admit, "If it's in front of me, I'll eat it!" so not presenting the food to oneself in the first place is effective to some degree. Many patients have difficulty with portion control, and for patients with clinical eating disorders this is a considerable problem. One helpful behavioral strategy here is that self-management procedures are most easily implemented early in a chain of behaviors (Rimm and Masters, 1974); that is, it is easier to stop oneself from buying a large container of ice cream at the grocery store than it is to refrain from gorging while one is seated in one's favorite eating spot at home, container and spoon in hand. Similarly, it takes less effort to control the size of a portion before the act of eating occurs, so making up a plate in the kitchen and immediately putting leftovers away can cue appropriate portion control. Those who wish to eat snack foods but are concerned about overconsumption generally eat less if they dole themselves out a handful of chips or nuts in a dish and put the bag out of sight. Alternative behaviors will be prompted by the provision of structured portion sizes and also by the availability of healthful and delicious food. For instance, packing a healthy lunch and snacks can help a person at work all day avoid the fast food lunch and the candy machine.

Another way to think about some of these strategies is that one is attempting to increase the effort required to engage in the problematic behavior and decrease the effort involved in performing an alternative behavior. The person attempting to quit smoking certainly can leave the cigarette-free zone of his house and purchase a pack at the nearby gas station, and the patient determined to binge eat will find no shortage of available foods at local fast food restaurants. However, it takes more effort to pursue these choices, and therefore decreases the likelihood that the person will follow through. Patients describing the effectiveness of this strategy note that they considered engaging in the target-problem behavior but "it was too much hassle" or "I just didn't want to bother." It is helpful if conditions can be arranged so that alternative behaviors are no hassle at all and that with minimal effort a healthier choice is available. That increased effort is required to obtain the craved item also allows a delay to be interposed between the impulse and the action, giving the person time to weigh the pros and cons of various choices. Denial and disavowal of one's actual intention and behavior become less probable.

That delay can be used for cognitive processing suggests one strategy for controlling antecedent conditions that involves modifying the patient's internal environment, not merely the external one. We are discussing problems that become more tenacious because reinforcement for the problem behavior is usually immediate, whereas reinforcement for the healthier behavior is delayed. Patients can profit from cognitive strategies designed to bridge this gap. For example, they can remind themselves of the benefits to be derived from adhering to their change program, and counter rationalizations such as, "I'll have just one," with more realistic self-statements. They can also reinforce themselves for their positive changes with self-congratulatory internal statements. Doing so not only helps counter the reinforcing effects of the undesired behavior but also strengthens the likelihood that one will treat oneself in an encouraging and nurturing manner rather than a berating one.

Controlling internal and external antecedent conditions can be extremely helpful, and patients are sometimes amazed that they have been able to be so effective in making changes using these strategies. However, these techniques are not magical. Patients need sufficient motivation and commitment to change so that they will take the trouble of implementing these tactics in advance and then resolve to persevere in their program. Patients whose lives are barren of a variety of sources of reinforcement or whose negative affective states are intense and unameliorated may not find environmental control to be very beneficial. In behavioral terms, an establishing operation is an event that changes the value of a stimulus as a reinforcer. Certain patients may require the establishing operations of increased affect tolerance or more positive engagement with the world if the reinforcing value of alcohol or pornography is to change.

The Premack Principle

Another way that patients can use principles of reinforcement to help them make positive changes is by implementing the Premack principle (Premack, 1959)—making a preferred behavior contingent on performing a less preferred behavior. Parents use the Premack principle when they tell a child that he must finish his dinner before eating dessert. The idea is that a lower probability behavior will become more likely if its occurrence permits a preferred behavior that functions as a positive reinforcer. Many people intuitively use this idea and reward themselves with social activities after they have completed their studying, or do Saturday chores before playing golf. However, many people have a great deal of difficulty in budgeting time, organizing, and figuring out a way to accomplish necessary although not enthralling tasks. Consequences for such problems may be quite serious for some patients, including potential school failure, loss of employment, and credit difficulties. The clinician working with such a patient might collaborate on the need to increase adaptive task-related behaviors by suggesting that one way to do this is to link the target behavior to a preferred activity in a "when . . . then" manner—"When I finish paying my bills, then I can see what my friends are up to" or "When I complete my two hours of studying per night, then I can check my e-mail."

Social Support

The social support for positive changes that can be supplied by friends, family, and members of self-help organizations can be an integral part of a self-management program. Patients may find it helpful to spend time with others who already engage in the alternative behaviors they are trying to strengthen, as in my earlier suggestion that someone quitting smoking would do well to pursue social activities with nonsmoking friends who help to cue the alternative behavior. People also benefit from embarking on a change program with a "buddy" who is also working to make changes; one study found that being paired up with a buddy doubled the chances that a person would successfully quit smoking (West, Edwards, and Hajek, 1998). Such an activity partner positively reinforces changes in the other. If one's motivation flags, the sense of responsibility toward the partner may be sufficient to keep the positive behavior up, as in "I really didn't feel like exercising today, but she was expecting me at the gym at the usual time" or "I wanted a cigarette so badly, but if I had one he might slip too." If such support is not available with any friends or acquaintances of the patient, he or she might pursue the option or finding a virtual partner through internet sites organized around changing particular behaviors.

The contributions of various organizations should also be considered. Organizations such as Weight Watchers and 12-step programs afford the benefit of contact with people who are working toward solving, or have successfully overcome, the problem on which the patient is working. From a behavioral perspective, such groups offer the opportunity for modeling, or imitative learning. A large literature supports the importance of live or symbolic modeling for learning and indicates that modeling is most effective when the learner can identify with the models' determined efforts to overcome problems rather than models who seem so perfect that their experience is perceived as irrelevant (e.g., Kazdin, 1973). These organizations encourage frank sharing of experiences, which enable members to think, "If she could do it, I can do it." For instance, many 12-step group meetings begin with a member's recounting her substance-abuse career, including a detailed disquisition of the regrettable acts she may have committed while under the influence. From a self psychology perspective, a combination of idealizing, instructional, and twinship experiences might be provided from interactions with sponsors, leaders, and fellow members.

Goal Setting

Goal setting is a remarkably effective intervention, which I first discovered a number of years ago when I was conducting research on the effectiveness of group treatment for bulimia. Very little was known at that time about treatment for this disorder, so my colleagues and I tried a number of ideas, one being to check in with each group member at every meeting about the goal she wished to work on for that week. Goals might be decreasing eating disordered behaviors, such as binge eating or vomiting one less time than usual, or increasing healthy behaviors such as exercising. To my surprise, goal setting was considered one of the most effective interventions by group participants. In addition to the social-support component of publicly committing to peers that one will change, members found it an absolute revelation that achieving small weekly goals was possible and, moreover, that such accomplishment over time could lead to recovery from an eating disorder. Most of these patients had felt quite helpless and hopeless about their disorder prior to the group, and, when they thought of the possibility of changing, they assumed that it would have to be total and complete. Unable to envision a normal relationship with food, these patients felt quite discouraged at prospects for change.

I found the work of Bandura (1977) to be very helpful in understanding my patients' experiences with goal setting. Bandura proposes that psychological procedures of diverse forms serve to create and strengthen expectations of personal efficacy, that is, expectations that one is capable of successful performance of certain behaviors. Such efficacy expectations affect whether or not people will even attempt to cope with a particular situation and how long and effortfully they will persist in doing so. Bandura suggests that individuals develop expectations of personal efficacy by drawing from four sources of information: their actual performance accomplishments, vicarious experience or modeling, verbal persuasion, and emotional arousal. The most potent source, however, is one's actual performance accomplishments. Successes raise efficacy expectations, and repeated failures lower them, particularly when the failures occur early in the sequence of events. Some implications for treatment that I draw from this work are that patients will benefit from the construction of conditions that facilitate success experiences of personal mastery that gradually can supplant previous experiences of failure. The therapist, as a presumably trusted and credible authority, may be able to raise efficacy expectations through verbal persuasion and encouragement and, in some circumstances, by offering techniques to decrease physiological arousal. Such procedures may enable a patient whose self-efficacy is initially quite low to feel motivated enough to initiate some new behaviors.

The idea that one can set short-term goals, intermediate goals, and long-term goals may not represent an epiphany for every patient, but the dichotomous thinking about change shown by my group members with bulimia is common. Decades of research on motivation and goal setting have shown that goals help people to direct their attention to goal-relevant activities (both cognitively and behaviorally) and increase the energy and persistence with which these activities are approached (e.g., Locke and Latham, 2002). Many patients can benefit from therapeutic assistance with goal setting. This has been recognized by Gedo (1988), who, discussing a patient who had incompatible plans for accomplishing various goals, states that the role of the analyst includes offering regular reminders about the need to reconcile wishes with goals consistently ("unification"): "Therapeutic activity of this kind amounts to teaching people how to plan goal-directed behavior" (p. 223).

When a patient is discussing a wish to change something, the therapist can ask what his goal might be and perhaps help him organize longer and shorter range goals. For instance, an out of shape patient might set a long term goal of running a marathon next year, with weekly training goals. The clinician can encourage both specificity and achievability. Specificity is essential in helping to translate vague aspirations into genuine accomplishments. For example, the person training for the marathon would be encouraged to specify such details as days of the weeks and times of day for exercise sessions, as well as their duration. The self-monitoring that I discussed earlier is often performed in conjunction with goal setting, so that one can see one's progress in goals over time. Setting goals that are achievable—neither too high to be possible nor too low to be valued—is essential, in line with self-efficacy theory. Patients may initially set goals that are overly ambitious and then feel discouraged at their perceived failure, often losing motivation at that point and abandoning any plans for change. The clinician can stress that success at achieving one's goals is a vital part of a workable self-management program and that it is better to start small and build one's confidence and sense of efficacy first.

Another element of goal setting is the need for commitment to one's goals. Setting a goal should be regarded as making a contract with oneself. Once the contract is made, there is no further negotiation until the next goal-setting period and there are no more decisions to be made. This commitment can help the patient to approach his goal in the same way that he might regard earning a living or paying his taxes; there is no point in being guided by the notion that he does not "feel like" doing these things at a particular time—they simply must be done. Excising the element of decision-making once a goal is set can help the patient to "just do it!" (barring emergencies, of course). Such a stance enables a patient to be undeterred by the effort required to meet a goal. It can be useful to inform patients that, as their new habits grow stronger, they will require less effort and in many instances will become intrinsically motivating. Consistent practice is, however, essential for this transformation.

Antiavoidance Techniques

Avoidance of threatening internal experiences by engaging in various defensive maneuvers is ubiquitous, as analytic clinicians are aware. The benefits of receiving assistance with such avoidance were demonstrated in a recent investigation into psychoanalysts' reports of what was most helpful in their own analyses (Curtis et al., 2004). The analytic intervention that was most highly associated with perceived positive change was "helped me become aware of experiences I was avoiding" (p. 183). Frank (1999) underscores the need for therapists to be alert to what he considers the central resistance demonstrated by patients—resistance to the initiation of constructive new behavior. As Wachtel (1977) pointed out, both analytic and behavioral clinicians have evolved methods to help patients expose themselves to anxiety. A number of behavioral techniques have been developed to assist patients with problems involving escape from or avoidance of anxiety-provoking stimuli that have limiting or destructive consequences for the patient's life. Some of these difficulties concern simple avoidance, such as phobias—a person with fear of flying may refuse to take an airplane and someone phobic of elevators will choose the stairs. Depending on the nature of the phobic object and how difficult it is to avoid, an individual's life may become cumbersome and circumscribed. A person with agoraphobia who feels unable to leave her house is an extreme example. Other problems entail avoidance of an aversive state of anxiety by engaging in another behavior, such as vomiting after one has overeaten, or engaging in obsessive-compulsive rituals such as cleaning. Such behaviors are negatively reinforced because the unpleasant state of anxiety is terminated, and thus the problematic behaviors are likely to occur more frequently.

One possible treatment for phobias and related problems of simple avoidance of a feared stimulus is called in vivo desensitization, or contact desensitization. This technique builds on the relaxation training described earlier, and successful use of it requires that the patient be able reliably to induce a relaxed state. The patient also must possess sufficient motivation to cease phobic avoidance and be willing to put concerted effort into dealing with the problem. This motivation is more likely if the phobic object is one that the patient would confront in the course of regular life if he did not take steps to circumvent such contact through avoidance; for instance, someone phobic about snakes who lives in a large city may not be bothered enough to deal with a fear so seldom activated.

In vivo desensitization requires that the patient place herself in the anxiety-provoking situation and call forth a relaxation response as an alternative to the fear response. This exercise is done in a graduated fashion, so that situations that evoke less anxiety are mastered before the patient attempts to confront the most frightening scenarios. Therapist and patient construct a hierarchy of fearful situations, perhaps 10 or so, ranging from the least to the most intense. The patient sets a goal of placing herself in the various situations one by one, while at the same time inducing relaxation through diaphragmatic breathing and muscle relaxation. It is important to select hierarchy items in such a way that the patient can relatively easily imagine herself tolerating at least the first few. For example, a person with an elevator phobia might choose as a first item spending five minutes in a high-rise building simply observing people enter and exit the elevators. A midrange item might be that the patient rides the elevator herself for a few floors before exiting; and a final item might be ascending and descending the entire span of floors in the high-rise building at a busy hour. The therapist can help to ensure that the items are indeed graduated so that the patient does not attempt overly anxiety-provoking items prior to the desensitization of lower levels of anxiety through exposure.

A technique used with persons who escape from or avoid anxiety by engaging in such problematic behaviors as vomiting or obsessive-compulsive rituals is called exposure plus response prevention. In exposure plus response prevention, refraining from engaging in the typical response exposes the person to anxiety rather than permitting the usual escape. This may be the only way to learn that catastrophe does not ensue in the absence of the dysfunctional response. Research and clinical experience suggest that avoidance responses tend to be very persistent (for instance, animals will engage in a response for hundreds and hundreds of trials once they have learned that shock can be avoided in this manner and will persist long after the aversive possibility has ceased to exist [Solomon, 1964]). The negative reinforcement of anxiety relief or avoidance is extremely potent, but as long as the avoidant response is selected the patient does not have the opportunity to assess the reality of the situation and to learn to tolerate it. Exposure plus response prevention has very well-documented efficacy in the treatment of obsessive-compulsive disorder (e.g., Jenike, Baer, and Minichiello, 1998).

With this technique, the therapist explains that the behaviors patients wish to change have become habitual because they effectively relieve anxiety, albeit at a cost, and that people can learn to tolerate the anxiety instead and to see that the situation may not be as frightening as they have feared. The therapist encourages the patient to refrain from the usual escape behavior the next time the situation occurs. Alternatively, if the situation is one that fluctuates in intensity of anxiety, a less anxious time should be chosen to begin with, as with the recommendations for in vivo desensitization. For example, a patient with bulimia who habitually vomits after an eating binge would be encouraged to refrain from vomiting the next time she has a small binge or wishes to purge after a normal meal, rather than starting with the maximally anxiety-provoking event of a major binge. A person who engages in cleaning rituals might attempt to avoid washing after shaking hands with one person rather than after attending a reception. Another possibility for titrating the intensity of the anxiety is to suggest that the patient set a time period and simply delay the usual avoidant behavior. The period of delay can gradually be extended until the patient feels that it is possible to refrain completely from the anxiety-reducing measures.

During the time period in which the patient is attempting to eschew the usual avoidant behavior, it is very important that a suitable alternative activity be available. Often this activity will be evoking the relaxation response. In many instances, however, anxiety is likely to be high, sometimes more so than the patient can overcome by practicing relaxation. If this is the case, I suggest two additional components. The patient might augment the response prevention with a cognitive intervention, for instance, by adding some internal dialogue aimed at decatastrophizing the situation. She can reassure herself that the anxiety will gradually abate and she will be able to manage it. Moreover, an active alternative behavior, perhaps physical activity or interpersonal support, may provide much needed distraction and assist with calming. For example, a person who habitually checks her stove 10 times before going out might take a brisk walk with a supportive friend who helps her leave her stove unchecked.

At times very serious clinical situations result from habitual reliance on anxiety-reducing dysfunctional behaviors. Some eating-disordered patients purge everything that they eat or drink, and many patients with serious obsessive-compulsive problems spend hours each day performing their rituals. For situations this severe, an inpatient hospitalization may be necessary to interrupt the habitual behavior. Many cases, however, can be successfully treated on an outpatient basis, particularly when appropriate medication management is also provided (Jenike et al., 1998).

Use of these antiavoidance techniques can be challenging for patients, even if the outcome is very desirable. Clinicians trained in behavioral procedures who fail to develop a strong therapeutic relationship will find it virtually impossible to persuade patients with severe anxiety disorders to comply with exposure treatment, and the process is difficult enough when a strong alliance exists (Craighead et al., 2005). It may be useful to consider how the therapeutic relationship can help the patient to confront anxiety-provoking situations. This assistance might include the actual physical presence of the clinician as well as using the relationship more symbolically and internally. Occasionally a clinician may feel comfortable accompanying the patient into a feared situation. Obviously there are many concerns here, including potential discomfort for the therapist working with a patient in a situation outside of the office; worries about privacy and boundaries; and issues of scheduling, time, and fees. Yet in some circumstances the potency of being accompanied by the therapist into a feared situation is immensely helpful; from an attachment perspective, the presence of the attachment figure permits a level of security in exploration of the world that is not otherwise possible.

For example, I was working with a patient who had an elevator phobia. As we devised a hierarchy of fearful events for her, we decided that I would accompany her on some elevator rides in my office building. Managing the logistics in this situation was simple, as we could begin our session in my office and then step right into the elevator and continue. Privacy was interrupted at times when other people entered the elevator, but we would simply discontinue our discussion of her shifting anxiety level until we were alone again. This patient had already demonstrated some capacity to confront her anxiety because she was willing to consult a therapist with a 20th-floor office, but she found that my presence was extremely helpful until her anxiety attenuated. In another situation, which required more investment of time than a single session, an analyst I know accompanied a patient with fear of flying on a short round-trip flight. This activity was obviously more challenging logistically than boarding an elevator and required that the analyst be willing to spend an afternoon flying with a patient. However, he felt that the result was very positive.

Obviously in many situations it may not be feasible or comfortable to provide one's actual physical presence to an anxious patient, but some patients may find it helpful to invoke their sense of connection to the clinician, in line with Donnelly's (1980) concept of the positive introject. If I think that a patient would benefit from this I might suggest that she imagine that I am with her in the feared situation and to think of what I would be saying to her. I might also tell a patient that I will be thinking of her and wishing her courage as she confronts her challenges. With some patients I might encourage telephone contact after the event (often just a message on my answering machine) so that they can share their sense of accomplishment and be assured of my interest; or they can let me know something did not go well and we need to strategize further. The phone call is also helpful for patients whose motivation to confront anxiety tends to dissipate between sessions because it evokes a sense of our collaborating to make their life better and reminds them of their commitment to taking some action.

Self-Management of Our Own Countertransference

One potential challenge for the psychoanalytic clinician using these interventions is a possible tendency to overattribute phenomena to internal causes and minimize the significance of environmental factors. Psychoanalytic training historically has emphasized that etiological model; moreover, such a paradigm may buttress our own defensive structures. We may have some narcissistic investment in viewing ourselves as more free and agentic than as to be strongly affected by environmental contingencies. Many of the principles underlying such behavioral techniques as classical conditioning and operant conditioning were first understood in connection with research on animals, and humans may be prone to dismissing the idea that their behavior might in any way resemble that of a pigeon or a rat. Stolorow and Atwood (1992) write of how strongly "the myth of the isolated mind" permeates our culture, and our ideas about our own functioning may be imbued with disavowal of ways in which we are affected by the beings and objects that surround us.

That stance may contribute to an intersubjective conjunction (Stolorow and Atwood, 1992) in which patient and therapist are similarly organized around overvaluing personal attributes seen as located inside an inviolable individual, with a concomitant dismissal of the impact of interpersonal and environmental conditions. Stolorow and Atwood note that, when the patient's perspective coincides with the therapist's own worldview, the patient's ideas will tend to be regarded as objective reality rather than as manifestations of the patient's personality requiring exploration. Many of our patients dismiss the idea that environmental contingencies affect them, such as the patient who believed that conquering his gambling problems was simply "a matter of willpower," so that he should be able to go to the track and refrain from betting, or the newly quit smoker who decided to "test" himself at a smoky bar. The regrettable results indicate that insufficient appreciation for external factors and an overvaluing of the potency of internal resources are not conducive to realistic change. It may be useful for psychoanalytic clinicians to examine countertransference reactions to the self-management ideas presented in this chapter.

ASSERTIVENESS TRAINING

Assertiveness training has been a popular topic in self-help books since the 1970s, and analytic clinicians might feel that this is merely a "pop psychology" notion. I believe, however, that work on these issues is extremely important for many patients who suffer from conflicts or skills deficits in this area of interpersonal relating, and that some aspects of depressive and anxious symptomatology may remit as a result of that work. Essentially, assertiveness training assists people to express themselves in interpersonal interactions in a manner that is neither overly passive nor too aggressive. Assertiveness is behavior that is respectful of self and others, clear, direct, and sometimes limit setting. Difficulties with assertion are very common in a clinical population. Many patients are passive and submissive in interactions, are easily exploited, do not feel entitled to refuse requests, and have great difficulty stating their wishes. Some underassertive individuals develop passive-aggressive behaviors because more direct assertiveness seem impossible, but the frustration of unmet needs leads to covert attempts at satisfaction. Other submissive persons have occasional aggressive explosions when their anger at exploitation can no longer be contained. At the other extreme are those persons whose responses are consistently aggressive rather than assertive. They may have frequent uncontrolled aggressive verbal and sometimes physical outbursts and attempt to dominate others in this way.

Problems of underassertiveness are fairly common in an outpatient psychotherapy practice. Discussions of assertive responding are also useful for those with an aggressive response style, but, in addition, those people may require further self-managment skills in dealing with overarousal. Lack of assertiveness is particularly common in female patients and an overly aggressive style is more frequently seen in males because of traditional gender-role socialization. As important as gender roles that proscribe certain behaviors are, however, it is also necessary to consider early relationships with caregivers. Assertiveness problems often stem from insecure attachment relationships in which the patient's own needs had to be subordinated in favor of caring for a parent. Adults with considerable assertiveness difficulties frequently retain their childhood sense that the other in the relationship has all the power and that it is dangerous to do anything except placate. Moreover, patients whose parents behaved in ways that von Brombsen (1999) termed "usurping" or "colonizing" may have little idea as adults that people can refuse to tolerate certain modes of relating, since respect for their personal boundaries was never anyone's consideration. (The *Star Trek* series' depiction of the Borg, a "hive mind" collective that assimilates other species with the directive, "You must comply—resistance is futile," resonates with the experience of some of these patients, and fans may enjoy using this metaphor.)

Typically a therapist will observe a potential need for work on assertiveness as a patient relates examples of current interactions that strike the therapist as overly other centered, possibly exploitive, unsatisfying, and so on. (Of course, our own subjectivity, informed by our family experiences, gender, cultural background, and so forth, will influence how we perceive some of these exchanges.) The therapist might inquire how the patient is feeling about such interactions if the patient does not comment on them herself. Patients may be willing to acknowledge some dissatisfaction (sometimes requiring permission from the therapist to do so) but typically express resignation that interactions must be this way. The therapist might take this opportunity to question such a notion and invite the patient to consider some alternative ways of thinking and behaving in relationships. Work on assertiveness with patients typically has an instructional component in which the clinician describes the differences among responses that are passive, aggressive, and assertive and suggests that assertive responses are best for getting one's important needs met in a way that is respectful of others. Many fruitful discussions may ensue, including elaboration of genetic material concerning the patient's attachment-related experiences and observation of ways in which parents interacted with one another. The patient's organizing principles concerning expectations in relationships may be directly illuminated.

In addition to education and exploration, integrative work on assertiveness involves detailed discussion of current interactions that the patient finds frustrating and has some wish to change. It is helpful to discuss typical scenarios and then to begin generating alternative responses. The therapist might inquire, "Now, what do you think you might like to say the next time Jane asks to borrow your car?" Possibilities generated by the patient may range from a fed-up "Screw you!" to the habitual acceding, but here the therapist has an opportunity to remind the patient what assertiveness consists of and coach the patient in verbalizing such a response. Some patients need much support and many reminders that they are entitled to act on their own behalf and that being "selfish" has its place. It may help for the therapist to model a response and ask the patient, "What would you think of saying something like . . . ?" The next stages of the interaction can also be anticipated, so that the patient feels prepared for the other's response to the more assertive statement. Patients and therapists who feel comfortable with the idea of role playing may find it very beneficial; the therapist could both model the assertive response in the role of the patient and then take the role of the other so that the patient can practice.

Assertiveness training is a powerful technique for assisting patients who feel unentitled to their own point of view and are overly inclined to accede to others' demands and requests. Depressed females are particularly likely to believe that others' needs matter, not their own, and to "silence the self" (Jack, 1991). Unassertive persons are a heterogenous group, and no doubt temperament is a contributing factor to their lack of assertiveness in addition to familial and cultural learning experiences. I suspect, though, that many highly unassertive individuals come from rather traumatizing environments in which they were required to take care of others and neglect themselves. In adult life they fear that self-assertion will result in abandonment or retaliation and are careful to renounce it, carrying forward the pattern of insecurity in significant relationships.

Use of assertiveness techniques offers patients two potent therapeutic experiences. They gain insight into and perspective on the impact that various types of responses have had on them in the past. This knowledge is particularly useful for elucidating wishes for mirroring and other selfobject needs that were not met, and the ways in which the compensatory strategies of insecure attachment were required in their early environment. An analytically oriented treatment will be significantly furthered by such discussions. It can be liberating for patients to realize that, although they internalized certain expectations about relationships based on earlier experiences, now they have a much greater degree of control over how they treat themselves and permit others to treat them. As one patient said, "It's so true that no one was really there for me when I was little, and my family is still the same. But now I can be my own ally, my own protector, and it feels so good!" Patients may benefit, too, from actually having a new experience in the treatment relationship as the therapist demonstrates respect for the patient's wishes and validates that he or she should expect the same in other relationships. Female patients in particular may find it a novel idea to consider the legitimacy of their own wants and needs in relation to those of others, including the clinician. This process probably occurs in most analytically oriented treatments, but assertiveness training provides an opportunity for particular attention on such issues.

A significant aspect of assertiveness work for some patients is the way in which they might use the relationship with the therapist to titrate their anxiety about behaving differently in various interactions. Patients often report that the thought of the therapist's encouragement, specific words, and overall validation of their right and ability to stand up for themselves were immensely helpful in enabling greater assertion: "I remembered what you said and I knew I had to do it" or, "I pretended you were with me, cheering me on." I have also worked with some patients for whom the thought that I would be pleased and proud of them was very motivating in helping them make some risky changes in other relationships. For example, a patient might burst into the office when I open the door, excitedly saying, "Wait till I tell you what I did—you're going to be so proud of me!" I believe this situation often represents a combination of revived needs for mirroring coupled with idealization of the therapist. As Gedo (1988) has stated, "The acquisition of 'know-how' is greatly facilitated if the holding environment includes an atmosphere of confidence in and even admi-

ration for the analyst" (p. 171). Moreover, a developmentally necessary and positive experience is that of others' pride in one's mastery and accomplishment. So I might agree, after hearing the tales
of increased self-assertiveness, that yes, I am very proud, think the
patient showed much courage, am so pleased that the patient is
insisting on the respect she deserves, and so on, all of which is, in
fact, true. Ideally over time the patient will also be able to feel
pride in her own achievements, but those whose life histories were
relatively devoid of mirroring may experience this feeling only
after some period of recognizing the idealized therapist's pride in
their growth.

SYNERGISTIC EFFECT OF RELATIONSHIP AND TECHNIQUE

The application of specific behavioral and cognitive techniques is
embedded in a particular therapeutic relationship. Although these
measures can be efficacious when employed in a self-help fashion,
much of their potency is derived from their meaning within a particular relational context. Some of these interventions invite patients
to share more of themselves and display greater vulnerability with
the clinician; doing so may represent an opportunity to disconfirm some negative beliefs based on past trauma. Receiving assistance from the therapist in regulating affect and arousal may
powerfully address selfobject and attachment needs. Collaborating
in the accomplishment of a patient's goals and assertive behavior
conveys that the clinician is deeply interested in helping the patient
have a fulfilling life and believes that the patient is deserving of it.
Freud (1940), discussing resistance related to an overly severe and
cruel superego, stated, "The patient must not become well, but
must remain ill, for he deserves no better" (p. 180). We clinicians
have many ways of communicating to our patients that they are
deserving of care, respect, and self-respect and that we are committed to helping them attain their goals for themselves even when
their self-esteem and motivation flag, but mutual work employing active techniques conveys the message powerfully.

Discussing the use of such methods, whether or not they actually are implemented, has the potential to illuminate important
organizing principles that had their genesis in early relationships
and continue to appear in the transference. Themes of exposure,
vulnerability, embarrassment, fear of failure and criticism,

submission to the perceived requirements of others, and worry about their dangerousness if one does not accede are but a few that may become activated when dialogue about active techniques occurs. As Wachtel (1977) has stated, "The interventions make a difference, but they make a different difference for each patient" (p. 139). I am constantly struck by the unique ways in which patients experience events; my patients have disclosed important concerns about my views of them as well as experiences in other relationships in the context of discussing these techniques, which I am far from certain I would have gained access to in any other fashion, and these insights have furthered our understanding greatly.

The introduction of active techniques into the therapeutic dialogue contributes additional elements to the dynamic system of patient and therapist, and the state of the relationship and the use of various techniques ideally can advance positive shifts in both. A degree of trust and confidence in the clinician can enable a patient to have sufficient hope and motivation to try something different. Positive experiences foster greater determination and strengthen the relationship further, making it possible for the patient to attempt more anxiety-provoking methods. Curtis et al. (2004) found that analysts' good experiences in their own analyses were related to the use of positive, active interventions within a relationship that was accepting and supportive. Although those interventions did not include behavioral methods, the analytic and the behavioral literatures converge in reporting the efficacy of treatments that include particular strategies within a positive relational context.

My explanation of various symptom-focused techniques and my arguing for their inclusion in many treatments may create the impression that use of these methods constitutes a large portion of my therapeutic work. Let me clarify that I probably spend about 10% of my overall session time using these techniques (and much of this time consists of cognitive work that includes exploration of genetic determinants). I regard these methods as extremely effective and important, but their use need not expend more than a small portion of therapeutic time. Psychodynamic clinicians may experiment with incorporating some of these procedures without concern that this way of working will supplant their usual methods.

These techniques must be applied with sensitivity, creativity, and respect for the whole patient. Occasionally a relatively simple application of one of these interventions will produce powerful results, but each person's strengths and psychopathology are unique. The intricacies of conflict and deficit, current concerns, and historical factors suggest that active techniques are most usefully employed in a flexible manner with great attention to the current treatment relationship and a patient's most pressing concerns.

CHAPTER SIX

Suggestions for Intervention with Specific Symptoms

RECENTLY I SPOKE TO A GROUP of students about some of the ideas in this book. They listened thoughtfully, and one earnest student finally said, "But this isn't a 'cookbook,' is it? So how is a person supposed to learn how to do therapy like this?" As I told him, I hope that this book can be helpful for such learning. The correct "recipe" for each patient will, of course, be different. Here I offer some general suggestions for integrating symptom-focused interventions into dynamic treatment with four types of symptomatic presentation.

Thousands of books and articles have been written about addictions, anxiety, depression, and trauma, and in a single chapter my treatment of the complex issues involved can be little more than cursory. I hope, however, that it will be helpful to describe the ideas and interventions that I find most useful in working with specific symptoms and to provide some brief case examples. My discussion of addictive disorders is particularly detailed because persons with this symptomatic presentation tend to be more ambivalent about changing than most others with symptoms. The lengthier cases that begin in the next chapter further illustrate the points mentioned here.

ADDICTIVE DISORDERS

People with addictive disorders face a terrible dilemma. The substance or activity on which they rely for self-restoration is harmful to overall physical and mental health, so that what is experienced as a lifeline is also a destroyer. People deal with this conundrum in various ways: popular strategies include minimizing the nature of the addiction ("I can quit any time" or "I don't drink any more than my friends"), the potential severity of the consequences ("My uncle Bill smoked all his life and died at 95"), or both. Persons with addictions who have moved somewhat beyond this precontemplation stage of change might alleviate their anxiety with vague thoughts of quitting their addiction "someday." I believe that it takes great courage for someone to admit being in the throes of an addiction with potentially very serious consequences and to decide to make a change. Addictive behavior represents an attempt to manage painful self-states by engaging in certain activities, and successful treatment requires that we assist patients to confront and tolerate affects rather than avoid them through addictive behavior. This section focuses on ways in which symptom-focused dynamic psychotherapy is helpful to patients with addictions by increasing insight, building affect regulation, and facilitating action.

Patients preparing to change addictive behaviors are considering letting go an object or activity that has served an extremely important function for them. As I described in chapter one, their addictive choice has been reliable, available, soothing or enlivening as needed, and has dependably operated to ward off states of fragmentation. Patients are understandably fearful and ambivalent about doing without what has become such a vital mechanism in their lives. They may be frightened that by giving up the addiction they will be left with nothing, will have no means by which to cope, and will be helpless and overwhelmed. A combination of relational elements and symptom-focused techniques is optimal for alleviating patients' concerns that ceasing addictive behavior will leave them bereft of everything.

The quality of the relationship with the therapist is central to the successful treatment of patients with addictive disorders. The attunement, availability, and dependability of the clinician are crucial. Addicted patients are considering or actively working on turning away from a major, if not the exclusive, source of selfobject experiences in their lives (albeit selfobject experiences that stave off fragmentation without promoting growth). Patients will feel significantly more able to accomplish this objective within a relationship that provides some selfobject experiences of mirroring and idealizing through the clinician's attunement and expertise.

The honest disclosure of one's involvement with addictive behaviors can be potent and probably occurs only rarely outside therapeutic circles (announcement of one's status as an addict is part of a routine introduction in 12-step groups for good reason). Revealing rather than concealing one's preoccupation with the addiction creates significant vulnerability and can be fraught with shame. Considerable empathy for the plight of the person with an addiction is a requirement for successful treatment. Obviously an empathic stance is desirable in any therapeutic encounter, but patients with addictions are less likely than some others to remain in treatment and work successfully if the clinician is seen as judgmental. Too often patients with addictions are treated with methods emphasizing confrontation of their defenses by clinicians holding negative and disrespectful attitudes towards them. It is undeniable that persons with addictions not infrequently behave in appalling ways when they are under the influence or desperately seeking to obtain their substance through any available means, including illegal ones. However, some therapists err on the side of holding a pejorative "us versus them" mentality; they consider everyone with an addiction to be a manipulative sociopath who attempts to con the therapist with a sob story. It is important to be realistic about comorbid psychopathology in treating addictions and to be alert to a variety of challenging dynamics, but the true suffering and desperation of these patients must be recognized.

I do not consider "neutrality" to be the most helpful stance toward addictions. I do not find it appropriate to be neutral about destructive behaviors; I think my patients would be better off without shooting heroin, bingeing and purging, and being alcohol dependent, and I am frank with my patients about these views when I feel it is warranted. However, at the same time, I recognize that they have arrived at their particular adaptation for a variety of reasons and that it has "worked" in some fashion in their meeting important needs. Rather than taking a neutral position,

I strive for one that I feel is balanced in which I can appreciate how the patient experiences the positive aspects of the particular addiction. It is important to convey understanding of positiveness as well as its problematic aspects. At times both can be combined in an interpretation like, "I can really see that throughout your growing up, food was the way you tried to take care of yourself, and it was the best remedy for emotional pain that you found. But then turning to food created problems of its own, so that now you feel preoccupied with bingeing and purging in a manner that really gets in the way of the rest of your life." In my experience, patients tend to feel very understood by such interpretations that indicate appreciation of their motives for addictive involvement, rather than only judgment and condemnation. Ultimately, having a more positive experience in treatment with a new object might open up the world of relational possibilities for the patient in other ways.

The role of insight in addictions treatment is often neglected, but I believe that it is exceptionally helpful for patients to arrive at a comprehensive understanding of the causes of their addiction and the function that it has played in their lives. Patients often enter treatment having only the vaguest notions concerning the etiology of their difficulty. They may experience their addictive cravings and behaviors as having descended on them mysteriously, seemingly unconnected to their life history or current circumstances. The therapist plays a crucial role in helping patients to understand that their behavior is meaningful, motivated, and related to a variety of vulnerabilities that may encompass genetic factors and sociocultural messages in addition to the patients' developmental history. The field of addictions treatment has been plagued by theoretical constructs that are both overly simplistic and polarized, for example, "It's a disease" versus "It's a bad habit." More nuanced explanations, however, enable patients to attribute some responsibility for the development of the addiction to such factors as inherited physiological differences in processing alcohol and growing up in a culture that portrays drinking as a key component of an appropriate masculine role. Such conceptualizations can help to diffuse the self-blame and attributions for the development of the addiction solely to one's personal badness and weakness common in these patients.

Particularly important, of course, is the patient's gaining insight into the developmental vicissitudes that may have resulted in a nonrelational means of regulating affects. Careful exploration of the selfobject experiences and level of attachment security related to growing up in a particular family offers a broad perspective within which to understand oneself and one's family, facilitates processing of painful affects, and provides for the meeting of some important selfobject needs in the context of the therapeutic relationship. A patient's understanding of core themes resulting from earlier experiences can be expanded to include parallels between genetic experiences and the nature of current relationships and stressors. Finally, the patient can appreciate links between addictive behavior and painful affect states related to earlier difficulties, with concomitant increases in level of awareness and self control.

The way in which insight and action facilitate one another is evident when we consider the symptom-focused techniques of help to addicted patients. A patient's awareness of his particular triggers for engaging in addictive behavior might be expanded by the use of self-monitoring in conjunction with in-session exploration of genetic material and current situations. Therapist interpretations linking addictive involvement to the need for affective regulation within a specific interpersonal context, such as, "You learned by age 13 that drinking could numb your anger at your father when he hit you," render addictive behavior more predictable and less mysterious. Greater consciousness of one's addictive patterns increases a sense of mastery and control over the behavior, which now is seen to be related to discernable internal and external variables. This growth in self-efficacy fosters motivation to change, and the patient views change as more possible.

Another component that can be added to therapist interventions elucidating the function served by the addiction addresses patients' fears that without the addictive behavior they will have nothing. After some statement taking the basic form, "You learned to do X in order to meet your need for Y," the clinician can go on to say, "You still need Y, and we can't leave you with no way to cope if you stop doing X—but there are some ways we can help you learn to manage your life without it." In the foregoing example of the patient whose drinking was connected with the need to suppress anger in a threatening family milieu, the patient could be told that working on alternative means of handling anger will be a focus of therapy, along with helping him feel more resolved about his experiences with his father.

Patients in the preparation or action stages of change may derive great benefit from a number of the techniques described in chapter five. Self-monitoring can help patient and therapist identify particular situations and affective states that result in vulnerability to addictive behavior; then the dyad can begin to collaborate on a program to reduce susceptibility. Such a plan will typically involve self-management techniques for controlling the environment so that greater effort is required to engage in the addictive behavior and a healthier alternative is readily available. The therapist may suggest ways to modify the patient's internal environment, such as the patient's reminding him of the benefits to be derived from sticking to the change program. Setting goals related to the addictive behavior that are moderately difficult but achievable will help keep the patient's sense of efficacy high. Enlisting social support from significant others, friends, and self-help groups can be of great benefit, in addition to the support of the therapist. Certain affect states that a patient finds troublesome and has attempted to manage through the addictive behavior may require special attention. Common issues include anxiety, anger, depression, panic at being alone, and unresolved trauma.

Patients with addictions seem to have "need" beliefs, such as that they cannot stand their affective state and they "need" to engage in the addiction (Beck et al., 1993). I have already mentioned that patients may require assistance in generating and following through on alternative responses to various difficult emotional states that give rise to a craving for the addictive experience, but the craving itself may require intervention. Patients with addictions often feel helpless and frightened of intense affect states (as described by Krystal, 1988) resulting from insufficient parental aid with titrating affects. Such states, including craving a particular experience, can then seem overwhelming. Patients may mistakenly assume that such urges will simply continue to increase until resistance is impossible (Marlatt and Parks, 1982). When a person gives in to a craving of high intensity, however, the behavior is reinforced by the reduction in tension and is more likely to occur with the next craving. Marlatt and Parks suggest helping patients develop an attitude of detachment toward their cravings, so that they can observe the waxing and waning of the urges from a more decentered position. It is particularly important to reassure patients that urges and cravings will gradually cease when they are not reinforced rather than continuing to build ad infinitum.

Relapse is extremely common in the addictions. Marlatt and Gordon (1985) have identified factors related to relapse that have considerable implications for treatment. In an analysis of over 300 initial-relapse episodes across a variety of types of addictions, they found that about three quarters of the episodes were associated with certain sorts of high-risk situations: negative emotional states, interpersonal conflicts, or social pressure. It is very helpful to try to anticipate such high-risk situations and to discuss possibilities for coping in treatment. In the study, stressful situations frequently precipitated a return to the addictive behavior, but whether or not an initial episode of relapse remained a single lapse or escalated into a full-blown addictive pattern seemed in part to depend on the person's evaluation of the situation. Marlatt and Gordon postulate the existence of what they term the Abstinence Violation Effect, or AVE, in which the person assesses the episode in highly pejorative terms as a violation of the self-imposed rule of complete abstention from the addictive substance. A cascade of negative cognitions involving the characterization of the self as a hopeless failure ensues and prompts further involvement in the addiction. Patients may describe such thoughts as, "What's the use? I'll never quit this. It's hopeless, and since I've blown it already I might as well go all the way."

Dichotomous thinking tends to pervade this process in which a patient has a sense of being good, pure, and successful while abstinent. This self-evaluation may be so fragile that it takes only a single puff of a cigarette or a bite of nondiet food to shift the self-evaluation from all good to all bad. Marlatt and Gordon suggest helping the patient reframe the entire experience in a less harsh and moralistic way and instead view a relapse in the addictions as a common occurrence that should be seen as a learning experience. Patients can be taught to regard the episode of relapse as a single event related to some expectable stressors, rather than as catastrophic evidence that they will never overcome their addiction. Very importantly, patient and therapist can discuss the measures to employ following such an episode that will help the patient get back on track. A patient in A.A. may call his therapist, call his sponsor, and attend a meeting, whereas a person who has had a bulimic episode can commit to eating the next normal meal rather than starving and precipitating further binge eating.

A controversial issue in the field of addictions treatment inevitably arises when we consider symptom-focused changes: what constitutes an appropriate goal of treatment and in what time frame might this goal be achieved? Must the patient be abstinent from the substance entirely, or is moderation in use acceptable? Moreover, is it necessary to achieve abstinence from the substance, for instance in an inpatient facility, before "treatment" can really begin? This issue has been very polarizing within the field, and often professionals and self-help groups hold divergent views; the Anonymous groups insist that strict abstinence is always required and that a person is always "recovering" but never "recovered," whereas some professionals hold that moderation is an appropriate goal for certain people (e.g., Sobell and Sobell, 2000). Not surprisingly, many persons with addictions would elect to maintain some level of involvement in their addictive behavior, preferably with more sense of control and fewer negative consequences than they currently experience. Obviously we do not want to collude with a patient's wishful thinking that the relationship with the addictive object need not fundamentally change, yet, as Marlatt and Parks (1982) suggest, insistence on excessive restraint is not necessarily the solution for excessive behaviors.

My resolution of this abstinence versus moderation issue is that it is very individual, and that whether, in fact, a patient can practice moderation with an addictive object depends partially on the substance or activity itself and partially on the nature and intensity of the biopsychosocial vulnerabilities that the person possesses. For me the real starting point is not whether a patient accepts that abstinence is probably going to be necessary, but whether I feel I can usefully conduct outpatient treatment given the current state of the patient. Sometimes a patient is so immersed in the addictive behavior that it interferes too greatly with outpatient treatment, and she misses appointments, shows up high or hung over, and lacks the cognitive functioning necessary to benefit from such treatment. In that case, following a brief initial trial of outpatient therapy, the clinician would offer a recommendation that outpatient treatment is insufficient at this time and the patient requires a more intensive intervention such as inpatient rehab or a day program. The patient may or may not accept such a recommendation, but possibly the clear statement from the clinician that the addictive behavior is severe enough to preclude outpatient treatment will have an impact. Many other patients with active addictions, however, can engage in outpatient psychotherapy very usefully and would not be likely to contemplate or actualize any changes in their addictive behaviors unless this work continued over time.

The clinician can inquire as to the patient's goals concerning the addiction. If the patient wishes to abstain completely from the addiction, it is clear that treatment should proceed toward this goal. If, however, the patient's goal is to limit the addiction without giving it up entirely, I suggest working toward the goal the patient sets and assessing progress. The clinician can suggest to the patient that setting specific behavioral goals will be most helpful for motivating and evaluating progress. For instance, if a patient states that he would like to "cut back" on his drinking, I will ask him to define what cutting back means for him: how many times in a week is it acceptable to drink and how many drinks on each occasion would represent successful cutting back? The patient's use of regular self-monitoring will stimulate specific, rather than vague, discussions concerning the addictive behavior. A patient may prefer to believe that he is successfully reducing his drinking, but record keeping means confronting the reality of day-by-day behavior. A strength of this approach of accepting the patient's goal and evaluating progress toward it is that the evidence of trying and failing to be moderate is much more salient for a patient than any of the therapist's directives concerning abstinence. Patients are often much more willing to accept that they must refrain entirely from the addiction after they have experienced their inability to limit or control use even after a concerted effort to do so. The therapist, of course, must be able to work wholeheartedly toward the patient's goal rather than sit back and watch the patient fail while thinking, "I knew it!"

The therapist's countertransference issues may become quite activated concerning an addicted patient's symptomatic behavior and choice of goals. Many clinicians come from backgrounds in which a parent or other family member's addiction had a significant negative impact on family life, and strong feelings may be evoked in response to a patient with a similar addictive pattern. For example, a therapist with an alcoholic mother who never accepted treatment may find herself having an intensely angry reaction when an alcohol-dependent patient informs her that he really does not want to give up drinking. In addition, numerous clinicians have struggled or continue to struggle with various addictive behaviors of their own. Therapists who have successfully overcome their own addictions through certain means, for example, abstinence and active participation in Alcoholics Anonymous, may find it difficult to be at all flexible about the possibility that a patient with a similar problem may obtain more benefit with other methods or may seek moderation rather than abstinence. If the clinician is in precontemplation or contemplation concerning her own addictive behaviors, an intersubjective conjunction may result, such that both patient and therapist cultivate some lack of awareness about the true nature of their addictive involvement. Such an intersubjective conjuction is most likely to occur when patient and therapist share a certain defensive solution, such as concluding that neither patient nor therapist has a problem rather than that both do (Stolorow and Atwood, 1992).

Clinicians may experience intense countertransference when working with addicted patients in the absence of a personal or family history with addictions. The process of therapy can be extremely difficult, lack of success and relapse are common, and addiction can have obvious dangerous and destructive consequences for the patient and her family. An addicted person's central relational conflicts often include struggles around power, domination, control, and destructiveness (Director, 2002). Director views drug and alcohol use as a means of enacting and expressing unsymbolized experience; when such conflicts are no longer diverted into addictive behavior they will manifest in the treatment relationship. Bromberg (2001), discussing experiencing his patient's eating disorder as his adversary, states that a clinician may find himself hating his patient's illness and hating himself for failing to heal it. It is common for therapists treating addictions to feel impotent, helpless, and betrayed, and to experience patients' relapse as a narcissistic injury and themselves as failures (Gabbard, 2002). Gabbard states, "I have long felt that many therapists espouse the view that substance abusers are not treatable with intensive psychoanalytic therapy because those therapists do not want to face the painful cycle of raised expectations followed by deceit, disillusionment, and despair" (p. 583). Gabbard proposes that, if the clinician can find a constructive way to use the experiences evoked by that cycle, the patient eventually may gain insight into his relational patterns inside and outside the treatment; such recognition can be pivotal in making a commitment to behavior change.

ANXIETY DISORDERS

Most clinical practices include patients whose difficulties center on symptoms of anxiety. For some their symptoms are quite debilitating, and many patients lead lives that are dominated by panic attacks, obsessions and compulsions, ruminative worry, or agoraphobic avoidance. Even patients whose chief complaint is not anxiety may at times suffer from high levels of anxiety, often revolving around a particular event such as an examination or public speaking. As I stated in chapter one, anxious patients feel vulnerable and are prone to fragmentation without the active efforts to ward this off seen in addictive disorders (compulsions are an exception and function much like addictions). Anxiety symptoms are diverse and manifest in a variety of presentations, often with comorbid symptomatic problems and long-standing attachment difficulties. The vulnerability of the anxious patient with insecure ties to others may be transformed in a dynamic psychotherapy that strengthens the self and enables the patient to forge secure attachments. In addition, anxiety disorders may include two components that are particularly suited to some active symptom-focused interventions: physiological arousal, and irrational cognitions. Moreover, anxiety problems that also involve behavioral avoidance may be addressed with specific techniques. Psychotherapy outcome research has shown that use of such techniques with specific anxiety disorders produces long-lasting, successful results even in brief treatment (Westen et al., 2004).

That physiological overarousal interferes with optimal functioning in a variety of ways has long been known by performers worrying about "stage fright" and students hoping that they will not suffer impairing levels of test anxiety. The importance of regulation of such overarousal has increasingly been recognized in the field of mental health. For example, one of the five motivational systems discussed by Lichtenberg (1989) is physiological regulation. Gottman (1994) has found that conflictual marital interactions are much more likely to result in poor outcomes if one or both partners become "flooded" with overarousal. Memory, concentration, the ability to speak fluently, judgment, and impulse control are all affected when anxiety is too high. Moreover, people find the subjective experience of such anxiety and impairment to be quite aversive. Diaphragmatic breathing and relaxation training are particularly useful techniques for patients who suffer from physiological overanxiety.

The cognitive component of anxiety disorders often requires intervention as well. As an anxious patient of mind commented recently, "I did the breathing, and I could tell that my heart rate was getting lower—but it didn't matter much because I still had all these thoughts!" Anxiety disorders typically include negative thoughts surrounding potential future catastrophes. The combination of certain types of thoughts with physiological overarousal can be particularly deleterious, as in panic disorder, which seems to entail misinterpretation of somatic events as potentially disastrous and a physical reaction is mistaken for an imminent heart attack or other possibly fatal situation. Although the fight-or-flight response is being activated by the perception of something that threatens the self, "there is no place to run and no one to fight" (Borkovec, 2002, p. 76). The capacity to evaluate potential threats more realistically rather than catastrophically is necessary to avoid a continual state of physiological and mental overreactivity. Cognitive therapy is specifically tailored to enable individuals to employ a more rational and evidence-based approach to fearful situations.

The use of cognitive interventions to help patients process information in less catastrophizing ways need not be limited to panic attacks or phobias. I treated a patient who was prone to experience her most intense anxiety in the context of an intimate relationship with a man. This patient's father was extremely narcissistic, was often rageful, and displayed dismissive contempt for others and their needs. Her mother was very affectively labile and often exuded uncontained misery in the context of the marital relationship. Not surprisingly, the patient found intimate relationships to be quite anxiety provoking. She began a new relationship with a boyfriend who was rather critical and lacking in warmth, and the patient commented, "I feel as I did with my father—he doesn't like me; he doesn't want me around. I'm always monitoring our closeness and his mood, but if we're three feet apart I feel so disconnected. In every relationship with a man I feel like my mother—needy and anxious!" This patient's tormenting insecurity when her attachment needs became activated required long-term treatment. Nonetheless, she also found some cognitive interventions useful in helping her manage the acute anxiety she experienced when she and her boyfriend spent time together and particularly after he left. She would be assailed by worries that he did not really like her and that he wanted to be apart. She would remind herself, "It's OK. It's not that he doesn't like me—he likes me, *and* he has to do laundry." Reassuring herself of the ongoing connection and the many other reasons besides dislike of her that would motivate her new boyfriend to go to his own apartment helped this patient's anxiety stay at a manageable enough level to permit her to explore this relationship more fully.

Finally, many of those with anxiety disorders attempt to cope with the aversive experience of anxiety by avoiding situations that are perceived to be threatening. Behavioral avoidance, such as that seen in specific phobias or agoraphobia, may result in considerable restriction of activities. Much of the greatest life impairment and dysfunction seen in anxiety disorders occurs when anxious individuals attempt to reduce their distress by avoiding large sectors of life outside their homes. In addition to the need to decrease physiological reactivity and catastrophic cognitions, many patients require assistance with overcoming behavioral avoidance through antiavoidance techniques such as in vivo desensitization and exposure plus response prevention. However, for patients who typically organize their lives around avoiding anxiety, the idea of possibly feeling more anxiety temporarily as they approach the feared situation can be very daunting. As I discussed in the previous chapter, a significant level of trust in the therapist is necessary before patients are willing to attempt this.

A patient complained of an obsessive-compulsive problem involving checking. She came from a family in which there had been much financial instability and parental conflict concerning money. As a young adult she was extremely responsible and conscientious, lived frugally, and worried about her financially precarious family members. This patient worked as an accountant, which suited her very well, except that she felt compelled to triple and quadruple check her figures to avoid worrying that they might contain errors. She also felt the need to check multiple times to ensure that her clothing pockets were empty when she laundered or brought items for dry cleaning, and to check on all of her credit cards and identification cards whenever she used her wallet. She experienced much relief from sharing these anxieties and processing the family situation in treatment. I suggested that she experiment with trying to tolerate the anxiety of halting the checking sooner. This patient had a busy life, felt quite weary of the time taken up with checking, and was very motivated to work on response prevention in this way. We discussed the level of checking that would feel realistic and careful to her rather than excessive, and she decided that checking her figures carefully one time and examining her pockets once should suffice. She also decided that an environmental change regarding her wallet and purse would be helpful and that she should carry with her fewer items about which to worry. She reported very good success with this program. She told herself that, when she checked her figures and came up with the same numbers as the original computations, that meant she was accurate and the figures error free. She also found that telling herself, "You've already checked. They're empty. Let it go," helped her to stop checking the pockets of her clothing. She experienced some additional tension as she stopped her usual anxiety-reducing responses but found it tolerable and enjoyed the increased free time.

When considering any type of intervention, the clinician must be alert to the patient's level of anxiety within the treatment relationship at a particular point. Anxiety problems, like patients, are quite heterogeneous, but frequently an atmosphere of critical evaluation pervaded the family during the patient's childhood. Although this situation may have involved overt deprecation, in some families the interactional processes were much more subtle and were centered on the requirement that the child satisfy parental narcissism through perfect performance. Life histories of anxious patients are often characterized by significant deficits in both mirroring and idealizing needs. Identification with a critical other (Stern, 2002a) permeates the self-experience of many anxious patients. Not surprisingly, such patients may experience much anxiety in the treatment as they anticipate judgmental responses from the clinician.

DEPRESSION

Depression is perhaps even more ubiquitous in the typical psychotherapy practice than anxiety. As I noted in chapter one, some depressive presentations relate to unresolved conflict concerning self-strivings that are suppressed to preserve needed relationships.

However, depression is an extremely complex symptom with multiple etiological pathways. Other dynamic issues may be vulnerability to loss, disappointment in the self, and failed mirroring experiences. Many patients will respond positively to psychoanalytic psychotherapy with no additional interventions. Depressive symptoms can be disabling, however, and a patient's overall hopelessness and lethargy can undermine his ability to profit from treatment. Antidepressant medication often helps with depressive symptoms, but many patients do not wish to take medication or plan to discontinue it at some point. The use of techniques to ameliorate depressive symptoms can be easily integrated into a dynamic psychotherapy and may enable patients to feel a greater sense of being in control than they experience using medication. I rely primarily on three types of active interventions with my depressed patients: cognitive therapy, self-management planning for a balanced schedule, and assertiveness training.

A primary method of symptom-focused intervention with depression is cognitive restructuring. Beck et al. (1979) note the pervasive negative views of the self, the world, and the future that tend to characterize depressed patients. Such statements as, "I suck," "I'm such a loser," "I'm a nothing," and "I will never have a relationship" illustrate the global and absolutist cognitive processes discussed by Beck et al. For instance, a man in treatment for depression lost his managerial position in a reorganization of his company. This patient had been neglected in childhood and had an abusive father from whom no one protected him. The patient ultimately concluded that this all happened because he was not worth very much. In his adult life he worked hard in and out of therapy to come to a different perspective about himself and was relatively successful. However, the ways in which the job loss replicated his childhood circumstances were at least temporarily destabilizing; a weak boss had failed to protect his group, all of whom had lost their jobs, and in general systems issues impinged on his particular cohort in such a way that all felt unappreciated. He initially slipped into thinking, "It's all my fault—this happened because I have nothing to offer. I'm so incompetent no one wants me around." I continued to interpret the ongoing parallel between his current circumstances and his childhood and reminded him of his earlier assessment of his boss's deficiencies and this company's poor management. He soon realized that his personalization of the job loss was based more on childhood vulnerabilities than current evidence, and he began telling himself, "My performance reviews were excellent, and if everyone in my group lost their jobs it says a lot more about the company than about me." His usual level of functioning was restored after a few weeks, and he began considering how he might use this shift and his severance package to his own advantage.

Depressed people often have difficulty following a balanced lifestyle with a reasonable activity level. Many people become inactive, withdrawn, and lethargic in response to depressive symptoms such as fatigue, hopelessness, and poor sleep. Their effort to reduce stress and feel better by retreating tends to create further difficulty, however, in the form of disrupted attendance at work or school, frustration of significant others, and removal of sources of gratification as activities diminish. Beck et al. (1979) note the importance of helping patients to choose activities that can bring them a sense of mastery, as well as those that are pleasurable. Goal setting is useful here. Depressed patients easily feel overwhelmed but can be helped to include moderately challenging experiences in their schedule and warrant therapist support for attempting them. Such patients also may feel bereft of a sense of pleasure in any activities. It can be beneficial to inquire about what they used to enjoy prior to becoming so depressed and to schedule an attempt to engage in the previously pleasurable activity. Since some research suggests that aerobic exercise is as effective as antidepressant medication for relieving depressive symptoms (Blumenthal et al., 1999), I mention this to patients and suggest they consider making a priority of increasing their physical activity and assessing the impact on their mood.

A type of depression characterized by exhaustion, self-neglect, and overaccommodation to the wishes of others may result from a seemingly insoluble conflict between one's own self-strivings and the requirements of caregivers. Cultural expectations that women take care of others selflessly along with early attachment vulnerabilities combine to render women particularly at risk. In addition to the important exploration of early and current interpersonal issues, some focus on assertiveness training may be very helpful. This training might be coupled with goal setting about scheduled activities that are enjoyable as well as much support and permission-giving from the clinician about the importance of treating oneself well. Finally, cognitive work examining the catastrophic cognitions patients may experience at the prospect of being "self-ish" may help them to integrate care of self and care of others in a more balanced fashion.

Susan, a married female patient, sought treatment complaining of fatigue, poor concentration, loss of pleasure in activities, and a constant feeling of being burdened. It was clear that she was in the midst of a major depressive episode, and that in addition her life had been depleting for some time. Susan had routinely worked sixty hour weeks at her sales job for the last twenty years, was active in local politics, and spent a great deal of time tending to the needs of various family members. She described a family situation in which her mother had "martyred herself" taking care of her own mother and expected the same from her adult children. Susan reported that her mother was extremely negative, critical, and embittered. When Susan was younger, her mother would disparage her with remarks like, "That was a nice looking boy you had a date with—he'll never call you again!" When Susan reached adulthood, her parents lived across the street, and her mother checked up on her activities constantly. Susan's mother was remarkably unboundaried and intrusive and seemed to think nothing of entering Susan's house and changing her curtains, taking things Susan did not seem to be using and giving them to Susan's sisters, and retrieving gifts she had given to Susan. Susan married a man who had lived next door since they were infants. He had suffered a brain injury when struck by a car as a child, and his social and emotional development were quite compromised. Susan had felt a sense of responsibility for him early in life and continued her caregiving as his wife.

As we explored Susan's life situation, it became clear that she had never felt entitled to her own wishes and desires and that she feared others would be deeply hurt should she fail to comply with their agendas. She experienced tremendous guilt if she did not accede to every request, but she also took very seriously my telling her that I thought much of her current depression related to her sense that her life was not her own and that neglecting herself in favor of accommodating others was taking a severe toll on her well being. Susan needed to take a leave of absence from her job because she was no longer able to function, and this shift, in conjunction with twice-weekly therapy, seemed to help her begin to

gain more perspective. She recalled that she worked with a colleague whom others liked and respected, "and she doesn't give
every last drop of blood!" With my encouragement, Susan began
to set a few more limits on her overactivity, such as declining membership on a political committee she disliked and suggesting to her
husband that he put his dirty clothes in the hamper rather than
Susan's continuing to pick up after him. Susan's mother remained
her most difficult challenge. Her mother enjoyed cleaning, and
expected that since Susan was not working the two of them would
spend her abundant free time cleaning closets and washing win-
dows. Her mother would become silent or hang up the phone on
Susan when Susan demurred in response to her mother's announcement that she was coming over for a day of cleaning. Susan would
feel intense guilt ("Would it kill me to spend the day with her? She
might not live much longer!"). Susan, however, could also see that
her mother's expectations of her were excessive and that in general she contorted her life to please others, who would not do the
same for her.

Susan's sisters and mother had married inadequate men whom
they disparaged. The family openly discussed their dislike of sex
and spent a great deal of time cleaning. They made fun of Susan,
who ended up feeling that she was odd because she preferred sex
to cleaning. Susan was relieved when I told her that some of the
family preferences were unusual. Susan told me, "I can't get myself
to spend a day cleaning closets!" I suggested that she was tired of
a lifetime of "shoulds" rather than "wants" and that, if cleaning
needed to be done, perhaps she could clean for an hour and then
do something that she enjoyed. Susan responded very positively
to my suggestions that she moderate her involvement in disliked
activities and make a priority of doing things that she liked. She
greatly enjoyed the sense of freedom and solitude she experienced
going for a drive alone with the music turned up and found that
her mood did improve if she concentrated a bit more on her own
pleasure. We continued to explore the origins of Susan's guilt, self-
sacrifice, and lack of entitlement in her relationship with her
unhappy mother. My encouragement to take better care of her
own self supplied a needed sense of permission in a different relational milieu. Gradually Susan realized that no amount of sacrifice on her part would really make her mother happy, and she
allowed more space for her own needs.

SYMPTOMS RELATED TO TRAUMA

It is notable that, after Freud (1905) repudiated his original theory linking premature sexual activity to pathology, classical psychoanalytic thought minimized the importance of real events in the external world in favor of inner conflict and fantasy. One consequence was a tendency to doubt the verisimilitude of abusive phenomena recounted in treatment. Herman (1992) notes that a propensity to minimize and deny traumatic events such as sexual abuse occurs at a societal level as well as an individual level and that the recognition of the prevalence and impact of such events is dependent on a supportive social milieu not available in Freud's time. She remarks that acknowledgment of such events confronts individuals with difficult feelings concerning personal vulnerability and knowledge of human capacity to do evil; thus, recognition of trauma tends to be followed by a backlash and a redirecting of attention away from traumatic events.

We are fortunate to live in an era that has permitted much less denial of such terrible and common events as sexual abuse and domestic violence. Freud's (1896) original paradigm of pathogenesis centered on seduction as the cause of hysterical symptoms. A century later we appreciate the brilliance of his discovery; such trauma as child sexual abuse constitutes a very significant risk factor for psychopathology. With a turn toward relationships and affects rather than drives and fantasies, modern psychoanalytic theory can reclaim the insights of Freud's early work and of such pioneers as Bowlby (e.g., 1969), who proposed that the way in which we are treated by other human beings has a lasting effect. Trauma and the relational context in which it occurs must be understood as significant elements of developmental history that tend to be carried forward into the present by means of an individual's organizing principles.

The evidence is overwhelming that trauma is a major risk factor for psychopathology of various sorts. For example, one type of trauma, childhood sexual abuse, has been linked to depression, anxiety, substance abuse, revictimization, suicidality, self-mutilation, impaired self-concept, dissociation, somatization, interpersonal difficulties, eating disorders, and obsessional behavior (Neumann et al., 1996). Emotional abuse and neglect may not inflict the same sort of damage as physical and sexual abuse, but their deleterious impact has increasingly been recognized (e.g.,

Sroufe, 1996). Societal recognition of the potentially damaging consequences of trauma was clearly demonstrated following the September 11 terrorist attack, when counseling services for rescue workers and survivors were viewed as essential. And, although our increased awareness of the impact of trauma has generated a few excesses, such as simplistic connections between particular abusive experiences and pathologies, overall it has been immeasurably useful for patients and clinicians.

Survivors of sexual trauma constitute a heterogenous group, depending in part on such factors as the type of trauma, age of onset and duration of the trauma, identity of the perpetrator, and degree of violence or threat of violence involved. Those aspects of trauma, however, cannot be separated from the relational context in which the trauma occurred. The most serious problems seem to result from situations in which attachment figures such as parents were abuse perpetrators, and sensitive parental response to the disclosure of abuse perpetrated by someone else is associated with better outcomes. The overall relational milieu may be more important than the actual occurrence of a particular event. One patient abused by a sibling commented, "The sexual abuse was bad, but the way my parents were every day was much worse." The essential feature of trauma is the experience of unbearable affect (Krystal, 1988; Stolorow and Atwood, 1992). Very difficult events, such as parent loss, are not necessarily traumatic if the child is able to be comforted, soothed, and regulated in the context of another attuned caregiving relationship. Parent–child relationships such as those classified as disorganized attachment tend to leave a child with literally nowhere to turn for responsiveness; in such cases, dissociation is likely as the child must find an internal method of precociously regulating affects that preserves the sadistic but needed attachment relationship.

Defensively compromised functioning in the wake of trauma represents one pathway to symptom formation, as I suggested earlier. Two major recommendations have emerged regarding the treatment of trauma. First, a major contribution of trauma theorists is the suggestion that the original trauma itself must be dealt with in treatment (e.g., Herman, 1992). As Freud (e.g., 1896) posited in his early writings on abreaction, recollecting and articulating the trauma, and reexperiencing some of the original distressing affects, may be relieving and curative. Current theory highlights the need to reintegrate disavowed affects in the context of a supportive relationship (e.g., Cortois, 1988; Briere, 1992), as the work of Alexander and French (1946) presaged. The importance of a treatment relationship in which the patient experiences a certain measure of safety and trust cannot be overestimated. A recent study found that improvement in PTSD symptoms was associated with the establishment of a strong therapeutic alliance early in treatment (Cloitre et al., 2004). A second major recommendation regarding trauma treatment is the acquisition of additional self-calming skills. Cloitre et al. found that good outcome was associated with patients' improved ability to regulate difficult affects as they participated in exposure-based treatment. Trauma experts recognize that this process is inherently painful and destabilizing, and they typically recommend a phase-oriented treatment, in which much work is done on strengthening coping skills and self-regulating abilities before exploration of the trauma is attempted (Briere, 1992; Herman, 1992).

A number of the patients that I discuss in this book have trauma histories. Because traumatic experiences in the context of insecure attachment relationships and a paucity of selfobject experiences tend to produce complex psychopathology with numerous secondary manifestations of the original trauma, many of the specific techniques discussed here may be of use to trauma survivors, depending on the particular presentation. Later I discuss techniques for dealing with the two aspects of trauma most specifically associated with posttraumatic disorders: one aspect is the numbing and dissociation characteristic of efforts to avoid the traumatic material, and the other is hyperarousal associated with immersion in the traumatic contents. Some people may experience alternation between the two, described by Horowitz (1986) as the "denial-numbing phase" and the "intrusive-repetitive phase."

Dissociative disorders, such as dissociative identity disorder, represent the most extreme example of attempts to sequester intolerably painful material among separate elements of the personality. Trauma suffered in adult life—such as being the victim of rape, assault, a vehicular accident, war, or terrorism may result in posttraumatic stress disorder. Numbing and avoidance are common outcomes; the survivor refuses to speak of the event and attempts to avoid thinking of it, taking the stance "It's over—what's the point of focusing on it?" Possibly for some this avoidant reaction has few drawbacks and should be respected. Other patients find, however, that they feel generally numbed and flattened in ways they dislike, or they experience disturbing alternation between numbing and immersion in the traumatic material. Still others begin to develop secondary manifestations of trauma such as substance abuse in attempts to buttress their avoidance.

Many of these individuals would welcome therapeutic help in dealing with their trauma. In this area, psychoanalytic ideas about the benefits of abreaction converge with the behavioral concept of exposure. Approach to, rather than avoidance of, the traumatic material is necessary if emotional processing is to occur and if the stimuli are to cease evoking intense reactions. According to Briere (1992), trauma patients are likely to become very conservative concerning what they think they can tolerate, and one therapeutic task is to assist them in gradually moving beyond what they believed they could not handle. Obviously, this path is best taken in the context of a trusting therapeutic relationship; a patient who has some degree of secure attachment will feel freer to explore difficult material and rely on the therapy as a safe base for doing so.

The technique of Eye Movement Desensitization and Reprocessing (EMDR) is frequently used in the treatment of trauma, and a good deal of research supports its efficacy (e.g., Shapiro and Maxfield, 2002). Special training is necessary to learn this technique, so I cannot include instructions for its use in this book. However, it is noteworthy that EMDR, a multicomponent treatment, includes elements of exposure to the traumatic material. Patients are asked to call up vivid imagery of the traumatic scene. Jaycox, Zoellner, and Foa (2002) report use of a treatment called "prolonged exposure," in which patients recount their traumatic event for some period of time, often with multiple repetitions. Since direct work on trauma may be distressing and destabilizing for patients, circumstances in the patient's life, his or her level of functioning, and the status of the treatment relationship all must be appropriate before the clinician invites the patient to work more directly on the traumatic material. If the patient accedes, the clinician might ask the patient to describe the traumatic event in detail, with attention to visual and sensory experiences both past and present. Reactions to this technique must be carefully processed to ensure that the pace of the material is tolerable and that the patient's self-soothing abilities are not overwhelmed. The high levels of arousal that the patient initially feels should extinguish gradually, provided the patient is not retraumatized by experiencing something that feels catastrophic.

Intense immersion in the traumatic material represents the opposite pole of the posttraumatic experience. Patients may experience flashbacks in which they vividly relive traumatic events; sometimes they feel unmoored from the present time and disturbingly lost in terrifying scenes. Traumatic material may also be reexperienced in vivid nightmares, which can make patients fearful to fall asleep. Patients suffering from flashbacks may benefit from techniques that help them to feel grounded in the present. Paying attention to current sensory details, such as breathing, the feel of the ground underneath one's feet, and any sounds occurring in the environment can help to interrupt the frightening intrusive experiences. If flashbacks ever occur in the clinician's office, it can be very helpful to provide some verbal orientation for the patient, such as, "You're safe now, you're here with me in my office, and you're 34 years old." Patients can be taught to ground themselves in a similar fashion. A frequently recommended and very helpful technique is the internal construction of a "safe place": the patient visualizes a mental image of a secure refuge. This process is similar to the evocation of a favorite relaxing place described in the section on relaxation methods, but patients may require additional elements to achieve a sense of safety (for instance, the peaceful garden may require a moat and an impregnable wall). Finally, a patient might attempt to attain a greater sense of distance from the traumatic events, such as imagining that those events are being projected on a video screen while the patient holds the controls. Ideally, these techniques facilitate gradual desensitization to the traumatic material and foster the capacity to process and integrate the painful experiences without rigid avoidance or overwhelmed immersion.

After a patient has achieved some degree of resolution of the traumatic events, attention should be paid to the patient's cognitions about the traumatic situation and its impact on her organizing principles. Illusions of safety, control, and human goodness are often brutally shattered when one's trauma is caused by other persons. Survivors frequently struggle to make sense of their experiences, to attribute blame and responsibility, and to integrate the traumatic event into their overall view of self and others. It is useful to ask patients to articulate their views of self and the world before and after the traumatic experiences as best they can and to discuss how some painful new information might be integrated into the previous worldview in a nondichotomized way (for example, "You can trust people," reversed after an assault into, "Everyone's out for themselves and you can't trust anyone" ultimately resolves to, "You can trust some people").

Sam, a college student, sought treatment after a car accident. He reported that he tried not to think about the accident but since its occurrence frequently had had attacks of anxiety and nausea that would make him wish to go home and lie down. Sam was driving a friend's car and had been speeding. He and his friends suffered some injuries and the car was totaled. Sam described feeling fine before the accident ("My life rules!") and was frightened and dismayed at the change in his functioning ("I just want myself back; I don't feel like myself"). He found it very difficult to talk about the accident and made only brief comments such as, "It sucked" and then changed the subject. His usual present-centered focus was very disrupted after the accident, and he found himself having many thoughts about death, including that he could die and his parents could die. Sam was very fearful concerning his new sense of vulnerability and worried that he would "lose it" and not be "cool."

He gradually became more able to talk about the accident, with much reassurance from me that his reactions were normal and that he was quite stable, but that part of the healing process involved getting temporarily upset about going through a traumatic event. Sam and I worked on cognitive restructuring concerning his fears about his current condition and formulated some self-statements that his reactions were normal and temporary. He began to feel better, but commented, "It's scary not being able to shut my brain off from always thinking bad stuff." He was referring to images of the accident, as well as to the more severe consequences that might have ensued, such as someone's death. Sam was struggling to integrate experiences that, as Epstein (1994) describes, could be neither ignored nor assimilated. I taught Sam diaphragmatic breathing so that he would have an additional means of calming himself when he began to feel inundated by frightening thoughts and images. Sam was no longer avoiding the traumatic material as he had previously. Eventually his most disturbing symptom was depersonalization; he would begin viewing himself from an observer's perspective and feel that there was a wall between him and others. He also feared that he would never get over this perception of himself and that at age 60 he would still be feeling as troubled. I continued to normalize his experience as an expectable response to trauma and suggested that he do cognitive restructuring daily, reminding himself that he was normal and that he was healing. Eventually Sam reported that his experience since the accident of "living to die," or expecting that death was imminent, was shifting ("Death is going back to the proper place in my mind"). He decided to try to use the accident as a way to enrich his appreciation of living fully, "but without fear."

Another patient, Becky, had a much more complex trauma history dating back to childhood sexual abuse with two different perpetrators. She entered treatment in her 20s after her physician had ruled out organic pathology as the source of her abdominal pain and recommended that she explore possible psychological factors. Her symptomatic compromise involved experiencing physical pain while lacking conscious awareness of much of her traumatic history. Her history included molestation by a high school teacher, as well as a very problematic family situation, in addition to earlier abuse. Becky's primary concern early in treatment was the abuse in high school, and this was a major focus for a few years. Becky ultimately mobilized other victims of this teacher, and together they took effective action against him with the local school board. Occasionally memories of the earlier abuse would surface, but most of this material was quite dissociated. We discussed the pros and cons of exploring her childhood experiences, and Becky decided that for the time being she would prefer to leave this material alone.

We terminated at this phase of treatment, but she maintained sporadic contact with me over the next several years, mostly when she found herself experiencing a powerful attraction to someone other than her husband and felt confused. Finally she called in a panicky and fragmented state, and we began another phase of intensive treatment. Becky reported that she had become preoccupied with thoughts of the high school teacher and was carrying on a flirtation with her older, married boss. I interpreted the parallel between the dynamic with the teacher and the boss, and how in both situations she felt special in being chosen by a powerful male. I told her I could also see that she felt very drawn to reenacting this situation, but that I did not think that it was in her best interests to do so.

Becky was able to get more perspective on the compelling nature of this scenario and, aware that she had more freedom to do so now than she had earlier in her life, decided to exercise her ability to decline sexual involvement. However, her boss was persistent. She began to panic about going to work and ultimately quit her job. Becky got more fragmented, and began calling me multiple times a day sobbing. It became clear that the dissociated childhood abusive experiences were breaking through. Becky was unable to eat, felt frightened to leave her home, and found that even her sleep was being disturbed by nightmares from which she would awaken screaming. We considered hospitalization but decided to try several sessions with me per week and some medication first.

Becky became more stabilized and began to talk in some detail about her memories of the childhood abuse. Sometimes, as she did so, she would experience physical phenomena that probably related to aspects of the abuse; for instance, a couple of times Becky said in a frightened tone, "I can't move my arms!" The first time this happened I had to contain my own anxiety about what was going on but managed to respond in a manner that seemed helpful—I reassured Becky that she would be able to move her arms in just a minute, and that she should take several deep breaths. I also told her that she might be remembering something scary but that she was safe here with me. My reassurances did seem to enable her to feel more grounded in the present, and she was able to move her arms again shortly. As she processed painful memories, Becky also experienced a variety of other somatic symptoms, including headaches that seemed to be related to new memories' surfacing, and jaw and genital pain associated with various traumatic events. These symptoms generally dissipated soon after she felt reoriented to the present.

Becky felt constantly immersed in images and memories associated with the abuse, and she began to experience severe depression related to feeling overwhelmed, horrified at what had been done to her, and despairing about ever getting over her trauma. In addition to our frequent contact and adjustments in her medication regimen, we tried to construct a schedule of activities for her that would be distracting but not overly demanding. When she needed to escape from the intrusive imagery, she found it helpful to imagine that the scenes were recorded on videotape and that she could just "hit the pause button" until we could discuss them at our next session. She listened to relaxation tapes and practiced breathing. Gradually her most acute distress subsided, and we decreased our session frequency to twice a week but continued to process early experiences for the next year.

Now, four years after Becky's return to therapy, intrusive memories or nightmares are very occasional rather than continual, she has made a number of life changes that she experiences as extremely positive, and her overall functioning is excellent. When I told her about this book and asked her if it would be all right to discuss our work, she eagerly acceded, hoping that it would be useful for other trauma survivors. I went on to inquire if she had any thoughts about what we had done together in our work that had especially helped her, and she broke into tears, immediately saying, "Availability! You were always there!" Becky's security in my ongoing presence and responsiveness helped her to tolerate the terrifying and disorganizing immersion in traumatic material that ultimately proved necessary for her reintegration.

Standard psychoanalytic psychotherapy is very well suited to many trauma survivors who require a safe and supportive relationship in order to process traumatic material. Such patients benefit greatly from an expressive treatment in which their experiences can be discussed in detail. Secure attachment to the therapist will enable greater exploration of frightening material. Selfobject needs that may emerge during such a treatment might include self-delineating selfobject needs, as many trauma survivors have relied heavily on dissociation and may be confused about aspects of their identity and history. Patients whose posttraumatic manifestations revolve around numbing and avoidance usually improve with exploration of defensive processes and gradual exposure to feared material. Cognitive interventions might be considered as well. Individuals who suffer from overwhelming immersion in traumatic contents particularly benefit from the containment offered by relaxation methods and cognitive restructuring. The specific grounding techniques mentioned here may also merit consideration.

THE NEED FOR FLEXIBLE APPLICATION

I have offered some general suggestions concerning active techniques that I find particularly useful with various symptomatic presentations. Patients with addictions may find self-monitoring and self-management strategies helpful in increasing awareness and affect tolerance while decreasing addictive behavior. The functioning of anxious patients may be enhanced with use of relaxation training and antiavoidance techniques. Many depressed patients benefit from self-management techniques that further a more balanced life, and assertiveness training can be helpful as well. Patients suffering from posttraumatic states require therapeutic aid in confronting traumatic contents while titrating overly intense affect states; relaxation methods and specific grounding techniques support such a balance. Cognitive interventions may be helpful with all four of these symptomatic presentations. These techniques are most effective in a therapeutic context that includes a positively toned relationship with at least some degree of trust in the clinician and a clear recognition on the part of the patient that he wants to change.

The wishes of the patient and the collaborative evaluation by patient and therapist concerning therapeutic response to various interventions should determine what elements of treatment are attempted, continued, or discarded. The specific nature of each unique patient's situation and the individuality of each treatment dyad take precedence over the general ideas suggested here.

CHAPTER SEVEN

A Patient with
Compulsive Behaviors

WHEN I FIRST THOUGHT ABOUT discussing longer cases, I had some discrete categories in mind: different chapters would depict the four pathways to symptom formation, a particular patient demonstrating each one, or perhaps I would order the material by specific symptomatic problems as I did in the last chapter. The complexity of working with real human beings rather than general concepts has confounded all my proposed organizational schemes. The patients I present here typically have multiple symptoms originating in more than one pathway. They are quite varied in their symptoms, the level of need and usability they demonstrate pertaining to symptom-focused interventions, and their overall functioning, including self-cohesion and attachment style. None of these conceptual formulations, however, provide a useful heuristic device by which to differentiate one patient from another in isolation. Therefore, my discussion of the following four cases does not delineate neat categories, but it does underscore the complexity and comorbidity of psychopathology and the fact that symptoms must be understood in relation to the whole person who suffers from them. I hope this case material conveys some measure of the individuality and specificity of each patient, our relationship, and the ways in which I tried to tailor interventions accordingly.

Writing about symptoms, Freud (1917a) stated, "The main damage they do resides in the mental expenditure which they themselves involve and in the further expenditure that becomes necessary for fighting against them. Where there is an extensive formation of symptoms, these two sorts of expenditure can result in an extraordinary impoverishment of the subject in regard to the mental energy available to him and so in paralysing him for all the important tasks of life" (p. 358). The patients I describe illustrate the truth of Freud's understanding. Their symptomatic "solutions" to problematic self-states and insecure relationships often required considerable time and energy, which were then rendered unavailable for other pursuits. The resulting preoccupation, countermeasures against symptomatic expression, and secondary elaborations of the symptoms resulted in an adaptation that largely "worked" to keep potentially intolerable experiences in abeyance; however, my patients were left with significantly constricted lives. These individuals tended to avoid certain experiences of painful internal states and anxiety-provoking external behaviors and to overrely on their preferred means of managing themselves in a relatively inflexible fashion. Their development was compromised, and in some fashion the symptom both encapsulated and maintained the status quo.

Numerous possibilities for intervention exist in every moment of the therapeutic encounter, and our own subjectivity (including our theoretical preferences) dictates which opportunities we are likely to seize and which particular points we are prone to emphasize. As I reflect on my treatment of these four patients, it is evident that I tended to prioritize helping them to recognize and change their avoidant tendencies, whether they were escaping from internal events, close relationships, or challenges in the external world. Exploration of organizing principles leading to avoidance, such as expectations of mistreatment from others, was facilitated by a focus on transference, particularly in the longer term cases. I also concentrated on the ways in which these patients related to themselves. I pointed out excessive harshness and absence of compassion which I linked to the relational milieu in which they grew up, and suggested questioning these attitudes from a more adult and balanced perspective. Many additional foci would be possible.

As I once told a patient who sought a consultation with me and had many questions about psychotherapy, what I could describe to her was not so much psychotherapy in the abstract, but psychotherapy with me. I invite you to reflect on the following case material and consider which elements of my treatment are congenial with your own individual style.

The first patient I present is Ken, whom I treated in once-a-week psychotherapy for about two years. Ken had multiple symptomatic problems probably corresponding to at least three different symptomatic pathways. He suffered from severe anxiety, representing vulnerability to fragmentation, and relied on a compulsive behavior similar to an addiction to ward off fragmentation. This compulsion probably also represented a compromise formation related to inflation and deflation of grandiose strivings. Additionally, Ken had a bowel problem that perhaps represented a compromise between impulse suppression and affective expulsion. Limitations in his functioning because of his symptoms suggested a high need for symptom-focused interventions, but the issue of usability was complex.

KEN

Ken was referred to me by his marital therapist for problems of anxiety and emotional regulation that were not ameliorated by his antidepressant medication. Now in his early 30s, Ken worked in sales and reported having held a number of jobs that ultimately left him feeling disappointed in the position and in himself. He had been married for a few years to a woman several years older and considerably more professionally successful than he. Ken reported quite a bit of marital conflict and frustration. He said, "She's realistic; I'm a dreamer." Ken's most prominent symptom related to bowel difficulties involving urgency; this symptom dated back to first grade. He reported that he tried to avoid using the bathroom at school because it had no doors, and he was embarrassed about asking the teacher for permission, so he would be uncomfortable on the bus ride home from school. He also related having had great anxiety on family road trips; his father would direct him to use the bathroom before leaving and become irate when Ken needed to stop along the way. He had a history of occasional bowel accidents, in adulthood as well as childhood. Ken was fearful of being trapped in places without access to a bathroom, particularly the train and in traffic. The bowel difficulty created much life interference in his daily activities and added to marital tension. Although Ken's wife tried to be understanding about the ways in which he circumscribed his activities, she longed for the two of them to do things like take a cruise together, which Ken felt was out of the question in his current state.

Ken reported a very difficult experience growing up, comparing his father to "the great Santini." His father was physically abusive and would hit or kick Ken about once a month. The verbal abuse, however, was relentless: "He landed on me all the time, I was always wrong." Ken said his father never gave explanations for things; he just blew up. For instance, he would ask Ken to shine a flashlight while he tried to fix a tire and would yell at Ken when the task went badly. Ken was poor in math and his father insisted in working on his homework with him, but, when Ken failed to understand something despite diligence, his father would shout at him and blame him for not paying attention in school. Ken considered his mother "more laid back," but she could "get to her breaking point, yell and scream and hit me with a yardstick." His primary resentment toward his mother, however, concerned her passivity. She seemed not to interfere with or protest his father's domination of family life and mistreatment of Ken, and he commented, "She got yelled at all the time, too."

Ken related that in some previous psychotherapy he had worked on his issues concerning his father and had found it helpful, and stated that he felt better about his father now. He knew that his father had been abused by his own father. Ken was also aware that his father had hated his job for many years but passively remained "and took it out on the family." Ken read me a letter that he had sent to his father several years earlier in which he expressed his anger at the man "for beating me black and blue." He had also protested his father's psychological domination and in our discussion demonstrated much insight about ways in which the constant abuse had led him to be both perfectionistic and afraid to do anything. Ken reported that his father's expression of regret over his treatment of Ken had been helpful, but he still found his father very difficult.

Ken and his wife had sought marital treatment in part because he was aware that they had developed a pattern in which "she's always walking on eggshells, just like my mother with my father," and he disliked the notion that he might be recreating a similar negative dynamic. Ken reported that, like his father, he was frequently angry and that, although he had never hit anyone, he found himself "yelling a lot" and would at times hit a wall and other objects. He said that he typically got angry a couple of times a day and that often his anger seemed to have risen "out of the blue." I suggested that it might be very useful for us to explore those situations carefully and try to figure out what was going on. We discussed a recent event in which he had become angry because he wanted to go running and his jacket zipper was malfunctioning; first he got angry at the zipper and then at his wife for washing the jacket. We discussed the fact that feeling blocked in his accomplishment of a goal had been disruptive for him. Ken expressed interest in continuing to do this type of detailed exploration of distressing events and even suggested that he write some of these things down.

Ken revealed more of his marital issues. He was quite aware that he had been drawn to his wife Peg initially "because I wanted to be taken care of." He never got on very well with males, always found his mother more approachable than his father, and had usually dated older women. In a gender-role reversal of the typical pattern in our culture, he found the financial security that Peg offered very desirable "when I was a struggling waiter." Ken had many fantasies of an opulent lifestyle based in part on family tales about a wealthy relative, and enjoyed daydreaming about a million dollar salary, household staff, and the like. Peg's actual income fed these fantasies, as did her promises about the life they would live together ("She said we could at least *rent* a Porsche"). In reality, however, Ken felt controlled and monitored by Peg ("She's always saying things like, 'Do you have to get the most expensive entree?'"), as he had with his father when he was growing up, and made the connection explicitly.

After several sessions I believed that Ken was feeling comfortable enough with me to tolerate more specific inquiry into the nature of the bowel problem at present. He told me that he had received a tentative diagnosis of irritable bowel syndrome, but that he had not liked the gastroenterologist and had failed to return. His internist had prescribed some medications to slow bowel motility, which seemed to help, as did the antidepressant and anxiolytic he was taking. Ken reported that he made many bathroom visits daily whether or not he passed anything. He always visited the bathroom during transition times prior to the next activity or trip. Ken stated that the feelings of urgency were worst when he felt trapped and that during these times he tended to get "tunnel vision" and be completely focused on his bodily sensations. Ken also mentioned at this time that he had seen another clinician before me for one session, and that therapist had suggested that they do behavior modification to cut down on his bathroom trips and get him off his medication. Ken's response to this: "No way!"

Clearly Ken found the prospect of that sort of treatment intolerably frightening. I was aware that, although Ken had what I would consider a high need for symptom-focused interventions because of the constricting effect his symptom had on his life, the issue of usability was less clear. Although he wanted to feel better, he was not necessarily in the action stage of change about actually doing things differently. Moreover, he had a number of current concerns that he wished to discuss, particularly his new job and overall professional life, as well as his marital difficulties. His departure from the behavioral therapist after one session suggested that he would refuse an intervention strategy that threatened to interfere with his typical methods of coping with anxiety. I decided to suggest further assessment of the bowel problem, which his marital therapist was also recommending, and to concentrate on techniques that might help relieve some of his anxiety. Therefore, I planned to prioritize helping Ken with physiological relaxation and cognitive methods to reduce anxiety as part of an integrative treatment that would also focus on interpersonal issues and problems of narcissism. I thought that exposure-based interventions for his agoraphobia might become possible in a later phase of treatment.

Ken agreed to see another specialist, and it was determined that his bowel problem involved no organic pathology, which clarified for us that the etiology and amelioration of this difficulty related to psychological factors. We soon had an opportunity to focus on Ken's bowel symptom in a way that he requested. Ken had to travel to another city for a visit to his family and was very anxious about taking a taxicab. Riding in a taxi represented the quintessential "trapped" experience for him, including worries about rush-hour traffic and the fact that a stranger was driving. I taught Ken diaphragmatic breathing, with which he was already somewhat familiar from an anxiety workbook he had purchased in the past. We also discussed the frightening cognitions he anticipated experiencing in the cab, and talked about what he might substitute that could help him calm down. Ken decided that telling himself, "I'm in control, I can handle this," would be his choice. Following this discussion, Ken remarked that he thought he might need to be in therapy with me for a year and a half or so and that perhaps he could gradually wean off his medication. I understood him to mean that he was feeling more secure that our relationship over time would help him with his anxiety, and he could foresee the possibility of relinquishing some of his usual ways of coping as we worked together. My assumption was confirmed when Ken suggested as he left the session that maybe he could call my answering machine from the cab, and that whether I answered or not he could hear my voice and focus on telling me how he was doing. I encouraged him to call if he wanted to and told him that I would be eager to hear how he was managing.

Ken reported in the next session that the cab ride had been successful. He had experienced "a few bad moments of panic" but overall had been able to use the deep breathing and cognitive restructuring effectively. I had not heard from him since our previous session, and I asked if he had thought of calling me from the cab, as we had discussed. Ken said that he knew he could call, which was calming to him, but said it had felt fine to concentrate on using the techniques rather than telephoning. I did not process this revelation further with Ken then but found myself thinking that he was attempting to reconcile two conflicting relational themes—one of depending on another to seek needed security and reassurance, the other related to eschewing involvement because of the wish to escape dreaded criticism and control.

He went on to talk about the family visit itself, which had been predictably stressful and had included some confrontation with his father. Ken said that he had returned home "feeling triumphant" but then had resorted to a compulsive behavior he had not previously mentioned—picking at what he perceived to be ingrown hairs on his face. Over the next several sessions we discussed this obsessive-compulsive symptom in some detail. Ken related that he would become very bothered by the feeling that he had an ingrown hair and experienced a sense of urgency "to get rid of that bad thing." He began picking his face at puberty when he developed acne, which had cleared up only a few years prior with medication. Ken is a handsome man and his appearance is extremely important to him; the perceived ingrown hair detracted from the perfect image he wished to project. He reported that he could feel quite desperate about needing to remove it, going to such lengths as hunting for tweezers he had previously hidden in an effort to stop this behavior. Ken was also aware that he was most prone to pick at his face as a means of emotional regulation, particularly "to bring myself down when I'm feeling good." When I asked further about this behavior, he stated that his parents frequently cautioned him as a child that "if you get too excited you're going to go to bed crying!" Deflation of an expansive mood seemed safer. Ken said that he also thought there was a self-punishing element to his face-picking.

At about the same time that we were discussing this behavior, Ken reported feeling very disturbed about a recent incident with Peg. She had been sick during a visit they made to her family out of state, and Ken told me that he had been feeling helpless and trapped. At one point he grabbed her arm in anger and frustration, hurting her, and was then very embarrassed and upset with himself. I was concerned, although not surprised, to hear that tensions had escalated to the level of a physical altercation but felt it was positive that Ken was accepting responsibility for this behavior and seemed to be motivated to change it. We discussed strategies that could help ensure that Ken would manage his anger better, such as monitoring his anger level carefully in stressful situations, reducing his arousal through deep breathing, using strenuous exercise to discharge tensions, and removing himself from the situation if he feared loss of control.

I also interpreted to Ken that immediate action was his preferred way to cope with difficult feelings and try to get some momentary relief. He was quite bothered at this time by the face-picking. Now that we had evidence that his bowel problem was stress related, I drew a parallel between the two behaviors, saying that in both he felt intense urges to get rid of what felt like bad things inside of him. I had discussed with Ken in earlier sessions the possibility that the bowel problem may have arisen in part as an attempt to deal with angry feelings that could not be safely expressed directly. I remarked on his use of bowel metaphors when he was angry, such as "I don't give a crap." His bowel-related behaviors and face-picking represented his efforts to deal with anger, tension, and what might feel like unsafe levels of self-expansion.

At this point Ken was experiencing the bowel difficulty as much improved compared with three months earlier, although it was still very bothersome. He was most interested in focusing on the problem when a particular challenge involving transportation was looming, and we continued to refine strategies involving breathing, cognitive restructuring, and the use of distraction such as attending to his palm organizer while in the high-stress situation. Ken was aware that he would progress more rapidly with anxiety reduction if he regularly practiced progressive relaxation using his tapes, but he tended to alternate between setting ambitious goals for doing so and avoiding it completely. We discussed this behavior as an example of his all-or-nothing approach to tasks and his feeling compelled to perform them perfectly and, when perfection was not attainable, to avoid them entirely.

It also became clearer that there was something comforting about the restriction Ken placed on himself owing to his bowel anxiety. Feeling forced to curtail his activities helped him to titrate his overly high expectations for himself and feel his choices were legitimate. He reported that it would make him very anxious not to have the bowel problem or the face-picking and that he could not imagine his life without them. I continued to let Ken know that I could appreciate his anxiety concerning these symptoms and that we would concentrate on his agenda. However, he did express some interest in managing the face-picking to a greater degree. I suggested a few options for him to experiment with as he wished: environmental control, such as getting rid of his tweezers; cognitive restructuring: "It's normal for a man to have hairs," "I don't have to be perfect"; and response prevention: delaying acting on the urge and curtailing the time spent picking.

Ken was also more interested in discussing his marital issues with me. He reported feeling that the relationship with Peg was "all on her terms" and that her constant message to him was that he should be more like her and less like himself. He felt that there was little room for his style in the marriage: "My name is not on the house or the car or the wife—I feel like a renter," and "She wears the pants. . . . I don't feel like a man with her; she's the man." We discussed his great sensitivity to feeling controlled by another because of his relationship with his father, but that in addition he had married a particularly dominant woman. Tension and hostility pervaded most of the marital interactions. Ken disclosed that a very problematic aspect of the marriage for him was that he was not physically attracted to Peg, and although he had been aware of this from the beginning he had downplayed its importance in his drive for security. However, he now had to admit that it was central, and that he was craving experiences with women to whom he felt more attracted. Ken finally stated that perhaps he wanted a divorce and that he thought he would like to live alone and see other women, although this notion made him feel very anxious and guilty.

Ken was tearful when discussing his level of marital dissatisfaction, and he was aware that his own issues affected the way he felt about Peg: "Maybe it's me I don't like, not Peg." Having expected that divorcing people hated one another and he did not hate Peg, Ken felt confused about his wish for divorce. He expressed the hope that Peg would end it so that he would not have to and plaintively said, "I wish someone would tell me what to do." I internally debated my response to that statement. Certainly one possible response was to discuss Ken's wishes that another direct his life but that this kept him in his usual compliant or rebellious position. However, I felt that he was asking this particular "someone" for feedback about his current situation and that my eschewing advice-giving in the service of his autonomy might not be very helpful. I was also giving particular weight to two aspects of our recent discussions: first, my sense that Ken's lack of attraction to Peg and his wish to pursue women whom he found more desirable represented an aspect of his more authentic self (his primary subjective experience, in Stern's [2002a, b] terms, rather than his intersubjective self); and, second, Ken's admission to me that he would have left the marriage already had it not been for the financial security it offered him. I decided to be frank about how I saw the issues and to speak to the part of him that felt drawn to being an adequate adult man who acted on his own desires. I said that I thought it was very understandable that financial security was so important to him, given his overall lack of security growing up and his equating money and a good life such as that of his wealthy relative. I continued that I could see why he had jumped at the offer when Peg wooed him at a particularly insolvent point in his life, but that I thought he had developed a greater sense of security about his own self since then. I told Ken that I did not think that staying would be a good thing for him unless he could feel differently about being married to Peg and that, if he stayed primarily for the financial security, I thought that over time it would undermine his sense of integrity as a man.

Ken was sober and thoughtful after my comments and expressed gratitude for my honesty. I was uncertain about how his reaction might unfold over time, however, and expected that he and Peg would remain ambivalent about their course of action for some months to come. To my surprise, Ken came tearfully to the next session and reported he had told Peg that he wanted a divorce. They had made plans for him to move out in a month. Ken initially felt much relief, but as time went on he reported feeling very anxious and shaky. He could think only of all he was losing—their social circle (really her friends) as well as their affluent life style. Ken reported feeling quite scared and stressed, and retreated into avoidant behavior such as watching television all day when he had planned to go look at apartments. However, he did manage to find a place and move out. He and Peg dealt with the transition by continuing to spend a great deal of time together, and Ken expressed his ambivalent feelings about his marriage by wearing his wedding ring every other day.

Ken's mood and functioning fluctuated quite a bit over the next few months. He continued to spend most of his leisure time with Peg, who wanted them to be together despite her dissatisfaction with him. Ken announced one day that he had quit his job; he was aware he was not performing and that the situation was not right for him or his boss. He planned to take a couple of weeks off and then decide what to do next. Ken was feeling quite depressed at this point and experiencing himself as a failure in his marriage and in his career. Peg made him financial offers that were very desirable in his current vulnerable state, including that she purchase a new television for him or support him while he obtained an advanced degree. He told me, "I just remember the Porsche!" and found it possible to maintain his distance, saying that he knew it was the right thing although the security was tempting. It became more apparent, however, that Ken felt hopelessly lost professionally. He had a multitude of ideas concerning a career choice, which included rabbi, teacher, psychologist, writer, sports broadcaster, and entrepreneur. It was evident that he sought a life that would garner respect from others and he expressed the desire to work with people, but his lack of identity development resulted in his having little idea about how he might best use his own resources in reality rather than in fantasy.

I became concerned about Ken's regression at this time. The threatened loss of his attachment to Peg (ambivalent as it was) and the selfobject functions she provided resulted in increased disorganization and fragmentation. Moreover, directing anger and blame at her had deflected some from being targeted at himself; now, with less externalization, his self-hatred was unabated. As Ken felt increasingly disappointed in his lack of ability to meet his own expectations, he became more avoidant and his functioning deteriorated; he reported sleeping much of the time, eating junk food, and picking his face. Without the structure of his job, he seldom left his apartment except for our sessions. I decided that some cognitive interventions concerning Ken's excessive and harsh expectations of himself might help to limit the regressive behavior that followed his perceived failures. I asked him to tell me more about some of the ways he found that he was talking to himself about his behavior these days, and he reported a stream of self-talk in which he castigated himself in a way similar to his father's condemnation, for example, "You idiot! How could you be so stupid!" I suggested modifying the harshness, perhaps taking as a model the way he would want to speak to his own child who was having difficulty with something. We also examined some of his more regressive self-statements in which he would give himself permission to avoid adult functioning in a way that was destructive ("I don't want to do that, I don't want to. OK, you don't have to. Stay home."). I suggested that he might not want to cut himself total slack that way, just as he would not counsel his child that the boy did not have to do his homework; rather, Ken would have moderate expectations and provide needed help and support. Ken found this suggestion useful, and we talked further about what might constitute reasonable rather than extreme standards for himself at present.

Ken brought his tweezers to the next session and, handing them to me, said that he had had a "pickfest" all week and wanted to stop. We had not previously discussed instituting environmental control by using our relationship and bringing me his tweezers;

when I inquired about how he had thought of that and how it felt to bring them in, he simply said that it felt right and he was ready to do it. I took that as a sign of increasing trust in our relationship and greater readiness for at least some behavioral change in his compulsive behavior. However, I also expected that he would continue to feel ambivalent about such change and about my holding the tweezers. I asked him how he thought he might feel if he had an urge to pick but I had the tweezers, hoping that we could discuss any concerns he might articulate about being controlled by me or my withholding something from him. However, he denied any possible negative feelings about me, and asserted his freedom to continue picking with another implement if he felt desperate.

Ken related that he was most vulnerable to picking his face after shaving, and that he kept thinking, "If you just get this one hair . . . ," but would then find himself going on to the next and the next. He was finding that it helped to turn off the light so that he was less aware of facial imperfections, and I supported this environmental control strategy. I also suggested a cognitive intervention: reminding himself that he looked better without picking, because his search for facial perfection in reality resulted in obvious swelling and redness. The frequent picking diminished, and, when it occurred, it was clear that emotional issues were involved, specifically meeting attractive women in social situations and feeling ambivalent about pursuing the women. Ken purchased another pair of tweezers but brought them to me the next day, saying that he knew it would help again to leave them with me. I told him it was fine "to leave things here with me" but again invited him to discuss any feelings about this that he might experience.

Ken was finding that living on his own without a car forced him to confront his anxiety about public transportation more directly. He told me that he had been "scared of the el" since an episode a number of months earlier in which his elevated train had unaccountably stopped on the tracks between stations and he had felt panicky. I said that he could gradually decrease his anxiety by putting himself back in that situation with very small steps, such as standing on the platform for a few minutes but not taking the train, and the next time taking the train for one stop. Ken had been thinking about doing that but was feeling frightened. He then had an experience with Peg in which their usual dynamic shifted; this time she was saying she was ready for a divorce but was not sure that he could manage without her. Ken used his anger and his wish to "show her" that he would be perfectly fine without her to overcome his anxiety—he rode the train one stop to an event and then rode back. This success ushered in a period of less avoidance and more exploration for Ken. He rode the train a number of times and also began dating a few women whom he found attractive. He enjoyed dating and was willing to move a bit further from his comfort zone when his dates suggested various activities that he normally avoided. He was making the decision to get out of the bathroom sooner, and managed to weather a very difficult experience in which the gas station restroom he sought was occupied and he had an accident. Fortunately that occurred at a time of higher self esteem and activity for Ken, and he had some perspective on it that was quite interesting: "I think it actually helped me—I've been so afraid of this, but it's like fearing making a particular phone call. It's not as bad as you think—so having an accident in my pants is not the greatest, but it's not the end of the world either." In addition to finding that the feared event was not as catastrophic as he had anticipated, Ken felt more able to give up some control. "I don't have to hold my stomach sphincter so tight" (Ken typically referred to his bowel difficulties as "my stomach").

A new relationship twist occurred at around this time. The evening before divorce papers were to be signed Peg called Ken begging him to give her another chance. She promised to be different and swore that she had seen how wrong she was to treat him in the old manner. Ken wanted to believe her and continued to crave the security she offered but found the turn of events stressful (his bowel accident occurred a short time after this call). He wanted to continue dating and thought perhaps he could just date Peg as well. They decided to spend more time together with "no expectations"; however, Peg suggested they drive around wealthy suburbs and look at houses together. Ken believed that Peg was showing something of a different attitude, and thought she seemed quite apologetic about her past failure to include him as a full partner. As had happened with his father, Ken experienced Peg's contrition as very meaningful and was convinced that she had truly changed. He found the whole situation quite confusing, and described his state as "torment" over not wanting to hurt Peg, craving security for himself, and still wanting to date. Although I was very dubious that anything in their parent–child dynamic had really changed, I did not articulate my thought; this time I experienced no sense from Ken that my opinion on the relationship would be helpful. My feeling that another sort of response was needed from me at this point seemed confirmed when Ken mentioned being angry at a friend who had advised that he and Peg were better apart. I said that I could see that he really wanted others to be respectful of his decisions, and he agreed. I told him that he probably did not need one more person telling him to be with Peg or not to be, and I asked him how he thought I might be the most helpful to him at this time.

Ken seemed a bit embarrassed by all this and finally said that he wasn't sure; it was difficult for him to ask others for help, but it made him feel good to come and work on himself. He then switched to talking about his career dilemmas and how confused he was in this area as well. Seeing that he was less defensive concerning this aspect of his life, I took a few opportunities to suggest that other peoples' voices had been very loud in his head and that it had been hard to hear his own, but that I could see that he really wanted to find his own path and his own voice. He talked about the possibility that he ultimately might have to move to follow his path, that he could see himself living alone or with perhaps some other people along the way. As I emphasized "It's *your* path, *your* journey," he seemed quite moved. Our refocusing on the need for his own development to continue regardless of his decision concerning his marriage seemed to promote greater self-cohesion. It was also clear that further discussion of our relationship and his wishes and expectations about responses from me was very challenging for Ken. His framing our treatment in terms of his "work on himself" was much more comfortable for him than thinking about a relationship in which he might encounter the intersubjective difficulties with which he had become all too familiar in his family and in his marriage.

Over the next few months Ken made a decision concerning his career and opted to take some graduate courses in education. He reported some positive developments with Peg; for instance, she was not pushing him to go out as in the past and instead he was challenging himself more. He related that another woman he had been dating had become "too much hassle" in her efforts to get him to be more active, and he had ended the relationship. He and

Peg decided to move back in together. Suspecting that the relationship would be no more fulfilling than it had been before but convinced that there was little more useful that I could say, I continued to attempt simply to stay with his shifting feelings about all this. I believed that Ken had all the information that I could give him concerning the dynamics of the situation and knew that I would be available to help him with whatever happened. Indeed, as soon as he moved back in with Peg, Ken found himself resenting her and reacting against her perceived control. "I sometimes feel I have to be an asshole just to assert that I'm a man!" He ignored the household chores Peg wanted him to do and stayed up very late every night at the computer to avoid her. Ken reported much open conflict and told me that he was aware that their getting together again wasn't working. I commented to him that it seemed that they were still very much themselves. He decided he wanted to move out again, saying that a large part of his motivation was that he was meeting women at school whom he wanted to date.

Ken continued to find that his pattern of compliance and rebellion was in full swing with Peg; for instance, she left town on a business trip and he ate a dozen doughnuts and numerous candy bars. After several more weeks of conflict and rebellion, he moved out again. This time he found it "very freeing—I didn't miss Peg and I just pleased myself." Ken enjoyed movies, and I remarked that he wanted to be the director of his own movie. "Yes, and the producer, too, with the money!" he responded. Despite some anxiety and regression over the next few months, Ken knew that he needed to work to be a whole person: "I want to be the Peg." However, he had difficulty focusing on how to meet his immediate income needs and struggled with his all-or-nothing tendencies: "I plan to get up at 7:30 and get going and instead I sleep until 11:30," and he fantasized about the perfect job rather than setting up interviews with currently available ones. At this point he found it very helpful to construct with me a daily schedule of goals that seemed realistic rather than overly ambitious. I suggested that, although goals for the future included working with a career counselor, at present he needed a job rather than the ultimate job. We constructed a daily schedule of moderate goals; for example, Ken would photocopy his resume that afternoon and make two calls the next day to set up interviews. I asked Ken how he felt about my suggestions concerning all this. I suspected that, although he had needed the organization, his ambivalence about being controlled was operating on some level; moreover, my recommending moderate goals was at odds with his grandiose, narcissistic dreams. Ken continued to accent what he considered the most beneficial aspects of our work and to dismiss any concerns; he said he never worried that I was trying to control him and that I was very different from his father and Peg. "Thanks, this was very helpful. I was all over the place."

Over the next several months Ken and Peg finalized their divorce. Ken did reasonably well in his education courses despite quite a bit of procrastination, but he ultimately felt that continuing in a business career might be most suitable for him. He continued to ride the train at times and enjoyed dating several different women. Ken suggested that we reduce our meetings to once a month because his insurance was running out and finances were an issue. After a few more months he told me that he thought he was ready to stop in another session or so. He reported, "My stomach is good," although he continued to be frustrated with his procrastination at school and his difficulty following through on finding employment. In our final meeting he reported having found a job that he was excited about and stated that he really wanted to depend on himself, not anyone else, not Peg, not even me.

DISCUSSION OF CASE MATERIAL

This case illustrates some of the complexities of conducting symptom-focused dynamic psychotherapy with someone who has complex psychopathology. The trauma that Ken experienced throughout his childhood and the dearth of ameliorative experiences resulted in a fragmentation-prone self engaged in a desperate search for security. The most accurate descriptor for his attachment style is probably disorganized; Ken sought dependent connection and regressed without it, but found himself feeling intolerably trapped in a close relationship. Archaic narcissistic trends were apparent in his daydreams of limitless wealth and infinite career possibilities; however, he was also frightened by his grandiose strivings. His father, in particular, had behaved in a traumatizing fashion, not meeting Ken's needs for mirroring, and Ken soon learned to deflate himself when he began to feel dangerously overstimulated. Unlike many anxious persons who simply experience their anxiety without a means of managing it other than avoidance, Ken developed compulsive behaviors. Like persons with addictions, he found that taking some sort of action when he felt stressed alleviated his tension, and he became deeply attached to his preferred methods. Moreover, his giving himself permission to avoid anxiety-provoking situations because of his problems provided additional negative reinforcement ("I can't make that sales call because my stomach is so bad today" or "Now I can't go out to that club because my face is too red from picking") and considerable secondary gain. Ken's identification with his father's harsh judgments of him as a child resulted in relentless experiences of self-condemnation. He attempted to escape further castigation by avoiding activities that would subject him to possible evaluation and sought out regressed stuporous states through large helpings of sleep, junk food, television, and grandiose fantasy.

Ken felt most bothered by his symptoms when his involvement with them exceeded typical limits or when he felt internal or external pressure to travel outside his usual routine. Much of the time he was not in the action stage of change concerning his symptoms. I had to be alert to staying with his agenda concerning his symptoms while at the same time not minimizing their problematic nature. When Ken felt more motivated to reduce his agoraphobic avoidance, he was able to make some use of diaphragmatic breathing, cognitive restructuring, and in vivo desensitization. He found that environmental control, cognitive interventions, and exposure plus response prevention had some impact on his face-picking. He was also able to use our relationship with both problems; he initiated such suggestions as the option of calling me while in a stressful travel situation and bringing me his tweezers. Although Ken had fled an earlier treatment in which the symptomatic changes proposed seemed overly threatening, he managed to tolerate a gradual approach to symptom management in the context of our relationship as I offered the idea of his having moderate expectations of himself.

Much of the time Ken was more concerned with love and work than he was with his symptoms. His accommodation to an insecure and traumatic childhood environment had resulted in a derailed individuation process; he had learned to comply with or rebel against a dominant other, but had little idea of the nature of his own subjective wishes. I believe our treatment provided him with some opportunity to explore them further, although a much longer psychotherapy would be required for this process to be more complete. Probably the most dramatic change for Ken over the course of our therapy was his decision to divorce, and it is likely that my support during this time made it possible for him to leave a marriage in which his experience was one of gaining security but losing control. He also came to a more realistic approach to his career choices over the course of treatment. At one point I had mentioned to him a statement of Jung's that in order to become something in actuality, it is necessary to give up being everything in potential. These words resonated deeply with Ken. His tendency to resort to fantasy about limitless options and great wealth was less pervasive by the close of treatment, and the fact that his income needs had become pressing was probably useful as a real-world consequence to dreaming rather than doing.

An important element of this treatment pertained to Ken's experience of his masculinity. His father's sense of inadequacy interfered with his own ability to model and support positive images of maleness in Ken. Such events as fixing a tire together, which ideally could foster twinship experiences of being competent males in a shared endeavor, were instead traumatic. Moreover, Ken's fastidiousness and concern with his appearance were deprecated by his father, who called him "sissy prissy." Many of Ken's statements concerning his marriage related to his feeling that he was not the man of the house with Peg and that, rather, Peg was the man. I believed that exploring and supporting Ken's sense of himself as a man would be a vital part to the overall enhancement of his self-cohesion. That was one reason I chose to comment on Ken's reasons for remaining in his marriage as I did, framing as an important issue his sense of his own integrity as a man. I also referred to gender issues in helping Ken feel differentiated from Peg in a way that felt positive to him. For instance, Ken related that Peg liked to rise very early on the weekends and go look at real estate after doing her errands; he preferred to sleep late and watch football. Peg chided him for this preference, and he felt like a failure in yet another way compared with her. I said simply, "You're a guy! You have a lot of company in the world of guys enjoying that kind of weekend."

The intricacies of Ken's interpersonal issues involving control and expectations were difficult for him to focus on in the context of our relationship, and my inquiries concerning his experiences with me were usually dismissed with brief, positive answers. His response to my question about how I might be of most help to him when he was contemplating a return to his marriage was typical; he moved the dialogue away from the topic of our relationship onto the idea that therapy helped him work on himself. At various points I made attempts to direct his attention to his discomfort discussing his feelings toward me, and he responded with confusion. It seemed important for Ken to perceive me as a benign, noncontrolling figure whose role was to help him work on himself and to keep what must have felt to him like a safe level of distance. Some of this stance might also have been due to the nature of the material we were discussing—lack of bowel control, an obsessive ritual related to grooming, and numerous experiences at variance with our cultural ideals of manliness—and its potential to engender shame. Ken expressed no curiosity about my reactions to him or about my personal life, and when I asked him how he would feel about my discussing our work in a book I was writing, he readily acceded, saying he hoped it might help others, but displayed no further interest.

His ongoing comments to me about feeling very comfortable with me, my being his "best" therapist, and appreciating my "confidence" in him suggested to me that my effort to supply guidance, including symptom-focused techniques, while supporting his autonomy was one that he experienced as usable. It is noteworthy that, although Ken's comments regarding our relationship tended to be succinct, concrete, and somewhat impersonal, he did initiate bids for greater connectedness to me that were action oriented as we conducted symptom-focused work. Ken suggested calling my answering machine when using self-calming techniques in a high-stress situation before I thought to propose this myself. In addition, he brought me his tweezers as he attempted to achieve greater environmental control over his compulsive face-picking—a move I never would have suggested because of Ken's sensitivity to feeling controlled, but he seemed to perceive turning the tweezers over to me as enlisting my help while he worked on controlling himself. It is not surprising that someone with Ken's action-oriented symptoms would find it much more comfortable to enact aspects of our relationship rather than to discuss them.

At times Ken seemed to find symptom-focused techniques

usable and helpful. At other points, his immersion in internal conflicts and interpersonal dilemmas rendered those techniques irrelevant or contraindicated. I found that as our work progressed it seemed at least somewhat clear how best to proceed at a given time: "Central to psychoanalytic treatment . . . is the analyst's capacity to engage that dimension of the patient's self-experience that embodies the experiential foreground but not to lose sight of other parts or aspects of the patient's self in the background" (Ringstrom, 2001, p. 739). Ken let me know verbally when he was uncomfortable with his level of symptomatic behavior, for instance, when his facial redness exceeded his tolerance limit, or he was facing an unavoidable experience in which no bathroom would be readily available. At such times he would actively engage in discussions of symptom-focused solutions and later report back on his use of them. His wishes and needs for more instructional guidance from me concerning his interpersonal dilemmas varied as well, but his verbal comments and affective tone helped me gain an intuitive sense of when further exploration of his thoughts was needed and when offering some of my ideas might be helpful.

My countertransference experience with Ken included liking him, feeling empathy for his difficult childhood and current anxiety, and being glad that he was my patient and not my husband. Sometimes taking the "other-centered perspective" (Fosshage, 1997), I could easily imagine the anger, frustration, and disappointment he could provoke in a woman expecting him to behave as a competent adult partner. Ken met my lesser requirements of coming to his sessions, paying me, and talking without difficulty. I am not a very controlling person by nature, but I also think that in our treatment together the transference–countertransference dynamic did not evoke the pattern he enacted elsewhere involving themes of control, submission, and rebellion. I think that unconsciously Ken had chosen to engage in a limited relationship with me, to see me as one of a line of therapists rather than thinking of me more individually as a person or as a woman. Our relationship felt pleasant but without intensity. I observed that Ken was attractive, but I did not feel attracted to him. I suspect that (at least consciously) the same was true for him; our relationship did not seem to include sending and receiving on that wave length. This type of more constricted engagement with one another probably enabled Ken to discuss intimate topics with me and find our relationship usable without its being unbearably threatening, and it may have made it easier for me to tolerate with minimal frustration Ken's lack of consistent motivation for change, regressed behavior, and narcissism. The downside, of course, is that a more complete resolution of his problematic interpersonal patterns through analysis of the transference did not occur.

I chose Ken's treatment for inclusion in this book not because it illustrates a brilliantly successful treatment illuminating ways in which analytic and behavioral interventions further one another—it does not particularly demonstrate this, and success was rather modest—but it does describe a form of treatment that enabled an ambivalent patient to remain in treatment for close to two years and to express high satisfaction with therapy at its conclusion. At the close of treatment Ken had gained greater insight, a sense of adult responsibility, maturity, and direction, and he had managed to leave a conflictual marriage in which he assumed the role of a sulky but dependent child. His obsessive-compulsive picking symptom had diminished, he was less agoraphobic, and he felt more in control of his bowel problem. Ken's overall emotional regulation was improved, including his ability to manage anger.

I believe that Ken made greater progress in this combined treatment than he would have in a standard analytic treatment, because some symptom remission led to more possibilities for adult engagement with the world and some confidence that he could manage himself competently. Of course, it is possible that he would have experienced some reduction in symptoms with analytic treatment only. The intensity of his anxiety and the rigidity of his compulsive symptoms, however, lead me to believe that little symptom reduction would have occurred in the absence of concrete techniques to relieve anxiety. Moreover, Ken's ability to engage deeply in a treatment relationship and discuss transference issues is questionable. Although many analytic patients may share his propensity to engage in enactments and find verbal exploration of the treatment relationship challenging, it is noteworthy that his difficulty was relatively unchanged after two years.

An exclusively cognitive behavioral therapy would have had no shortage of problematic symptoms to treat, and the sort of anxiety symptoms Ken described can respond very significantly to behavioral treatments. However, Ken felt quite attached to his bowel and picking rituals. In addition to relieving anxiety, they both contained and expressed anger, and provided him with comforting rationalizations for limiting his activities. Moreover, such constraints on traveling and socializing probably also supported his wish to avoid domination and control by another, but in a fashion less likely to evoke anger; for example, he could communicate to Peg, "I can't go on a cruise with you" rather than "I don't want to." Ken really did not wish to do away with his anxiety symptoms; he just wanted them to remain within certain limits. Ken's investment in his symptoms and his ambivalence about changing them significantly limited his motivation for symptom-focused work. Exposure-based treatments, while quite effective, require high motivation. Ken's description of fleeing his previous behavioral treatment after one session indicated that his willingness to experience additional anxiety in the interests of symptom alleviation was slight. He was able to tolerate a degree of exposure-based work after we had developed a good alliance and his motivation was high because of interpersonal factors, for instance, riding the el because he wanted to "show Peg" or date a new woman. I suspect that, if Ken had begun a treatment that was exclusively cognitive behavioral, he would, again, have terminated it quickly. Our treatment enabled him to engage in symptom management when he was finding his symptoms bothersome, and to explore his identity and interpersonal issues as he found them more pressing.

Ken alternated between grandiose aspirations and minimal expectations for himself, and I sought to construct a treatment that did not err in such extreme directions. I was aware that Ken was prone to flee relationships that became uncomfortable, and I tried to engage him in interactions that would be challenging at a tolerable level. His evident discomfort with discussing our relationship ultimately led me to continue to invite him to engage in such discussions but not to persist in such exchanges. In attempting to meet him where he was and help him progress further, I had to titrate my ambitions of transference analysis and symptom remission in favor of a moderate blend of acceptance and change.

A much longer term therapy would be required for thorough resolution of Ken's combination of Axis I and Axis II psychopathology. Ideally, with more time to consolidate the treatment relationship, Ken would find it possible to access and discuss his ambivalence about intimacy as it occurred in the transference. However, his choice (largely but not wholly dictated by financial and insurance strictures) was to leave treatment following some improvement and to concentrate on being independent. Ken expressed great satisfaction with his therapy. Mindful of his early comment to me that he might be prone to get a little better and stop ("Don't let me do that here"), I carefully assessed his feelings about ending. Treatment already had continued for several months longer than his original projection of a year and a half, and Ken expressed confidence in his readiness to be on his own. I would have preferred to continue, but felt that I needed to respect his decision and what I saw as his hope for further individuation and freedom. I articulated the progress he had made, told him that I had really enjoyed working with him, and invited him to return for more treatment at any future time if he so desired.

In one of our last sessions, Ken commented that my new clock was not reflecting the recent change to daylight savings (I had been trying to figure out how to get at the mechanism, but with no success). Before I could reply Ken picked up the clock, and in one smooth movement popped out the clock face while I watched in surprised admiration. He made an adjustment, pressed the face back into the wooden base, and returned the clock to its position on my table, all in the space of about 20 seconds. I thought to myself of his father's failed "fix-it" experiences for which Ken would be blamed and of incidents Ken had related to me in which he felt inadequate in this realm compared with other men. Setting my clock seemed another way for him to feel comfortable initiating an action that related to our relationship, and as we moved toward termination I thought it was particularly fortuitous that Ken had had an opportunity to display his "manly" competence by fixing something of mine at which I had not yet been successful. I told him I had been trying to do that for days, and thanked him very much.

CHAPTER EIGHT

A Patient with
Generalized Anxiety

IN THIS CHAPTER I DISCUSS a patient whom I have treated for about 10 years. The first phase of my work with Ann involved intensive psychotherapy with three sessions per week; this stage was followed by several years of less frequent and sometimes sporadic meetings. The patient's chief symptoms related to generalized anxiety, with hypervigilance, physiological overarousal, and excessive worry. Ann had a history of anorexia nervosa, and, although her weight was normal when she entered treatment, she continued to experience some body-image disturbance and to restrict her eating. Ann's symptoms predominantly correspond to the pathway I have described as anxious vulnerability to fragmentation. More specifically, she attempted to cope with the inadequate selfobject milieu in her family by disavowing need altogether, including need for food and for relationships. Unable to trust, she tried to control interpersonal interactions. Hoping to disconfirm her pathogenic beliefs that she had to take responsibility for everything because no one else was competent, and that vulnerability would be punished, Ann engaged in many transference tests. A successful symptom-focused intervention early in treatment was instrumental in convincing this young woman who had abjured trust that I could provide her with competent help.

ANN

Ann was a 23-year-old graduate student in literature when she began treatment with me. A self-possessed young woman but obviously tense, she described a history of anorexia nervosa and current anxiety symptoms, including muscular tension, nausea, and vomiting. She reported two brief tries at psychotherapy in college that had not been successful ("We stared at each other"), after which she decided just to work things out herself. Ann stated her belief that seeking psychotherapy was a "wimpy" thing to do and that she ought to be able to manage her own problems so that she would not have physical symptoms. However, since she had begun vomiting from tension several times a week following her father's (successful) major surgery a few months earlier, she felt that she had to seek treatment. Ann told me that she had accessed my publications through her university library and was reassured to discover that I had written on the topic of eating disorders. Ann stated that, in addition to her anxiety symptoms, she was aware of a need to control everything and that she felt very small when unable to do so.

I suggested a once-a-week treatment, since I believed that Ann could not tolerate greater frequency at that point, and we agreed that longer term issues as well as specific symptoms might require attention. As Ann began describing her history, the anxiety, hypervigilance, and lack of trust that I was observing became understandable in the family milieu she described. Her father was alcoholic, behaved unpredictably, and was often enraged. Her father was not physically violent but there was much parental arguing. Her father, a successful entrepreneur, was often away from home during her childhood. When he was with the family, he found it amusing to tantalize the children by such means as asking if everyone would like some ice cream as they approached an ice cream stand, and, after they became excited, he would drive on past without stopping.

Ann's mother seems to have been depressed throughout Ann's childhood. She would sleep late in the mornings, nap in the afternoons, and doze off in her chair in the evenings. Ann's mother was erratic; for instance, she would forget that she had promised to go somewhere with the children and then would get angry at their upset reaction. The mother frequently criticized Ann; she particularly scrutinized Ann's physical appearance—her weight, skin, and hair. When Ann became an adult her mother apologized to her for some of these incidents, including one that Ann did not remember. Her mother told her that one Sunday when the mother was sleeping late Ann came into her bedroom to show her mother how she was dressed for church, and, although Ann entered the room beaming and excited, her mother criticized her appearance and Ann left in tears. Ann believed that her mother was completely ineffectual in controlling her brothers; she described ways that she and her younger sister were virtually terrorized by the oldest brother, who was physically violent with them and with their mother. He sexually abused Ann for several years when she was in grade school. Ann eventually was able to tell her mother, who said she would take care of it, but nothing changed. Ann reported a memory of asking her mother if she wished Ann had not told her; Ann believed that her mother answered yes.

Ann described feeling conflicted over seeking her parents' approval. Neither had gone to college and they did not understand her Ph.D. program. They wanted her to enter the family business instead. She also reported feeling great self-doubt whenever her mother questioned her judgment or taste or appearance; she said that her anger about this would surface as iciness and "analytical" questioning of her mother's comments. Ann noted that she had erected barriers to keep her family out but ended up taking a "my-way-or-the-highway" position with everyone in which she was always in control.

Ann's need for a certain safe interpersonal positioning was very evident in our relationship; from the beginning I experienced her as likable but difficult to be with. She was frequently confrontational, critical, and questioning, asking in numerous ways how this ridiculous and self-indulgent process of talking about herself and her feelings was supposed to help her. She disparaged my responses when I was feeling attuned to painful affect that she had to disavow. For instance, she told me to "calm down!" when I murmured "hmmm" in a sympathetic tone at her description of some difficult event. She conducted a microanalysis of many of my questions and comments to her, and I often felt barraged and anxious during our early sessions. Ann scrutinized me so vigilantly that, if I displayed a minor change of expression, she would ask "What?" and say she needed to know what I was thinking. She also commented that she thought she was overconcerned with my approval, but in the next session she was challenging and abrupt. Ann began reporting a series of dreams about therapy, mostly involving my unavailability. In one dream I had many good things to tell her but our time was up, and in another old people and children and my husband were interrupting us.

Ann's most acute anxiety symptoms, such as the vomiting, began to abate shortly after she entered treatment. I taught her diaphragmatic breathing and encouraged her to practice relaxation, and she found these techniques somewhat helpful. After several months of therapy Ann disclosed that she was fearful of flying and was dreading an upcoming unavoidable flight. When we explored this fear further, Ann explained that she found it unbearable not to be the one flying the plane, and that it meant that she had no control. In previous flights Ann had focused on keeping the aircraft aloft through sheer force of will from the passenger section and had found this effort to be frightening and exhausting. Ann was very eager for us to help her manage air travel more effectively. I told her that I thought her lack of trust in others and need to be in control were getting in her way in this situation, and that it was worth considering that some people really were very competent at doing their jobs, unlike her experience of her parents. I further stated that pilots go through a great deal of training and really do know how to fly, and that perhaps she could let go of a little control and permit the pilot to fly the plane. We constructed a multicomponent fear-of-flying program that included deep breathing, muscular relaxation, and probably most important for Ann, cognitive self-statements such as "The pilot knows what he's doing. I can let the pilot fly the plane. He has control, I don't have to."

Ann returned from her trip reporting great success with these techniques. She had felt much calmer than on previous flights and had experienced a sense of relief concerning the pilot's competence to be in control of the aircraft. Ann told me much later that my ability to help her with this situation was pivotal in her decision to trust me more and to remain in treatment. It seemed to increase her confidence that perhaps I knew how to fly the plane, too. But Ann really wanted to know just who her pilot was. She began asking me questions about my life and my experiences She wanted to know if I had a husband and a dog as I did in her dream, and I told her that I did. She also wanted to know if I cared about my patients and if I liked her, and was relieved when I said yes. She said she did not want to get "touchy-feely" or hear about my life, but that what I had told her helped. Her idealization began to emerge in her comments that she was glad I was so confident, had written a book, and was the most expensive therapist she had contacted. Ann also started to reveal her concern about loss by commenting how "weird" it would be never to see me again after we ended. I had a sense that Ann would now be able to agree to a more intensive treatment, and in this session we decided to move to twice a week.

Ann experienced intense anxiety following this change. She stated that she had "freaked" in one session when she thought I might be yawning, and criticized herself for using poor grammar and not saying anything "of substance." Ann described being extremely tense and wound up all the time, feared a return of anorexic symptoms, and claimed she was "not coping." I suggested that her increased anxiety was related to our greater involvement, and she reiterated her hatred of dependency. She felt that I "did this" to her, I was "in control," and she was "on the dissecting table." Ann described having become anorexic in high school when she was injured and had to wear a sling on her arm, stating that she had found the dependency intolerable. Ann also reported that, when she had knee surgeries in college, she found being bedridden so unendurable that she removed her own stitches rather than seek further medical care. She stated her belief that food and relationships were luxuries rather than necessities and described the "high" of asceticism. Ann also related some of her fears about our relationship. She found it difficult to believe that anyone cared or could be interested when she talked about herself, and said, "I don't understand why you're doing this, since you don't owe me anything." She also described fearing a loss of control or problems in functioning and stated that she did not know how to let herself feel. I continued to inquire about Ann's anxieties and to reassure her of my interest in her. Eventually she settled into the twice-a-week treatment.

Over the next few months Ann talked more about her childhood experiences, including the sexual abuse, for which she blamed herself. She described feeling trapped by her brother and trapped as well by the need to take care of her sister when her parents were "clueless." She realized that her sister was alcoholic in high school, and Ann got her into treatment with no help from their parents. When discussing family incidents, Ann occasionally cried, a rare experience for her. She called me one weekend, and, again, this display of need was followed by a session in which she was distant and sarcastic. She had more dreams of me, including one in which I was behind a counter (as in a store). She was unwilling to ask for help, and when I gave her something she refused it. She described her anxiety about what I might be thinking and not saying, reported feeling scrutinized, and told me how frustrated she was about the inequality in our relationship. As abuse-related memories became more prominent, however, and her anxiety and distress increased, she was able to ask for an extra session ("Is it justifiable?"). Ann also expressed worry about my impending vacation, and wished to know not only my destination but also what airline I was taking so that if a crash occurred she could know whether or not I was all right.

Ann continued to process painful family material. She reported images and dreams of herself in childhood, and berated herself for having let her family "get to" her and for having been abused and affected by it. She said she thought that her "inner child was a loser." She was also able to relate some of her anxiety to feeling more vulnerable and trusting in our relationship. She said that she had never needed anyone before, had never been in love, and worried that I would "dump" her or not like her. She described constantly feeling hurt by her parents when she was looking for empathy or support, and reported that her mother alternated between a pleasant demeanor and meanness, so that interacting with her was like getting kissed and slapped. Much of the time during these discussions Ann was haughty, icy, and confrontational but eventually was able to say that she thought she would like to try coming three times a week. Ann said she had had a comforting image before sleep one night: I was Joan of Arc with sword and shield. Ann told me how glad she was to have found me.

Ann continued to ask me many questions about myself. She wanted to know if I had suffered from an eating disorder, if I had had my own therapy, if I believed in God, what I liked to read, whether or not I had children, and how old I was. I told her that I would tell her anything about myself that I thought would be useful for our work together, although I might want to defer some answers until we understood better their meaning for her. I answered most questions directly at the time she asked, and we discussed her reactions. She seemed to enjoy learning from my answers and from such clues in the office as my magazine selections that we had some similar tastes and political leanings. She further commented that it felt good that I trusted her enough to let her know things about myself such as my having been in analysis.

Ann said that she had rarely let herself be comforted by her mother because, in addition to being inconsistently available, mother's nurturance had "strings attached." If her mother were emotionally supportive, then Ann would feel indebted, would have to answer her mother's questions, and might have information used against her later. She discussed her relief not to owe me anything other than my fee (which she always paid immediately, despite the financial exigencies of her graduate-student status). She also described how difficult it was for her to feel "one down" in therapy, how she felt competitive with me and saw things in terms of my winning and her losing. She complained about what a "big ego" I must have and how I must go around thinking I am great because I am "always right." Ann made these comments in a grudgingly admiring tone that connoted her hatred of "losing" but her relief that she could count on me to know what I was doing.

At my urging, Ann joined a therapy group for survivors of sexual abuse. The strong affects expressed by other group members frightened her because they made her think that people were out of control, and she denigrated other group members for their difficulties in functioning ("losers on Prozac"). However, she gradually became less self-blaming about her family experiences and increased her comfort with affective expression. Some interactions with me seemed central in this process. She experienced my empathy with her as condescending, wanted to know if I had been abused myself, and, if I had not been, asked how I knew what it felt like. I told her that, although I had not been abused, I was acquainted with suffering in my own life. I did not elaborate further, but Ann had a strong reaction to my response, felt tearful for me briefly, and later referred a number of times to being glad I had said this and noted that it helped her not to feel patronized when we discussed her pain.

Ann's chronically high level of anxiety was a frequent topic, and we focused a good deal on her constructing a balanced life style that helped her to regulate her anxiety. Ultimately she found that a regular program of running and yoga, moderate eating, spending more time with friends and less with parents, and getting a pet were all salutary. When we discussed painful memories in session, however, her anxiety escalated to levels that were difficult for her to manage. At such times she tried deep breathing, but often required further assistance and distraction. Ann found that getting up and closely inspecting my office plants offered a needed immersion in a different sort of experience. She also sometimes requested that I tell her about what I was growing in my garden or what my dog had been up to lately, and I was comfortable with complying. The "bedtime story" quality of these little tales seemed soothing for Ann and she was able to enjoy the notion of my taking care of my plants and my dog without the same level of conflict engendered by my nurturing her.

Ann's relationships outside of therapy deepened. Her previous relationships with men had been nonsexual or sexually manipulative, but, now, for the first time she entered a relationship that was characterized by emotional and sexual intimacy. She experienced intense anxiety about this and was not able to sustain the relationship, but became more aware of "options" in relationships. She also developed deep friendships with two women, one a graduate school peer and the other her martial arts instructor. This teacher became an idealized figure and would often appear in dreams together with me. Ann's anxieties about self-disclosure and dependency were features in these relationships, but less so than in the past, and she was able to be more honest about her vulnerabilities rather than icy and controlling.

Ann continued to inquire about my life. She said that, although she did not see me as very human much of the time, she felt she occasionally got a "foothold" into the "real me." She admitted to glee at my having a cold one day, because it showed I was human and "took you down a peg!" After close to two years of our working together, she stated that the struggle was over and that she finally trusted me. Ann asked to borrow my pen to write her comprehensive exams, for she believed that she would feel stronger with it (she did very well, fortunately!). Humor that felt friendly to me rather than hostile became a larger feature in our relationship. Ann described therapy as a mirror in which she saw herself reflected back, and that when she was away too long she would forget who she was, as a mirror needs a frame around it.

Ann still struggled with issues of power, control, and need, however. She would describe mumbling to herself after seeing me, "Who does she think she is!?" and blocking my words in session by singing a little ditty to herself about how "full of shit" I was. She showed me an angry poem she had written about me as "queen of nots" and how, of course, she did not love me or need me. She dreamed that I folded up the comforter on her bed and she told me not to. We discussed her wish not to "even get started" with what felt like an unfillable ache for mothering and how she never wanted to want what she could not have. Ann commented that, when she first came to therapy, she could barely say words like "incest" or "anorexia," but that later the most difficult things had to do with need and nurturance, and that she got agitated thinking about them. She said that she understood more clearly that it was dangerous to expect anything from her parents but she knew that did not have to be true in other relationships.

After four years of therapy ("An Olympiad! A marathon!") Ann's relationships with friends were characterized by depth and mutuality. Her relationships with her family caused her much less anxiety than in the past, and her self-esteem regulation had become more stable. Ann had attained a great deal of insight into her development, and had passed from self-blame to anger at her parents to some appreciation for the forces that shaped them. She was free of eating-disorder symptoms and major anxiety. Ann successfully concluded her doctoral program and prepared to relocate to take a faculty position. At that point she still wrestled with issues of trust and dependency with me, especially as termination approached, but she was able to tolerate her feelings and discuss them rather than act cold and hostile.

We terminated, but, as is my practice, I told Ann that I would be available for any future contact, short- or long-term. Our "termination" instead launched a second phase of therapy as Ann found that her new position entailed many challenges, including some dynamics that replicated issues in her family. She was dismayed to need further treatment, but ultimately accepted my framing this as expectable given the difficulties of her childhood experiences and the current stressors. Much of this work consisted of once a week telephone sessions while Ann worked at her out-of-state university, and we met in person when she visited the area for vacations and summers. This phase of treatment was much less focused on issues of trust of me, worry about my reactions, and fear of abandonment. Ann seemed considerably more secure at this point and had a much greater degree of confidence in my ongoing availability and good will toward her. She continued to enjoy a sense of my competence and self-assurance ("I met a psychologist on the plane who called your book the 'Bible' of eating-disorder treatment—you sure don't lack for confidence!"). In this period of treatment we concentrated primarily on Ann's current relationships and on her professional life. She had developed a number of relationships that were very important to her, although intimacy continued to be a considerable challenge. Ann pursued relationships with both women and men, and ultimately decided that women probably met her needs better. Ann was able to tolerate some disappointing experiences, and eventually began a serious relationship with a female partner. In the professional realm she was extremely successful, but concluded that her chosen profession was not as fulfilling as she had hoped.

Ann reported feeling much more resolved concerning family issues at this point, and we discussed them for the most part in relation to current situations triggering organizing principles developed within her family. She wanted to react differently to situations that activated issues of control, vulnerability, and competence. I believed that doing so would be much more possible for her now because of the degree of resolution she had already achieved. I suggested that in these situations Ann remind herself of the contribution of the past to her reaction and that she employ internal dialogue that would facilitate her responding in a new way. For example, some aspects of her partner's approach to household tasks and career-related issues resulted in Ann's becoming over-controlling, related to the activation of fears that Ann had found a partner who resembled her incompetent mother. She found it helpful to remind herself that Mona was not like her mother, that she got things done but had her own style, and that Ann did not have to do everything. Gradually she found herself able to be less reactive. Ann continued to struggle with chronic anxiety, however, and constantly had to work on calming herself through deep breathing, exercise, and self-talk.

Ann decided that she needed a profession that was more "hands-on," and sought my opinion on her becoming a physician, her original career choice in college. I thought that medicine would be a very good fit with Ann's talents, and I encouraged her. My approval of this professional choice was very important to her, probably because it met some mirroring and twinship needs that had been unavailable in her family. As Ann took the prerequisite courses and studied for the MCAT, she felt stressed, but also experienced a greater sense of being more settled in her professional and relationship life. She no longer needed weekly sessions, and our contact became more occasional. Ann ultimately was accepted at a medical school in Chicago, and she moved back to the area with her partner. They purchased a home, and her partner began a graduate program as Ann started medical school.

DISCUSSION

This case illustrates the complexities of treating a patient who had become defensively self-sufficient and overcontrolling, while at the same time requiring help with anxiety management. The paramount issues in the early years were Ann's insecure attachment style and need to achieve greater resolution of a traumatic childhood. Stolorow and Atwood (1992) describe the dynamic unconscious as containing unintegrated affect states that have been defensively split off because of poor responses by caregivers; those responses are then experienced as threatening to psychological equilibrium and needed relationships. Much of Ann's energy was aimed at keeping affective states of fear, anger, and sadness out of consciousness, but she was only partially successful; her desymbolized experiences (Bucci, 1997) broke through in the form of vomiting and muscular tension. Ann greatly feared my responding to her emotions in the same traumatizing way that her family had, and she also dreaded the affect states themselves because they made her feel out of control.

We repeatedly explored Ann's anxieties about my responses and all the ways in which my actual behavior was different from what she expected; ultimately some of her organizing principles as well as the contents of her dynamic unconscious were transformed. To Ann's surprise and relief, I did not show contempt for her vulnerability, but instead tried to provide her with a new experience. Bucci discusses the positive changes possible when a patient experiences an emotion schema in a new interpersonal situation that does not match the old traumatic expectations. According to

Spezzano (1995), "The patient and analyst co-create and co-sustain a joint consciousness that holds and thinks about affects that previously were simply felt by the patient" (p. 35). As Ann shared detailed information with me concerning her childhood experiences, her tolerance for feeling long-suppressed affects grew. Anxiety symptoms such as vomiting and muscular tension improved as verbal processing in the context of a new relationship affected what Bucci (1997) terms the somatic and sensory components of emotion schemas. In addition to the vital importance of disconfirming Ann's pathogenic beliefs about my reactions, I believe that my being able to offer her specific techniques to manage affect states facilitated her willingness to explore difficult material. The overall relational context plus anxiety management strategies reduced her panic about feeling vulnerable and out of control.

Ann's attachment style had many dismissive elements, including an excessive focus on work, lack of trust of others, and an insistence upon emotional self-sufficiency. Our successful employment of symptom-focused techniques early in treatment to help her resolve her fear of flying was central to her assessment that I might have something to offer her. The defensive dismissal was, however, only a thin veneer covering profound anxiety about her needs for approval and understanding from others and her expectation that vulnerability entailed further trauma. Ann's typical strategy of repudiating such needs in favor of controlling interpersonal interactions worked only to a limited extent in our relationship, and her sense of control diminished as she found that I was becoming important to her. My efforts to remain consistent, reliable, and nonretaliatory seemed to help her tolerate the treatment process. In addition, after Ann's having experienced her parents as incompetent, it was very important for her to be able to idealize me. A powerful idealizing transference was uncovered after some of Ann's defensive distancing attenuated and she recognized my ability to "fly the plane." Mirroring and twinship selfobject experiences were central in this treatment as well. Ann found my understanding of her, my appreciation of her intellect and wit, and our similarities of taste and intellectual interests to be very healing.

I believe that my willingness to self-disclose constituted another central element in this treatment. I have suggested elsewhere that a clinician's self-disclosure may facilitate a shift from a defensive posture of repudiation of need to one in which a patient is more able to tolerate vulnerability (Connors, 1997a). Patients such as Ann are prone to interpret ambiguous information in a negative way; for instance, a fleeting expression on my face must mean I dislike her rather than something more benign. My willingness to be as transparent as I could with her about my thoughts and feelings concerning her provided an antidote to her anxiety-ridden organizing principles and pathogenic beliefs. For example, she stopped worrying that she was boring me one day when I explained that a back problem was acting up and that was why I was moving around in my chair more than usual.

I also acceded to Ann's requests for information about myself, and she informed me directly that my willingness to be human with her and answer questions such as what I liked to read made her willing to risk letting herself be more open with me. My provision of personal information helped to titrate her frustration at the asymmetry of our relationship. With a move away from the old ideal of the anonymous "blank screen" analyst, numerous relational authors in recent years have written of the potentially mutative aspects of self-disclosure. Burke (1992) has emphasized the utility of therapist self-disclosure as forming a bridge between an old and a new object experience. Patients who lack trust may particularly benefit from information about ways in which a new attachment figure is different from previous ones. Shane, Shane, and Gales (1997) posit a dimension of intimacy concerned with interpersonal sharing, which relates to a capacity to be with another in a mutual and connected fashion and with appreciation of the other. These authors suggested that when this dimension of intimacy is present certain clinician responses such as answering questions may be appropriate that would not necessarily be indicated at other times. Benjamin (1988) and Hoffman (1998) have addressed the need for mutual recognition in relationships and the positive, growth-oriented aspects of patients' wishes to have access to their therapists' subjectivity. Frank (1999) calls for an "authentic analytic attitude" to replace the anonymity that was valorized in a one-person treatment model, and suggests that we permit ourselves to be accessible to patients in a nonimposing and genuine fashion (p. 128).

Ann always treated the information I gave her with great interest and deep respect. Some information I shared fostered selfobject experiences of twinship with me and lessened the alienation that resulted from her feeling so different from others in her family. Ann probably knows more factual information about my life history, views, and preferences than anyone else with whom I have worked, and my providing such information at her request seems to have helped foster the type of relationship we have developed over the years, which is characterized by deep mutual respect, appreciation, and warmth. My being something of a real person to her seems to have been vital in her gradually developing trust in me. Such self-disclosure offers a special kind of recognition of the patient as a human being when the therapist is willing to share some measure of the self that he or she is outside of the office (Hoffman, 1995).

My countertransference experience with Ann evolved considerably over time, as did my decisions concerning what to contain and what to share. In the first several months of our once-weekly treatment, I consistently felt anxious, scrutinized, and criticized. I believe that my experience was connected to Ann's identification with critical and sadistic aspects of her parents and constituted a transference test for me in which she turned passive into active. I found this experience unpleasant but manageable and had no difficulty retaining a sense of my own competence. I tried a few times to draw Ann's attention to ways in which she might be relating to me as her parents had to her, but she found this disorganizing, stating that she couldn't stand thinking that she was like them. Eventually I concluded that interpreting her style of relating to me was ill timed and that I should simply try to contain the experience until she was more secure with me. I believe that I passed this test by delaying, which helped to initiate the next phase of treatment, in which Ann became aware of intense wishes for my approval and availability while fearing my criticism and abandonment.

The test here involved a need to disconfirm her pathogenic belief that vulnerability would be responded to in a traumatic fashion, and Ann feared my scrutiny and criticism more than she subjected me to hers. This phase was much easier for me, as I seldom felt anxiety during sessions. Her assumption of a cool and superior manner was now more sporadic than constant, and when she became icy and challenging with me I was able to interpret her attitude as the result of increased anxiety about dependency and vulnerability in our relationship. Most of the time she could accept this interpretation and become more self-reflective. We had an interaction after about a year of therapy that seemed pivotal in this regard. She had adopted her haughty critical manner and said something snide to me which I cannot recall. I was concentrating on interpreting the defensive aspects of her behavior, but she told me much later that what really affected her in that exchange was seeing a hurt look on my face. Instead of feeling satisfaction at her ability to get to me, she felt miserable, and vowed to herself that she did not want to treat me like that. Since that time, with very minor exceptions, she has not. Ann's experience of my vulnerability and her capacity to cause me pain, at a time when she had some evidence of my competence and trustworthiness, helped her relinquish part of her identification with the aggressor. My countertransference experience with her continued to evolve in the direction of less anxiety and more enjoyment of our engagement.

Ann's formerly insecure attachment style is now quite secure. She has had a stable and satisfying committed relationship for several years. Although she found medical school a trial, she was able to maintain perspective and not permit her sense of herself to be defined by her interactions there. When Ann has sought contact with me in recent years, she has specifically requested pragmatic help with present-oriented issues on a more time-limited basis, in contrast to our earlier work involving intensive exploration of genetic material and our relationship. A blend of dynamic and cognitive work that involves the recognition that certain organizing principles are becoming activated and a restructuring of internal dialogue in the direction of less personalized responding has proved quite effective for her. Moreover, my comfort with Ann's oscillating between seeing me and not seeing me seems to have provided her with a sense that she can turn to me without the "strings attached" that she experienced in seeking her mother's care. It has seemed developmentally appropriate to maintain this stance rather than insist that Ann be in regular treatment or terminate. Ann reported finding it very helpful in recent years to be able to consult with me on an "as-needed" basis.

In one of our most recent sessions, Ann observed me closely for a few minutes and then asked if I had a headache (I had a terrible one and was soon to be diagnosed with having migraines). I answered that I did, and she asked a few more questions about my symptoms, demonstrated an acupressure technique, and advised me to seek medical attention. I told her I appreciated her perceptiveness and her concern, and it was clear that we both enjoyed the temporary role reversal as she practiced her new profession on me (and provided some symptom-focused treatment!). The mutual comfort and trust that permitted such a flexible interaction to take place attests to the major shift in relational style that took place over the course of this long-term integrative treatment.

CHAPTER NINE

A Patient with Binge Eating and Depression

THIS WAS A RELATIVELY SHORT-TERM treatment (nine months). Carol entered treatment suffering from a major depressive episode and binge eating disorder. Carol's depression quickly remitted with a combination of medication and psychotherapy. The chronic binge eating problem was a major therapeutic focus with this highly motivated patient. She demonstrated a high need for symptom-focused interventions and found them very usable. Carol's symptoms conformed to the addictive pathway in which fragmentation is warded off by the patient's engaging in some active mood-changing behavior. As she developed greater affect tolerance and sought more selfobject experiences in the relational world, her need for food as her primary selfobject diminished. Carol permitted me to audiotape sessions, so I can present some verbatim exchanges here.

CAROL

Carol, an attorney in her mid-20s, entered treatment wishing to overcome a problem with binge eating that dated back to grade school. She described being a "latch key kid" who would come home from school every day to an empty house. She would fill the time with eating and watching television. Family life was often conflictual, but "although the dinner table might be chaos, food never disappointed." Carol had experienced numerous weight fluctuations as a result of binge eating and dieting. She reported that she was always either in "good mode," such as counting Weight Watchers points, or "binge mode." When the latter prevailed, she would eat anything well beyond the point of hunger, including foods she did not even like, but generally preferred to binge on high-fat foods such as ice cream and pizza. Her binge eating was invariably done in private, and Carol noted that she experienced few cravings when with others. However, she reported that recently she had found herself withdrawing and eating on the weekends rather than socializing. Carol told me that there had been a time in her life when she had done without food; in college she had successfully dieted and lost weight, but during this process a close relative had died and she had been rejected by a boyfriend. She refrained from overeating as she dealt with these events, but reported that she had been severely depressed and experienced much difficulty getting out of bed. Carol said that she often felt insecure and not liked by others and that her eating was a shameful secret. She expressed a deep wish for a normal relationship with food in which she felt more in control.

We began a once-weekly psychotherapy with an explicit agreement to work on Carol's goal of controlling her relationship with food. Further exploration of Carol's history and current experience suggested chronic struggles with depression as well as with binge eating. She reported that she had always hoped that the next event in life would make her feel better, but that no transition ever really had. She could feel good for perhaps a week, but rarely more, and she described a life in which everything took great effort, even hanging up her coat. For years she had had to "psych" herself to get out of bed and begin the day. Her family history revealed that depression was prevalent in family members, including bipolar disorder and a few suicides. Very harsh with herself concerning her depression, Carol chided herself because "I should be so happy—it's not like anybody died or something. My family is alive. I have a great job—what's my problem?"

Further discussion of family life revealed, however, that although Carol's parents were physically alive, their emotional availability was quite compromised. Carol described her mother as an excessively cheery woman who refused to acknowledge painful events and went through life "wearing blinders, thinking prayer will solve everything." Carol's mother worked long hours outside the home when Carol and her siblings were growing up; the mother failed to attend to Carol much of the time. At one point in high school Carol was eating only 400 calories per day and was getting up to eat cereal in the middle of the night for a full year before her mother asked her if she had an eating disorder. "She just wants it all to be OK." Carol reported that her father was "useless" and that her mother had really been a single parent. Carol's father was alcoholic, and although he went to rehab and stopped drinking when she was 10, it made little difference—"He was still mean, he still ignored us, and basically we have no relationship." Carol expressed much pain concerning her family relationships. She commented that she knew intellectually about her parents' limitations but that she was aware she needed help with all the feelings. She said, "If your family is defective, then you feel defective too."

Carol had entered treatment with some awareness that her binge eating stemmed from emotional issues, and as we discussed her depressive experiences I suggested that she might have been using food as medicine for her depression, an idea with which she readily agreed. We also explored other functions that food had served for her: it felt comforting when she was lonely and longing for attention, and it helped her feel distracted and distanced from other painful feelings. We discussed the severity of her depressive episode in college, when she had been confronted with major losses and had not turned to food, and how frightening it was to contemplate managing her feelings without the usual buffer. I suggested that our therapy could include a focus on other ways for her to cope so that she would not be left with nothing. In addition, I recommended that Carol seek a medication evaluation so that her difficulties could be addressed in every possible way.

Carol began taking an antidepressant, and reported a marked change in her experience after about a month of therapy and a week of medication. She described being less preoccupied with food and noted that stress at work was no longer making her want to eat. In our first few discussions of her binge eating I had commented that, in addition to the impact of emotional factors on her eating, I thought that her behavior might be exacerbated by the "all-or-nothing" judgments she made about her eating. I suggested that she experiment with trying to have a moderate portion of a "binge" food at a time that she was feeling good. Intellectually she thought this made sense but felt so immersed in constant depression and food cravings that moderation did not seem possible. Now that she was feeling a bit better, however, she was letting herself have a "normal" portion of cookies or a brownie, and in her improved mood state she had found it satisfying. She also seemed to be experiencing less general difficulty tolerating affects, and gave the example of her usual experience of driving a car and feeling an urgent need to escape from boredom by smoking and making phone calls. Now she simply felt the boredom without desperation about changing it.

As Carol's depression abated and her food cravings became less constant, she could easily observe ways in which various situations and her emotional reactions to them provoked urges to binge. She noticed that she felt angry at a rude person in a store and immediately felt cravings for food. Telephone calls with her mother proved to be a frequent trigger. Carol would share some of her thoughts and activities with her mother in the hope that her mother would be interested and responsive. Most of the time, however, her mother would switch the topic to herself or to one of Carol's sisters, or tell Carol that she shouldn't feel or do what she described feeling or doing. Carol was left feeling angry and disappointed. These conversations were likely to prompt a "bad eating night," whereas some other stressors were more easily tolerated. It was clear that Carol would require further resolution of her painful family experiences and the conclusions about her own worth that she had drawn from them, in addition to some focus on her present thoughts, feelings, and behaviors. We spent much time talking about her feelings of not being valued and appreciated in her family. Carol related numerous incidents when she sought her mother's care and attention, only to be disappointed. Carol stated that she had always wanted her mother to take her side and be her ally but was constantly disappointed in this wish.

Carol: I could start talking about a serial killer and she would turn it around and take that person's side. I think she just has a chip in her brain that makes her play the devil's advocate, but I just want to shake her and say, "Don't do that!" When someone is upset about something, think about how you would want someone to react when you're upset.

MC: Exactly.

Carol: When you call me and tell me how big of a dick Dad is being, do you want me to defend him or take your side? God, it's so frustrating!

MC: It must be incredibly frustrating.

Carol: Never—I am not exaggerating—never take our side, never once have I heard this from her. . . . I can see myself fighting with my husband someday and he backhands me and she would somehow justify that. It's just the most frustrating characteristic someone can have! I don't know why she feels she has to be on the opposite side of me all the time—and it's not just me, it's everyone. My sisters and I all talk about it, and she's always been that way.

Carol goes on to relate an example in which she was treated unfairly by a difficult teacher and her mother predictably took the teacher's side, in contrast to the mother of a friend who listened to the girls and commiserated with them.

Carol: She took our side—that's all you want from your parents, to think that you can trust them to be on your side like my friend's mother was. If parents only knew what is important to kids—the number one thing that would have made my childhood so much happier is if she just would have listened to me when I talked and then taken my side. I don't even think that my dad being an alcoholic would have been that big a deal if you can feel that kind of ally in your parents.

MC: I think you're right.

Carol: That's all kids need.

MC: This is what kids need more than anything, isn't it—for you to get to feel listened to, understood, that your mother was your ally and would stand up for you.

Carol had enough awareness of the impact of all this to be able to say, "How are you supposed to value yourself if you were never treated as valuable?" Her mother also refused to intervene in any conflicts among Carol and her siblings and would just tell them to stop fighting even if a particular offense kept occurring, such as a sister's taking Carol's clothes. Carol commented several times that there had been "no justice," and acknowledged that becoming an attorney had probably seemed so desirable because she wanted to be able to resolve conflicts in a fair way and see that justice was in fact done. As the oldest of five, Carol was frequently asked to sacrifice and accommodate, and referred to herself as "the brown lollipop kid—the other girls get the purple and red lollipops, and that's what's left."

Carol's relationship with her father appeared to be much less important to her than that with her mother, both in her childhood and at present. Carol described her father as either yelling at the children or ignoring them; she seemed to consider him an aversive nuisance. Her family life while she was growing up was dictated by him and his rigid preferences. She commented that her mother "probably doesn't even know what she herself likes anymore, because it's always been about him." How Carol might have regarded her father in earlier childhood is not clear; possibly there was a time when she directed greater longings toward him than was the case later. By her report she had very low expectations for him as far back as she can remember, and she developed a dismissive style of attachment with him, which was probably adaptive in minimizing her anxiety and disappointment concerning his reactions to her. Carol noted that with her mother she kept hoping and trying to get the response she wanted. Overall, neither mother nor father nurtured Carol's sense of herself as worthy and lovable. Carol excelled in school and received mirroring from teachers, which did foster her perception that she was smart and might be valued by some for this attribute. However, although popular with peers she was also teased for being fat, and her early development only exacerbated her sense that her body set her apart in a negative way.

As Carol and I discussed her painful experiences with family members and peers, she was very affectively engaged, becoming alternately tearful and angry. She reported much relief at being able to talk about these events and to feel that I understood her point of view. She described feeling like such "an oddball" at times with her friends because they love their families, and why didn't she feel that way? "Am I just hard to please, like my mother says?"

It was very meaningful for Carol when I said that her parents had many of their own issues and limitations, which really got in the way of their being tuned-in parents, that she had suffered greatly because of it, and that she had a more difficult family than many. She acknowledged that growing up in her family had left her "hungry" for love and attention. As we talked about the various issues in her family (including such factors as extensive substance abuse in the extended family), she was able to gain a broader perspective on the dysfunction in her family and feel more detached from it. I suggested to her that some of her views of herself had formed many years earlier on the basis of her parents' limited ability to respond to her because of their own problems, and that perhaps some of these attributions about herself could now be reevaluated.

The aspect of Carol's life that she considered the most painful was the absence of an intimate relationship. She had never felt attractive to men and had considered herself fat since third grade. Carol reported great popularity and many boyfriends earlier in her life, but in college and later she had felt like "the fat girl" and had lacked confidence. She described a repetitive thought that summed up her view of herself and relationships: "Boys don't like me. I'm fat." Although Carol had dated in college and had a relationship of a few years' duration in law school, she had not really had any involvements in the last two years. She found this lack shameful and horrifying and wondered if others thought there was something wrong with her. She tearfully said that her greatest fear in life was of living and dying alone. Carol stated that the content of her most painful depressive thoughts revolved around her worries about never being attractive to anyone and never having a relationship. At times this pain was so unendurable that she considered suicide, although she said she knew she would never act on this urge. As her depression lifted, she experienced the most distress from relationship worries when she went out with friends to clubs and bars and did not meet anyone. Being back home alone at the end of such an evening feeling lonely and hopeless (and having had a few drinks) tended to disinhibit Carol's otherwise better controlled eating.

As Carol and I continued to discuss her relationship concerns in the present, it because apparent that her belief that men did not find her attractive and her sensitivity to rejection resulted in considerable filtering of information. For example, a friend that she went out with told her later that several men were "totally hitting" on her, but Carol had not noticed. She also casually mentioned to me that during another evening out at least five men had bought or offered to buy her a beer, but since she had her eye on a man who was paying no attention to her these offers failed to register as evidence that men found her attractive. In addition, she observed that men often seemed to be looking at her, but she always just assumed they were thinking that she was fat. I decided at this point to give Carol my perspective, although I was not sure that she would be able to take it in just yet. I told her that, in fact, she looks extremely attractive and that I suspected that, when she noticed men looking at her, they were thinking positive things about her appearance. I pointed out that she may be interpreting situations in terms of her conviction of being unattractive but that we could examine the evidence for this in various circumstances.

I also broached the idea that much of attractiveness has to do with fit, and referred to an earlier discussion in which I had asked her what she was looking for in a man. I told her that, just as she was most attracted to certain physical and emotional characteristics in a man, men were looking for their preferred type as well. I emphasized that, although our current culture idealizes a model of female beauty that is extremely thin, this did not mean that all men were searching for a size zero and that, in fact, I thought that there were any number of men out there who would be very happy to date someone just like her. However, I also stressed that, since everybody has a certain template in mind, she might not be the right match for a particular man—he might be looking for a petite redhead rather than a tall brunette—but this choice does not have to be seen as total rejection and failure.

Carol could see that on an intellectual level, and, although I thought it might be some time before her emotional sense of her own desirability changed, she reported a very positive development just a few weeks later. She and a few friends had taken a vacation together to a resort with many singles, and she found that she was feeling less intense and desperate about finding someone and enjoyed herself more. She said, "I heard your voice in my head—I would think when some guy looked at me, 'Oh, he thinks you're fat,' but then I'd remember what you would say, that so many guys go for exactly what you are, and it helped!" She reported that the "boys don't like me, I'm fat" cognition was much less frequent and that she was having a couple of dates.

Our work on Carol's binge eating continued. We focused on her tendency to binge in response to distress about her relationship situation, and we also discussed helpful general strategies for managing her relationship with food. Carol observed that she often ate more than she intended in the evenings when she came home tired, hungry, and lonely after work, so she decided to get rid of most of the "junk food" in her house, such as bags of chips that she would pick at and ultimately consume. We discussed the desirability of controlling her environment in this way and in planning ahead so that she would have a real meal for dinner that could be prepared quickly. She observed that eating carbohydrates often prompted the urge to eat more carbohydrates without reaching satiety and decided to attend more to the composition of her diet regarding protein and carbohydrates. She enjoyed feeling very much in control of her eating during a two-week period when she decided to try eliminating most carbohydrates. We discussed some upcoming social events at which she anticipated eating some carbohydrates, and we did some problem solving about how she could view doing so without considering herself a failure. I introduced the concept of the abstinence violation effect and suggested that, after she ate some carbohydrates, she remind herself of this discussion and that she had not "blown it." The following exchange illustrates a realization concerning the role of certain environmental cues.

Carol: The other day I realized I hadn't eaten before bed in four nights. . . . It's probably helping that I'm so tired from training and work—I see my bed and I want to get into it with a magazine or a book and just fall asleep, and I've been making my bed every day so that it looks really appealing, and it gets me off the couch . . .

MC: Did the couch signify eating more than the bed?

Carol: Yes, oh yes, I wouldn't dream of eating in my bed. I have this beautiful white bed with an expensive comforter—I would never bring food into my bed.

MC: OK, so the couch is a signal for relaxing with food, and the bed is a signal for something very different.

Carol: If I could get out and do things and not sit on my couch in front of the TV, I wouldn't eat nearly as much. I'm fine all

day—I don't even eat with stress being the trigger now. . . .
But that's comfort for me, curling up with ice cream or
whatever and just sitting on my couch, and that's the only
time I ever overeat, truly. . . . So being so tired and getting
into bed really helps.

MC: I think you've hit on something helpful here—if you can
orient yourself toward relaxing on your bed rather than
on your couch with food you are much better off.

Carol was able to use these self-management strategies quite
effectively, but continued to struggle with painful affective experiences, eating in response to them and feeling bad about herself
later. She ate a large quantity of pizza following another disappointing Saturday night out, and we discussed how much better
she might feel if she responded differently to such an experience.
I suggested that simply reminding herself to try an alternative was
the first step and that it might help to cue herself with something.
Carol thought of tying a ribbon around her refrigerator. Next we
discussed what besides food might comfort her in that particular
emotional state. Carol recalled reading magazine articles about
things like taking a bath or keeping a journal, but to her this type
of alternative seemed "boring"; she was aware she needed something of higher intensity, such as playing music loudly and reading a magazine. We agreed that for now nothing was going to seem
anywhere nearly as desirable as what she termed "the total experience of being on the couch with limitless comfort food." A
coworker became engaged, which Carol found extremely upsetting. She went to bed soon after coming home from work but did
not binge, and tearfully said that she couldn't stand feeling things
like this, that it was so hard without food. She also said, "It's so
overwhelming to feel your feelings when you've always suppressed
them!" I agreed but told her that it would become easier with more
practice. I also told her that, although her feelings could seem overwhelming, in fact they would not continue indefinitely but would
crest and move on, just like a wave. I recommended that she do
some diaphragmatic breathing during the process.

The exchange that follows illustrates a type of intervention I
used with Carol concerning her painful affects. The intervention
combined a focus on physiological relaxation and an attitude of
self-compassion rather than harsh judgment. Carol described being
haunted by regrets concerning the past, particularly that she did

not obtain help for her depression and binge eating sooner and that she sought attention from men in ways she now considers demeaning. These thoughts sometimes kept her up at night, and she wished there were "a pill that could wipe out your memory." This subject came up near the end of a session prior to a several-week break due to a trial.

MC: This is an area that you and I will continue to work on. But in the meantime there is one thing that you might try when some of those thoughts come up about regrets from the past and you're feeling sad. I recommend that at those moments you pay a lot of attention to making sure that you are breathing deeply and that you're trying to think about those things with compassion for yourself—to try and get away from any kind of self-blame and just see if you can approach this with an attitude of compassion for the suffering person that you were. The suffering you were going through led you to make certain choices that you wouldn't make now . . . but to have done something different at that time I think you would have needed a kind of help that nobody was giving you.

Carol: (very quietly) Yep.

MC: And that's not your fault . . .

Carol: I know—I think I'm just mourning the time I lost . . .

MC: It's sad that you suffered as much as you did, and it makes sense that you would feel that sometimes. When you do, just try not to tense up and just keep doing some deep breathing and try to be compassionate with yourself—and it will pass. You won't be immersed in it forever.

As Carol continued with therapy, medication, and the marathon training she referred to earlier, she did find it easier to manage her affect states. She reported, "Between this [therapy], the medicine, and the training, I must have so many good endorphins going through me! Because nothing has changed. I'm just dealing with it so much better. I still had no phone calls last night and I have nights where there's nothing going on and I'm lonely but it bothers me so much less. . . . It's so funny to think back to the winter, how hard it was for me to do anything at all and I just ate everything to medicate myself. . . . All those things that were so hard are so easy now—I'm a much happier person." She also noted that gradually it was becoming more possible to refrain from eating in difficult situations. "Saturday night we went out, I had a really good time, and on the cab ride home I just talked myself through . . . 'OK, go home, get right into bed and don't eat, you'll fall right asleep' . . . and I did. I was even hungry, because we hadn't had much to eat, but I really didn't want to eat that way. I wanted to go to bed, get up and eat a big breakfast because that's better for you." However, food still played a central role in her life, and in my interventions I tried to find a balance between promoting positive changes and supporting self-acceptance about using food for emotional reasons at times without harsh self-judgment. In the following exchange I refer to harm reduction strategies as "damage control."

Carol: I stayed in Saturday, and Sunday I had to go into work and I just need something to get me excited again—because what got me excited was going home and having a little pizza and getting some ice cream. That got me excited and it got me through work. I don't have . . . and I hate that, that it does that for me, and I know if that boy had called I wouldn't have eaten the pizza. I would have had something else. I would have called my girlfriend to tell her that he called and think about what I'm going to wear and where we're going to go and all this other stuff . . . but I have nothing, that's why pizza is what I have and it made me happy.

MC: You had a date with your pizza. You didn't have a date with this guy, so you had a date with your pizza.

Carol: Yeah! And I don't want that to be the case, and it's not even so much anymore that I'm lonely and I'm going to eat. It's like I've got nothing else to get me excited and food really does it for me so . . . I know I shouldn't need things like this to make it but I do, I need that little . . . give me that phone call! . . . so I can have something to be happy about to make me not want to eat, to give me that determination . . .

MC: We both hope that your romantic life, soon, can feel more satisfying and exciting, but in the meantime it seems to me that there are going to be times when you will need the excitement of knowing that little pizza is waiting for you. I think the trick would be to let yourself do that sometimes and do damage control—minimize the number of calories you're eating so it's a little more contained, not "anything goes"—like it's low fat ice cream and you can do some portion control.

Carol: That's a good idea—I think you're right. I know my eating always ties in with how I'm feeling, it's never about the food, the taste or the texture, I don't miss things like chocolate, I like healthy eating, I don't miss it because of how it tastes, it's just the emotions that go with it . . .

MC: And there's something about pizza and ice cream that sometimes fills those emotions . . .

As Carol felt generally better and also more in control of her eating, she was able to focus on issues concerning her motivation for change and the ways various rationalizations about her eating blocked her from reaching her goal of weight loss.

Carol: I can so rationalize what I put into my mouth at times to where I think it's OK for me to do it—it's not OK and I need to remember that . . .

MC: And to think about the cost in the same way the Weight Watchers point system encourages . . .

Carol: I do need to do that! It's almost like . . . I don't do my time at work if I know my hours are low because I don't want to look at it and I don't want to see that yesterday I was there for 10 hours, and I only billed 5 so I don't want to . . . sometimes I don't want to count my calories because I don't want to know the truth—if you eat mindlessly out of the thing of ice cream I don't know how much I ate . . .

MC: It feels better sometimes not to know . . .

Carol: A portion of it, I know how much, but even if I don't know I still billed that few hours and I still ate that many calories.

MC: That's right. So maybe part of this . . .

Carol: Denial!

MC: . . . is convincing yourself that it's in your best interest to know the truth even if the truth is unpleasant—but at least then you know where you are.

Carol: When you write things down, you are amazed at how much you put into your body! At Weight Watchers they call them BLTs—bites, licks, and tastes, and they all count. I know I can do it. Why am I not doing it? It's all within my control . . .

MC: You know exactly what it takes and you realize what you haven't been doing lately, and that you can—it just takes effort and a different mindset than the one you've had since you started your training.

Carol: I know it's within my control and I've just been rationalizing about it . . .

She then talked about noticing some automatic eating when out to lunch that could be changed but also said that being able to eat and drink freely when out for an evening was very important to her.

MC: You have priorities, and on some evenings you want to be able to eat and drink with friends and in your mind those calories are well spent, but at other times it isn't so crucial. And what you would like to do is just exercise more consciousness about the choices you're making in the moment instead of rationalizing that it's all OK. So you want to try to be more aware and ask yourself, how badly do I want this food? If I really want it badly, I can have it, but let me just think about the cost.

Carol: And that's where I need to get—because, if I got there and I looked at pictures of myself thinner or thought about how none of my clothes fit, I wouldn't eat it. But I don't know how to get there, to get that yellow light in my brain, I just go green and go, so I'm trying to get better about that—I have some times when it happens and I feel really strong and I'll say go to bed, don't eat that. But at other times it's overwhelming temptation. I almost can't—I rationalize it: it's my entertainment, it's my friend, and it's my thing I curl up next to, you know. But I do want weight loss really bad—I have to remember that . . . I think what I'm going to do tonight after talking to you is I'm going to gather up pictures, ones where I think I look good and ones where I want to throw up, and put them on my refrigerator and computer at work, so I can stop and look and remind myself I want to look like *this*, I don't want to look like *that*!

As Carol continued to make changes, she found herself feeling excited about the possibilities, but her sense of efficacy wavered. As we explored her fluctuating feelings, I highlighted the need for her to move away from dichotomous thinking, and I underscored the fact that perfection is not required.

Carol: I've never told anybody this before, but sometimes I have this wave of excitement come over me, like let's just do this, let's lose all this weight. Oh my God, I get this very excited feeling like, what if you lost all this weight? What if you did? And they say your life doesn't change that much; but I know it must, like a different level of confidence I'd have, not just with men but in all areas, like certain things will happen and I'd want to be assertive about it. But I'd worry what someone's going to say back, and I worry most that they're going to say something about my weight and then I won't.

MC: It makes you feel vulnerable . . . you could be attacked on the grounds of weight.

Carol: So I know that your life must change in a lot of ways, and you don't have that vulnerability as much anymore . . . so I get excited and think, yeah, let's just do it—but then doubt starts creeping in.

MC: Tell me about the doubt.

Carol: I start thinking about all the times I've failed and why do I think it's going to be any different—I get all excited and motivated, I even get chills. But then I think, what are you going to do the next time you're lonely or have to work on a Sunday? You haven't been able to deal with it before, so what makes you think it's going to be any different now? And instead of saying, OK, it's going to be different now, I don't take that excitement and hold on to it; it comes and goes. What makes you think you can pass the jelly bean jar without sticking your hand in because you always have? One cheat leads to two cheats to three, and I'm off the diet . . . I can't think positive all the time, I'm too rational, I'm a lawyer!

MC: I do think that you can succeed at your change program and that it won't require positive thinking all the time . . . but one thing to remind yourself of when you say what's different this time is that a lot of what's gotten in the way in the past has been your depression, and you are taking care of your depression through treatment in a way you've never done before. When you don't feel the same level of intensity about needing to binge, it really puts you in a different place about how much you use food to manage your emotions. There will be times that you want to eat and times that you will eat, but if you can keep in mind the damage control we talked about earlier so you're doing it somewhat less—but you don't have to be perfect and not have any of what you call cheats in order for your program to succeed. It's not humanly possible to do that, but the way people succeed is by persisting even if they have periods when they say, well, I wish I hadn't eaten that but instead of saying oh, forget the whole thing, I've blown it, to say what can I do now to get back on track?

Carol continued to discuss with me her challenging family relationships and gradually found herself less preoccupied with the dissatisfactions of relating to her mother and siblings. In addition to the relief afforded by treatment, she very resourcefully found a way to interact with her mother that minimized her mother's frustrating features.

Carol: I've been e-mailing my mom nearly every day, and that's been going really well—I'm not having as many negative thoughts about her, and we've been getting along a lot better.

MC: I was very struck by what you were telling me last time about how close you were when you were in England e-mailing a lot and how that closeness continued for some time after you came back—it seems there's something about the process of e-mailing rather than being on the phone that your mother is better at.

Carol: Yes, infinitely better, unbelievably way better. She just isn't a phone person and so it's fine . . . I think it's the process of asking what's going on with me. When you e-mail someone you don't have to ask them, they will write you back and tell you what's going on with them—when I'm on the phone with her I'll talk to her and it feels awkward to then say, "So this weekend I did . . ." without having someone ask you. And I noticed that because I called her on Saturday and she was telling me about her weekend and I kept kind of waiting for her to ask me what I had done and she didn't and it felt awkward telling her and it just didn't work . . . I didn't get that upset about it and I just got off the phone really quick and thought, well, we just shouldn't talk on the phone.

As Carol and I discussed her attempts to relate to her mother in a more satisfying fashion, I wondered if it might be worthwhile to work with Carol on being more assertive with her mother concerning her wishes for responsiveness. I understood her response to my inquiry in the next exchange as indicating that she currently felt that she was tolerating all she could of increased vulnerability with her mother. Work on assertiveness would have required further displays of need to her mother, and, as she says, "I don't even want to broach it." Her preference here is so clear that I did not pursue the idea further, even as a future possibility.

MC: And if you had shifted the conversation, gotten over the awkwardness and said, "Well, this weekend I did such and such"—would she then express interest?

Carol: I don't know how to answer that, because if you tell someone what you did all weekend and it's your mother and they don't express any interest and it can just be such a blow that I'll get angry and say, "Well, you know what? I'm going to let you go because you obviously have other things on your mind," and then I feel hurt . . . I don't know . . . I don't like feeling like that, and I don't even want to broach it, and I don't want to risk feeling bad.

MC: I see what you mean. It's just too unpredictable—sometimes it might be just fine, she'd be able to focus on your weekend; other times she might be too wrapped up in herself.

Carol: Exactly.

MC: And you won't get the response you want and that will feel lousy.

Carol: And sometimes she will express interest and we'll get along great; other times not so much. But realizing how to limit the phone conversations and stick to e-mail, that helps some, and trying to get off the phone as quickly as possible when it's not going well . . . I'm having fewer upsetting feelings about it. I just don't like feeling that way when you can't stuff it down with food or something else and you have to feel it so strongly, and I hate that, so this is better.

Carol's experience of food continued to change, despite the difficulties of managing intense affects without it. The following comments near the end of treatment illustrate her perception of the transformation in her sense of control over her eating.

Carol: That's been so big. I have to tell you, when I came in here I never thought that could change. There's no way I thought that would ever change. It just felt like it was out of my control. Now I just don't think about it. I can eat what I want; I go hours and hours without eating, and I don't even think about it anymore like I used to.

MC: I know that was just unimaginable—you couldn't conceive of having a different relationship with food than you always had.

Carol: It's nice too—I probably don't eat as healthy as I used to (laughs) in the sense of I don't eat as many fruits and vegetables as I used to, but, before, I'd eat all these fruits and vegetables and then sit down and eat an entire bag of chips at night. I have bags of chips in my apartment that have been there for months, and boxes of cereal that I'll probably have to throw away . . . I never had to throw away cereal! So I have better control over it and it's just food!

DISCUSSION OF CASE MATERIAL

I view Carol as having suffered from significant deficits in selfobject experiences in her family, most particularly in the area of her mirroring needs. Carol's father seems to have provided few selfobject functions for the children, and her mother appears to have actively frustrated mirroring needs much of the time by responding in an oppositional fashion. Carol managed these frustrations from an early age by developing a selfobject relationship with food that was of central importance in her life. She referred to food as her friend, something to curl up next to when she was not obtaining sufficient attention elsewhere. Carol's family experiences equipped her poorly for dealing with her own affects; her mother seemed to disavow and deny all her own negative emotions, and her father's surfeit of untitrated anger contributed to Carol's fear of strong feelings. She turned to food to perform a range of affect-related functions: she could "stuff down" angry feelings, feel insulated from sad ones and obtain comfort, and become excited when she was feeling empty. Her recent comment that "It's just food" represents a considerable shift from experiencing food as a powerful selfobject.

Empathy was painfully lacking in Carol's family experience, and she responded very positively to my efforts to be empathic in the treatment. Carol's mirroring needs were a prominent feature in the transference. She tended to speak with much animation and some degree of pressure when recounting difficult events. It was clear at such times that she just needed to be listened to and not argued with. Little more was required for her to feel relief. Carol had learned at an early age to redirect most of her emotional needs away from the relational world, but a sector that remained available (and caused her much anguish in her relationship with her mother) was her wish to be mirrored. My invitation to Carol to share whatever was on her mind with me was very welcome, and she thrived in the context of my prioritizing her feelings and views. Carol responded immediately and positively to my inquiry about whether I might tape our sessions for inclusion in this book; my taking her words so seriously that I wished to record them perhaps contributed further to some satisfaction of her long-frustrated mirroring needs.

At the point in treatment when Carol began to focus more on weight loss, she seemed to experience some revival of long-suppressed grandiose strivings ("I've never told anybody this before, but sometimes I have this wave of excitement come over me . . .") as well as some anxiety and vulnerability concerning them ("Then doubt starts creeping in"). Those feelings likely related to parental quashing of any expression of such strivings early in life. Carol learned to deflate herself ("What makes you think you can pass the jelly bean jar without sticking your hand in because you always have?"). However, the increased self-cohesion she experienced as a result of more attention to her mirroring needs (interpretively as well as experientially) enabled her to have greater tolerance for her deepest wishes and to persist in actualizing them.

Carol seemed to benefit from interpretations that underscored and clarified the much less than optimal conditions in her family and her understandable response to them. She achieved a wider perspective on ways in which she had internalized her parents' neglectful responses to her as reflections of her worth, and this insight, in conjunction with her feeling mirrored in the treatment, resulted in heightened self-esteem. Stern (2002b), writing of the importance of identificatory processes, noted that patients seek out self-facilitating experiences of identifying with the view of the other toward the self, and that this search for an ameliorative experience might be directed toward old objects, such as parents, as well as the new object of the clinician. Carol was able to identify to some degree with my positive feelings toward her, as when she described hearing my voice in her head regarding her desirability and experienced herself as more appealing. Carol also found that communicating with her mother primarily by e-mail seemed to limit the possibilities for a hurtful interaction and enabled her to enjoy a more mirroring response.

My work with Carol has included a number of cognitive behavioral components, including control of the environmental, self-monitoring, restructuring of dichotomous thinking, instruction in diaphragmatic breathing, goal setting, and a concentration on alternatives to engaging in the addictive behavior. Because Carol was in the action stage of change, it was possible to move ahead quickly with action-oriented strategies without a great deal of work on motivation. We spent much time talking about the specifics of Carol's eating and helping her to structure it to facilitate moderation. This focus on moderation included a number of dimensions. From a cognitive perspective, we were attempting to modify dichotomous thinking. In Carol's polarized view of encounters with food, she was either overeating or dieting (her "binge mode" versus her "good mode") and tended to conceptualize food itself as good or bad. In addition, Carol's instructional selfobject needs were mobilized, and she sought my advice in constructing a way of eating (and living) that had greater balance than she had previously known. My suggestion that a food which Carol typically perceived as "bad" and associated with binge eating could be included in her regular eating was intended as instruction in a non-depriving and flexible mode of eating. My later suggestion to her that she could eat anything that she wanted, and that she should also consider the "cost" as it related to her weight loss goals, further promoted the idea of respecting her internal wishes and at the same time being mindful of the impact that meeting such desires might have on her goals. I felt it was important to balance support for symptomatic change with respect for the ways in which Carol had relied on food for many years and would continue to do so at times.

Earlier in the treatment we had focused a good deal on the fact that Carol ate as her primary method of dealing with painful affects and often felt overwhelmed by emotion. Gaining control of eating was central at this point. As Carol began to feel better, her goal of weight loss became more feasible and we could focus on her motivation for that objective. As is often the case with persons who have addictive behaviors, Carol suffered from a comorbid condition, in her case depression, and management of this problem through psychotherapy, medication, and exercise has been of crucial importance in her overall improvement and in her relationship with food. Her situation illustrates a common issue in conducting integrative, symptom-focused treatment: a person may have more than one symptomatic difficulty, and decisions must be made concerning how and in what order to undertake interventions. Such factors as the relative debilitation caused by each symptom, the patient's attitude toward each, and the ways in which the symptoms are related to one another must be considered. In Carol's case, her depression initially was quite impairing and made everything seem effortful, in addition to being a primary cause of her binge eating. I believed it necessary to address the depression at once so that Carol's overall experience of life could improve and so that she would have sufficient energy and motivation for treatment. Focused work on her eating was much more feasible after some amelioration of the depression.

These changes in a treatment of fewer than nine months suggest that Carol is a resilient and motivated woman with much resourcefulness in her approach to life. Despite the relational difficulties in her family, she seems to have achieved a decent measure of attachment security. Although there were insecure elements in her relationships, both dismissing and preoccupied, Carol related to me in a relatively secure fashion that enabled her to use treatment quickly for significant change. I suspect that her earlier relationships with teachers may have provided a model for engagement with an older mentoring person that is mutually beneficial. I enjoyed working with Carol very much. She was highly verbal in a fashion that was often amusing and unusually expressive, and I felt I could easily connect with her affectively.

Although I try not to have overly ambitious expectations about how patients will respond to psychotherapy, I do find it particularly gratifying when a patient changes in ways that give her great satisfaction, as Carol did. Carol had a specific goal for her psychotherapy with me and felt no need for further treatment when the goal was achieved. As with Ken, I had a sense that Carol was interested in relating to me in a relatively limited fashion for a particular period of time, without much interest in a deeper or longer engagement. It has obviously been highly adaptive for her to figure out how to get maximum benefit out of her relationships while attempting to limit ways in which her longings might be unsatisfied, as in relating to her mother by e-mail. A more complete treatment would have enabled us to explore these relational dynamics as they infused our relationship, but at this time Carol found a way to have an uncomplicated positive transference to me, do some work, and move on.

In chapter three I discussed the idea of the usability of symptom-focused techniques based on issues such as the patient's stage of change and the state of the therapeutic relationship; that Carol was in the action stage of change and related to me in a securely attached fashion resulted in high usability. Carol responded very positively to engaging in a relationship with me and eagerly made use of symptom-focused techniques, creatively tailoring them to suit her individual needs. Her rapid improvement illustrates that dramatic change is possible when a patient can use both the treatment relationship itself and the proffered techniques in a resourceful and relatively unconflicted fashion.

CHAPTER TEN

A Patient with a
Relational Dilemma

THE FINAL CASE IS THAT OF a woman whom I treated for about four years in weekly psychotherapy, with continuing sessions at lesser frequency over the last few years. Her symptomatic presentation revolved around prolonged indecisiveness concerning an intimate relationship, which ultimately was revealed to be part of a longstanding pattern of anxious avoidance. Bridget's symptoms seemed to connote vulnerability to fragmented states and avoidance of potentially threatening situations. They also reflected a compromise in which she found herself unable to move closer or get more distance and tried to negotiate this crippling ambivalence by attempting to stop time.

BRIDGET

Bridget sought treatment in her early 30s because of frustration concerning a relational dilemma. In her late teens, she had begun dating a young man and 17 years later felt unable either to end the relationship or to marry him. Bridget's distress concerning this ambivalent relationship grew with every passing year, particularly as she saw more of her friends marry and start families while she and Joe seemed to stay in the same place. It was very difficult for Bridget to imagine the current situation ever changing, but she hoped that I could help her feel able to make some decisions about the relationship. In our first meeting Bridget told me that she had had a couple of sessions with male therapists in the past but that therapy "had not worked" for her with men, and that she knew she needed a female therapist. She said that she had been worried about seeing a happily married therapist who would be sitting there judging her, but that I did not seem like that. In the second session Bridget found herself able to discuss some issues that she could not imagine sharing with a man, and stated that she felt committed to doing this work with me, although it was very difficult to focus on the relationship problem rather than just avoid thinking about it. She asked me if I thought that I could help her, and I told her that I believed that, by working together, we should be able to help her clarify her situation. Bridget expressed much relief at this.

The youngest of eight children born to Irish parents, Bridget described a very difficult family background. Her mother seems to have suffered from chronic depression, and Bridget depicted her as extremely passive and unwilling to offer any sort of guidance on life. Bridget said her mother would listen to her, for instance if she related a tale about something that happened at school, but would provide no feedback. Bridget's father was hostile and devaluing, and everyone in the family agreed that Bridget more than anyone else was the target of his wrath and deprecation. He called her a "slovenly slut" when she experimented with eye makeup as a teen, and frequently informed her that she was a loser and was so incompetent that she didn't know how to "wipe her own ass." Not surprisingly, Bridget's parents were miserable together. Her father would openly say that marriage is awful, and Bridget felt that she had observed her mother wither over the years. Bridget reported that her father was at his worst at the time she met Joe.

When I asked Bridget to tell me more about her relationship with Joe, she immediately said, "He's everything to me—he's been like a parent." She described him as very loving and available, said that he had rescued her and took care of her and was a great listener. However, like her mother, Joe was extremely passive. Joe was anxious and lacked confidence, and Bridget had always "called all the shots" in the relationship. Bridget expressed extreme guilt for often having treated Joe in a "mean and hostile way" earlier in their relationship and said that, although her behavior was much better now, she felt very burdened by this guilt. It was especially troublesome to her that Joe seemed to have no goals other than those she suggested to him, such as taking some college courses. Bridget herself had been an underachiever despite high intelligence but she finally had figured out her life was going nowhere with short-term jobs. She pursued higher education with no help from her family, graduated from college, and was now performing very well in a career as a special education teacher. Joe's apparent satisfaction with his high school diploma and routine position were at variance with Bridget's evolving aspirations for her life. She reported that it had been very gratifying to achieve and to be recognized for her achievement in college and on her job. Although she knew one major factor in her achievement motivation was to prove her father wrong about her competence, she found it very difficult to respect someone like Joe, who seemed utterly lacking in such drive.

I had a sense very early in treatment that Bridget was longing for contact and dialogue that would add something new to her understanding of her situation, despite her anxieties about being criticized. I began to share my preliminary ideas with her. I told her that one thought I had as I came to learn more about her family situation was that the model of marriage she had grown up with involved one partner who was very dominant and one who was extremely passive, and that, if those were the only roles that she knew, it would make sense to choose to be the dominant one. In addition, I told Bridget that her terror of marriage was quite understandable given her perception of the unremitting misery of her parents' life together. She responded positively to these ideas, and in the next session told me that she was finding it a bit easier to think about different possibilities for her life without panicking or becoming tearful. Bridget told me that she had felt very alone and tortured with these concerns for a number of years and that she wished she had seen me long ago. I told her I was sorry that she had suffered for so long on her own, and that I could see that sharing was beginning to help. She also wondered if other people ever had problems like hers. I told her that sometimes they did, and she expressed relief, saying that she frequently worried that "I'm not normal."

We continued to discuss Bridget's family. Her father's method of interacting tended toward the sadistic; Bridget remembered that he would tickle her and her siblings until they were crying and screaming. Her mother managed to perform the household tasks for a large family, but was so conflict avoidant and uninvolved that she seemed physically present only. Bridget related that she was becoming more aware that her background was affecting her in ways she had never thought and that this new awareness was very painful. We spent a good deal of time discussing her siblings, most of whom as adults were having considerable difficulty with alcoholism, relationship problems, and various psychological disorders. Bridget was tearful over their situations, but also felt more confirmed in thinking that things had been very inadequate in the family. I told Bridget I could really see that her parents' ability to meet her needs growing up had been so limited that she was left desperate for some of the understanding and support that people ideally get at home and that she had found that in Joe. As she described his background, which also involved the stresses of immigration and very critical parents, it seemed clear that, like Bridget, Joe badly needed a new attachment figure to help compensate for some deficits in his family.

Bridget came in tearful for a session in the first few months of treatment. She was feeling very negative, worrying that she was not normal and never would be and that nothing would ever change. The precipitant for her more acute distress was a difficulty with a work colleague who criticized Bridget for failing to take care of something in a shared teaching room. Bridget thought that the colleague was still cold after Bridget had apologized. She worried that the colleague disliked her and that she would lose her job. A midyear evaluation was coming up in the next month, which always made Bridget highly anxious. We discussed the fact that her current position felt precarious and that catastrophe seemed imminent, and related that circumstance to her worry that her father was correct in his assessment of her as a dislikable loser. I explained a little about cognitive therapy at this time and suggested that Bridget might focus on the question, "What's the evidence?" when she found herself worrying that she would receive poor evaluations and lose her job. I also told her that her father's voice was loud in her head making all kinds of negative comments about her, and that I thought she should send in an internal defense attorney who would object to such criticism and speak up on her behalf. Bridget liked this idea and found herself excited about starting some cognitive work. Having an active technique to try at this time seemed particularly helpful as she was wrestling with a sense of hopelessness about the dysfunction in her family and whether she could ever change.

Shortly after this session, Bridget experienced what felt like a "real breakthrough" for her. She had a long conversation with her father concerning what to do about her brother, who had psychotic features. Bridget reported that she no longer felt reactive to her father as she had before or so affected by his critical comments. "For the first time I didn't believe it—I knew it was his problem!" Bridget noted that, even when she had fought back with her father in the past, "I would crumble inside," but that it had not happened this time: "I was a cool competent adult all the way!" Continuing to experience this shift with her father as highly significant, she said a few sessions later that she was less angry at him and that he did not have the control now as he had when she was a child. I believe that Bridget's engagement with me had resulted in her ability to feel more secure and to retain a more cohesive self-structure so that she did not "crumble inside." She found herself able to use the cognitive work we had discussed as she interacted with her father, and its efficacy was probably enhanced because it also evoked her connection with me.

Bridget expressed appreciation for therapy and for me at this point, as well as some longing for more contact than the one session per week for which her insurer would reimburse. "If I won the Lotto, I'd want to book all your time. I'd come three or four times a week for long sessions!" Bridget also reported a talk with Joe in which he had commented that therapy left her with more questions than answers, that therapists just wanted to make money, and that it was a good scam to keep people coming back for more therapy. I asked her what she thought about those ideas, and she replied, "I don't think you're like that," but it was clear that her mistrust of others' motives (shared by Joe) was in conflict with her emerging wishes for more connection with me. Some of this tension seemed to resolve in favor of more trust of me the next week when Bridget called me between sessions; she was extremely upset about having been criticized by the assistant principal, but as she related the incident to me it was clear she had handled the situation very well. I told her this, and, quite proud of herself for being professional but not letting herself get pushed around, she commented that she felt stronger as well as more fragile since starting therapy and that she was grateful.

Bridget now felt able to focus on her relationship with Joe in more detail, including expressing her longing to be single and to date other men. She described a terrible weekend with him during which she finally screamed that she hated him. She said that she felt awful about herself for treating him in this fashion. I told her I understood that she did not want to behave that way but that she must have been having very intense feelings about the situation with him. "He's so passive I can't stand it—here's the sum total of his conversation: 'I don't know' . . . 'Maybe' . . . 'I'm not sure' . . . We'll see' . . .". I asked her what Joe did when she screamed that she hated him, and she replied that he said nothing. She thus described a cycle in which she sought a reaction from him, failed to get it, and then became more exasperated and provoking as he remained silent. "But I can't leave him. He was there for me, always, when I really needed him. It would be so cruel to leave him; it would be like pushing a person in a wheelchair into the river." I told her I was struck by this image. She replied that she had seen it in a movie and that it really conveyed how she felt about him. "I can't see him standing on his own two feet. How would he manage? Don't you think I owe him? You think I should leave him, don't you? Oh, I know you can't tell me . . ." I responded that, of course, it had to be her decision and that her own values really had to determine her choices, but that I would tell her how I saw the situation. I told her that I thought she owed Joe a great deal of appreciation and respect, but that she could not force love and passion no matter how she might try. I went on to say that I believed, if she remained with him simply out of obligation, he would perceive it and this would not be a good basis for a marriage and family life. Finally, I told her I thought that, if the relationship were not able to change in the direction of more satisfaction, then she would be better off leaving and that perhaps Joe could manage that eventuality better than she anticipated.

Bridget was very thoughtful and said that she had never really realized before that she felt no freedom of choice about remaining with Joe. I pressed her about what it would mean if she were to leave him, and she immediately replied that it meant she was bad, because he loved her unconditionally and she owed him that too. I raised the possibility that love in adult life might not be so unconditional. Ultimately Bridget was able to say that she found Joe's love burdensome at times but still thought that perhaps they belonged together. I agreed that maybe they did but that I thought she would know that only if she felt more free to leave rather than believing she must serve a life sentence. We also talked about her feeling paralyzed to decide whether to leave Joe or to marry him. I suggested that she consider a few moderate courses of action that could move the relationship in the direction of more closeness or more distance—for instance, they could take a planned break from the relationship to experiment with greater distance, or they could pursue couples therapy to work on intimacy. Bridget particularly liked the idea of a planned break from the relationship and believed that she wanted to implement it. As she thought about the future, however, there were always various events affecting her and Joe together, such as a family wedding or holiday that made a break seem impossible. As she reflected on the possibility of a break, she found that she relished the prospect of "having no one to answer to" but also realized that she would be very lonely: "I can't count on my family—only on Joe. He's always listened to me like I don't have two heads!"

Although I liked Bridget from the start, I found working with her challenging at times because she was so cynical, angry, and stuck. She would frequently make comments like, "I have to marry Joe—no one is happily married anyway. I need to have a baby and there's nothing more to say," and then angrily reject any comments or questions I might raise about the validity of those assumptions. "If I don't marry him, can you guarantee I will meet a nice guy who'll love me and that I'll have a baby? Well, can you?" In one session her anger and sadness were intense from the beginning, and she launched into the following: "I'm just never going to be happy. That's OK. It's too late. I'll marry Joe because that's what you have to do, you have to have a baby. I don't want to really but you have to . . ." Bridget completely avoided eye contact, and I found myself frustrated at her unreachability. I commented that she was very angry at her family, at Joe, and probably at me too, but nothing I said seemed to have much impact. She went on to say in a denigrating tone, "Next I suppose you'll say that Joe needed me like I needed him . . ." Quite irritated at this point, I rather uncharacteristically said, "No, I wasn't going to say that, and I think you're being kind of snotty, aren't you?" She responded, "Even you are reacting to me—I think I'm really sad but I'm getting mad to cover it up."

We were not able to process our interaction much until the following session, when Bridget came in apologizing: "I was a real bitch last week, I don't know why . . . I told Joe that you were mean to me." I suggested that we talk more about what had happened and told her I did not want to be mean to her but that I had become irritated at her tone about what I would say next and that I felt unable to reach her. She said that she thought she had been very angry with me, although she did not know why, and that she had also been extremely angry with her family all weekend. She had raised the idea of a break with Joe, and he had been unresponsive. I told her I thought she had continued to be very upset with his being so passive and wondered if she might have wanted to provoke me to react to her in some sort of way. "Well, it did stop me! I want him to stop me. He doesn't. I'm like my father in a way, constantly creating conflict." I said, "You have a short fuse. Joe has a long one—when things are good, he calms you down and you enliven him, but when it's not good, he's like a rock and you want to light a fire!" This comment really struck Bridget, who turned bright red and said, "Exactly—it's awful to think you'll never be happy with a person!" and began crying.

That incident seemed to represent something of a turning point, and in subsequent sessions I never again felt irritated with Bridget in the same way or experienced her as unreachable. It was not unusual in later sessions for her to feel angry and hopeless at the beginning of a session, but then her mood would shift as the session progressed and we would typically be laughing together by the end. A few months after this interaction she remarked that we have a great deal in common, including that we are both Irish, share the same middle name, and own property in the country. She discussed how relieving it was to be able to talk about the anguish she experienced in her relationship with Joe and to feel that I really understood it.

Although Bridget continued to feel at an impasse with Joe, she made great progress with other areas of her life, showing increased insight and changed behavior. Becoming less risk averse in some areas, Bridget purchased the vacation property she referred to as something we had in common and going on a Habitat for Humanity trip to a Third World country. She realized that she was very prone to avoidant behavior because it increased her short-term comfort, "but it makes a long-term mess!" She also became aware that her procrastination about such issues as paying bills (she would hide them when they arrived to avoid seeing the due dates) related to a profound wish to deny that time was passing, that she was aging, and that she and Joe would have to make some decisions about the future.

Bridget's insight into how her family experiences had affected her continued to grow. She realized more about how neglected she and her siblings were. She related tales about falling out of a moving car as a young child, unnoticed by her father, who had to be alerted by her brother, and how her mother frequently became absorbed with her shopping and lost young Bridget in stores. She noted the effect on her siblings as well: one sister had been molested but not believed by their mother, and another had to have her stomach pumped several times after she ingested medicines. Moreover, Bridget became aware that her mother had communicated some powerful messages to her concerning marriage; she had conveyed that Bridget should stay single and have her own free and exciting life by doing so. "I got the idea that young, single, and free were all lumped together with a lilt in my mother's voice—and on the other side was married, old, unfree . . ." This message gained additional importance because Bridget's mother typically offered little verbal guidance and daily modeled the depression Bridget learned to associate with the married state.

At times I felt moved to make interventions with Bridget that involved disclosing aspects of my own life experiences. I suspected that she would find references to our shared Irish heritage usable when she was proposing avoidant strategies I thought were likely to fail. For instance, in one session she was disappointed and angry with her siblings and told me of her plans to respond by withholding Christmas gifts from their children. I talked with her about its being very Irish to respond in a passive-aggressive fashion in the hope that others would get the message and be sorry, but that to do so was not likely to be the most effective way to communicate one's feelings. She said she could see that, "But I could never tell them I'm hurt or I have a need, it isn't me!" I told her that, since

I was Irish too, I could really understand this and that growing up in my family I was noted for my "sulking" but that I had had to learn to communicate more directly. She was fascinated by my revelation and commented, "Oh, I thought of you as being totally together in relationships!" I told her that I had had to learn. She was very thoughtful after this disclosure, and a few sessions later told me that she had talked with her mother, who tended to get overburdened and martyred with holiday chores. Bridget informed her mother of what I had said about the Irish way of indirect communication and advised her mother that if she needed more help with things, she should be sure to tell her children!

Bridget's confidence in herself continued to grow. Several times she found that she was able to be assertive with colleagues at work and felt very pleased with herself for not letting her anxiety lead to avoidance. She reported feeling more "normal" and having a sense that she would survive even if something catastrophic happened, such as losing her job or Joe: "I'd be OK—people like me!" I agreed, telling her that I liked her too. "I know!" She reported pushing herself more at work to be friendly with peers after having always felt like an outsider in groups. She found it very helpful to consider that, although she suffered from shyness and social anxiety, she was normal, likable, and "cool in my own way." I had told her during one discussion of social interactions that anxiety was contagious and that, if she managed her own nerves during tense encounters, others would relax too. She found this idea extremely helpful, worked very hard to calm herself with self-soothing statements about being competent and likable, and was amazed at the beneficial effect on her social interchanges.

Bridget remained quite vulnerable, though, to dichotomous thinking; she considered herself a disliked loser in response to any slight criticism or rebuff. We came to understand that Bridget thought others disliked her if they failed to initiate interactions in certain ways. I asked her if she felt the same with me, and she blushed and replied, "I know you like me. I do believe that, but I kick myself that I can't call you Mary. I hear your next patient doing that and I think, 'That's the cool way!'" She associated to her mother's social anxiety and inability to call a neighbor by her first name when invited to do so. "You don't think I'm weird?" I told her that I didn't, and that I thought she had to struggle very hard with social anxiety probably as a result of genetic vulnerability and what she had learned in her family. I assured her that we would keep working on this, including her comfort level with me. A few months later Bridget began calling me by my first name. She expressed great pleasure at being able to do so and remarked that it felt so natural.

Bridget's anxiety management and assertiveness were severely tested by several incidents that followed. She needed to respond to some critical feedback from a colleague and wanted to avoid the extremes of being overly submissive or too aggressive. I suggested that she relieve her anxiety first with a few deep breaths, then let her colleague know she understood her point of view while explaining her own. Bridget had to contend with the old internal voice saying she was bad and no one liked her, but managed very well: "I didn't want to be super nice and kowtow, or take her on, and I didn't do either!" She also had to tell her principal that she would be unable to attend an important meeting because of a prior commitment. Bridget became highly anxious in session as we discussed this situation, and we took the opportunity to help her focus on diaphragmatic breathing and self-calming statements. I also normalized the fact that it was expectable that she have more intense anxiety at times because she was taking on so many new challenges.

Bridget seemed to find our work on assertive behavior quite beneficial. These discussions often had an instructional aspect; I might offer alternative possibilities for understanding others' behaviors and suggest ways that Bridget might communicate her ideas. Over time Bridget's confidence about her interpersonal knowledge and behavior increased. She came in one day stating that she had had a miscommunication with an administrator concerning whether she would proctor a standardized test session. She asked if we could role play the situation. I acceded, pleased that she felt comfortable taking such initiative with me about the use of session time. She explained the relevant interchanges, and we discussed likely responses from the character I was to play. We began our role play, and in character I chided her for failing to inform me of her plans about this test. She responded in a highly professional and poised manner, stepping out of role for a moment to tell me that I was doing a pretty good imitation of this person, "But you need to have a more mean look on your face!" I did my best, and we continued to role play until we agreed that she was very prepared to handle the situation. I complimented her for her assertive skills as well as for her courage in proposing to confront the situation rather than avoid it. She was very pleased with this feedback and found herself quite able to handle the subsequent interchange much as she had in the session.

Bridget's challenges continued. Some related to renting out her cottage, which involved property held in common with a few other owners. A phone call with a new male owner triggered many issues related to her father; she feared that somehow this neighbor would have power over her and interfere with her rentals. She found herself disliking him intensely and overreacting to his suggestions. I proposed some cognitive work on this reaction, and she found it helpful to remind herself that her place was her own and that he did not have any more power than she. As she began to feel less threatened she was able to have greater perspective on interactions with him, which quickly deescalated in intensity for her. Following this positive development, however, she came to a session more enraged with herself than I had ever seen. "I'm scum . . . I'm a loser . . . I'm so stupid . . ." She had misplaced a large rental check and was unable to find it after tearing her place apart for hours. She started to calm slightly as we talked, and I told her that I could really see how something like this had triggered her agreement with her father's old point of view on her, but that her disorganization had to do with not having been taught certain skills as well as her wish to stop time by ignoring her bills and paperwork. I urged Bridget to practice self-talk along the lines that she is not a loser, that the worst that can happen is not a catastrophe, and that she does not deserve this kind of treatment. She responded very positively to this suggestion, was laughing by the end, and asked if she could call me to tell me what happened. I invited her to do just that, and she called a few hours later to report that she had located the check.

Although Bridget continued to contemplate both taking a break from the relationship with Joe and pursuing couples therapy, she found herself ultimately deciding to do neither. Couples therapy seemed frightening; Bridget worried that somehow engaging in joint treatment meant they would definitely get married, and she said that although she knew it was immature they might both have a tendency to use couples therapy "to tell on each other to the therapist." As is so often the case, she and Joe arrived at a course of action that would not necessarily have occurred to me but with which they felt very satisfied. After seeing some news coverage of fertility difficulties for women in their 30s, Joe encouraged Bridget to go ahead and have a baby. They both found this idea very compelling, for they felt that their relationship would not have been "a waste" if they had a baby together. Bridget's anxieties about marriage's representing a miserable loss of freedom were not activated by the idea of having a baby. She came in excitedly talking about this plan and asked me what I thought. I was aware that Bridget's wish for a baby was deep and genuine and that her earlier diatribes about the obligatory nature of childbearing probably reflected disavowal of an authentic desire she could not imagine actualizing. I told her I could certainly see the sense of it, that she did want a baby and she felt much more comfortable separating the issues of baby and marriage rather than putting them together. I also encouraged her and Joe to give themselves more time to continue thinking and talking about such a big decision.

Bridget returned the following week still excited about the idea, but also with some worry about whether to tell family members that a pregnancy was accidental or planned. "Oh, I know what you'll say—be honest!" (In Bridget's family lying was common, as was indirect communication, and in many of our interactions I had advised her in the direction of greater honesty.) A bit later she commented, "Joe says you just have to agree with your patients or they'll leave—so what do you really think about us having a baby?" After all our discussions about honesty, I was aware that Bridget knew me better than that, despite Joe's cynicism, and I let myself show my genuine reaction, which was to start laughing. She joined me, and I told her that she knew that I value honesty and that it is my responsibility to tell her the truth, so that if I thought this was a bad idea I would tell her so, tactfully but clearly.

Bridget soon became pregnant, and reported that she and Joe were extremely happy about the prospect of having a baby. Bridget began to experience Joe in a much more positive way since he had suggested getting pregnant. She noted that he had been taking initiative and behaving in strong and competent ways that she found very appealing. In recent months she had also been using her newly developed skills at assertive communication with him, letting him know more about what she wanted from him and feeling much more satisfied with his responsiveness. Their joint focus on becoming pregnant and then parenting appears to have assisted both Bridget and Joe in breaking out of their old relational routine of dating in a way that seemed frozen in time. Bridget began to think that she would like them to live together and perhaps become engaged. She started discussing Joe in a very different way, with comments such as, "It feels so nice to share and collaborate on things—we're a 'we,' not a 'you and me'" and "I don't like 5% or 10% of him, but the rest is so great!" Bridget also reported a powerful experience of empathy for Joe after spending time with his family and noticing their relentless criticism of him. She told me that it was no wonder he was the way he was and that she very much wanted to treat him in a loving and supportive way and help him to be his best.

As Bridget's stalled development began to resume in the context of the therapeutic relationship, the original relational dilemma, as well as her anxious avoidance, ameliorated. In the span of a few years, her life changed dramatically. She and Joe had their baby, moved in together, and then got married. Bridget related how she had worried that being pregnant and married would somehow mean she would not be herself, that she would be a different person, but that these experiences had not been at all as she had imagined or how her mother's life had been. With relief she described feeling exactly the same as before, only with nice additions to her life: "I'm moi!"

DISCUSSION

When I asked Bridget for permission to discuss her in this book she readily gave it, pleased that I thought of her as successful enough to wish to write about her. I believe that Bridget's progress in life and in treatment is quite remarkable, and that she has shown exceptional resilience in being able to attain her current level of personal and professional development. Bridget's intellect, engaging personality, and sense of humor are great strengths, and despite her aversion to risks she has taken a great many of them over the last several years, not the least of which was engaging in therapy.

A number of aspects of this treatment seemed to further Bridget's development, the therapeutic relationship being particularly central. Bridget's background of abuse and neglect had left her mistrustful and wary, but she also had some positive experiences in early relationships with siblings, extended family, and friends' parents, as well as with her own parents when they were less depressed and preoccupied. Her attachment to Joe had been healing as well as stifling for both of them. I became a new attachment figure for Bridget, and, developing security with me, she became more able to explore her internal states and dilemmas without immediately feeling overwhelmed and becoming avoidant. Later in treatment her more secure attachment to me helped her to venture further out into the world and feel safer trying some new behaviors, such as buying a new home, that previously had seemed intolerably risky.

Bridget entered treatment longing for a positive connection as well as fearful of retraumatization, and her sense of security with me deepened over time as she gradually perceived that calling her tone snotty was about as "mean" as I got. She commented at one point that, after growing up with her father, she was always worried that in the next minute another person would explode or become abusive. It is likely that Joe was appealing as well as frustrating because of his extreme nonreactivity. My having called her on her provoking behavior rather than remaining passive or becoming punitive seemed to help her feel more secure with me and broke through some of her defensive anger. Bridget entered treatment in part because she horrified herself by enacting her father's sadistic stance with the masochistically passive Joe, and it was reassuring to her that I proposed and modeled a less polarized set of roles. My temporary shift into the "other-centered perspective," that is, a focus on my own experience that her behavior was annoying, seemed to enable Bridget to reflect on herself. My choice of the word snotty is interesting; it is not a word I tend to use as an adult, but it was common parlance in my childhood. Bridget knew what I meant right away. This comment is not one on which I reflected much before speaking, but I had no doubt at the time that I wanted to say it. As Hoffman (1998) states, "A certain specific kind of spontaneous interpersonal interaction may be the least of the various evils the participants have to choose from, or, more positively, the healthiest of the various transference–countertransference possibilities that are in the air at a certain time" (p. 130).

As Bridget experienced greater security with me, her self-object needs emerged more obviously than was the case earlier in treatment. Mirroring needs were evident in her comments about how much better she felt talking to someone who really seemed to understand her dilemma. She reacted powerfully to positive feedback from me, as when I would talk about her courage handling something difficult or tell her that I thought she was very smart or funny; she would usually blush deeply and say, "Really? You really think so?" At such times it was evident that, despite the harshness of her earlier life, Bridget had retained (or was able to revive under sufficiently supportive conditions) strong mirroring needs and openness to their being met in a way that promoted internalization. Gradually Bridget became less identified with her father's negative view of her and more able to identify with my perception of her as likable and competent.

Twinship needs were also paramount in this treatment. Bridget experienced enhanced self-cohesion by feeling similar to me in such areas as our shared Irish-American cultural background and love of nature. She also found it helpful to think that we were alike in having to learn to communicate more directly than our families did, and my having managed this inspired her to believe that she could as well. Finally, instructional selfobject needs were very important in our work. Bridget's early longings for maternal guidance were continually frustrated by her mother's passivity. She eagerly sought direction from me and relished the idea that she was learning things about conducting herself and handling interpersonal issues that she had not known before.

Bridget's insight into the impact that her family experiences had had on her was a major curative factor in this treatment. Prior to therapy Bridget knew that she had been angry at her father for many years, and more recently had come to consider her mother as inadequate as her father, although in different ways. However, she did not focus on (and often actively avoided) making connections between her current struggles and family life. She found it extremely painful, but also validating and liberating, to understand much of her anxiety, anger, and ambivalent relationship with Joe as consequences of a neglectful and abusive childhood. Her self-esteem increased as we discussed the fact that so many skills, values, and approaches to goals that people learn in childhood had been hard won for her in adult life through her own efforts. Over time her anger at her parents diminished, and she became able to enjoy their company when they were behaving pleasantly and to take it less personally when they were not. Bridget appreciated her mother's obvious love for her baby and found that her mother was relaxed and happy when they spent time at Bridget's country property without Bridget's father. Bridget came to treasure these experiences.

The symptom-focused techniques that I used most with Bridget were cognitive restructuring and assertiveness training. Her vulnerability to concluding that her father was correct in depicting her as an unpopular loser was high in reaction to even the mildest criticism. Bridget's self-state would become fragmented, and she would temporarily lose perspective. Bridget found it stabilizing to engage in self-talk about being a normal person whom others liked. Assertiveness training was also of great help to Bridget as a needed supplement to the indirect and passive-aggressive communication style that characterized her family. She had many experiences of learning that her wishes were better met and that others responded to her positively when she spoke assertively. Moreover, she found that some sources of anxiety in her life were removed when she dealt assertively with an interpersonal issue rather than worrying about the situation's worsening at some future point. Bridget's view of assertiveness training as beneficial is illustrated by her initiation of our most recent use of this method and her request that I role play her colleague.

Unlike Carol, Ken, and Ann, Bridget did not enter treatment complaining of a symptomatic problem that seemed readily amenable to active techniques. Her relationship dilemma precipitated her entry into therapy, and it was only over time that such issues as social inhibition and avoidance surfaced as potential points of intervention. I found that I employed more active techniques with Bridget in the middle phase of treatment. We did some cognitive work relatively early in therapy when Bridget experienced acute anxiety concerning a colleague, but most of our first year of treatment involved a standard psychoanalytic focus of establishing an empathic connection, processing issues in the therapeutic relationship, and exploring historical events and their relationship to current problems. Only after Bridget had established greater security with me and had begun to feel more resolved about her family did I sense that she could benefit from additional cognitive work and assertiveness training. I believe that Bridget found these techniques very usable because she had developed a powerful transference to me and gained confidence that I liked and valued her. As her security and cohesion increased, she found it easier to identify with my positive view of her rather than her father's devaluing attitude and to retain this experience as she interacted with others. Assertive behavior and affirming self-statements seemed much more plausible and legitimate in the context of her experience of our relationship, illustrating the fact that symptom-focused techniques are most powerfully employed within a particular kind of therapeutic relationship. Bridget would bring up positive self-statements that she and I had constructed together; the combination of the self statements and the way in which they imbued her current state with a reminder of our connection and my positive view of her proved a potent antidote to fragmentation Moreover, Bridget wanted to please me and make me proud of her. As our relationship grew more important, she became increasingly willing to engage in previously avoided behaviors and modes of interaction, and relished regaling me with tales of her new ways of being while I responded with pleasure and pride.

Bridget's transformation over the last few years demonstrates that small changes in dynamic systems can ultimately have large effects when the system is in a sensitive state. By the time Bridget entered treatment with me she had spent many years in stasis and was desperate for some movement. Her ability to use our relationship for growth enabled her to initiate changes with Joe to which he responded, and their dyadic system became much more expansive. In the last few years our work has centered on all the changes in her life and roles, including her enjoyment of parenting and a new and very satisfying closeness with her own mother. Bridget still uses symptom-focused techniques but requires little instruction, and our attention to them in sessions largely surrounds discussing Bridget's experiences employing them in various situations with family members and work colleagues. We have often spent time laughing together in the last few years; Bridget's relief at feeling like a normal person with a husband and family has enabled her droll humor and pleasure in life to dominate her mood much of the time. Both having come from large families, Bridget and Joe's idea of family life called for more children, and they now have three. Our sessions are currently intermittent because of Bridget's child-care responsibilities.

DEVELOPMENTAL PROGRESSION IN SYMPTOM-FOCUSED DYNAMIC PSYCHOTHERAPY

Shane et al. (1997) have postulated the existence of three "relational configurations" that describe a developmental progression in the nature of the bond between analyst and patient. The first is the *old-self-with-old-other* configuration, wherein the patient experiences both himself and the clinician in accord with organizing principles based on past traumatic experiences. In the second configuration, *old-self-with-new-other*, the patient's view of self remains largely unchanged, but he begins to experience the analyst as different from past figures. In the final configuration, *new-self-with-new-other*, the patient is able to view both self and other in new and positive ways, with increased freedom from the limited views associated with prior painful life experiences. These authors do not minimize the rigidity with which all relational events may be assimilated into entrenched organizing principles, but they emphasize the possibility that new experiences with the analyst can have impact. They suggest that at some point the analyst does something (consciously or not) that illustrates a difference between herself or himself and past traumatizing figures, and that at a certain time the patient becomes able to appreciate that this experience is in fact different, ushering in a shift to the *old-self-with-new-other* configuration. Ideally, the accretion of novel experiences in the treatment relationship, coupled with continued exploration and resolution of painful material, ultimately results in a transformed view of self and an openness to new possibilities in the interpersonal world.

The development-facilitating novel experiences offered by the clinician may at time include interactions related to symptom-focused techniques. With Ann, for example, my suggestion of effective strategies to reduce her fear of flying seemed to permit a tentative view of me as competent, in contrast to her experience of her depressed mother. The original relational configuration involving expectations that others will be self-preoccupied, inadequate, critical, and sadistic began to loosen. Bridget, on the other hand, eventually came to trust me not on the basis of any active techniques but because in a variety of interactions she experienced me as sensitive, nonretaliatory, and not overly passive. For her, symptom-focused techniques in the context of a selfobject transference and a more secure attachment facilitated her developing a new perspective on herself as normal, likable, and capable.

I would like to elaborate further on ways in which dynamic treatment that incorporates active techniques fosters the development of a consolidated and integrated self and promotes secure and balanced relationships with others. I suggest that several aspects of relations with the self and with others evolve in a successful treatment. Regarding the self, I propose that three aspects of self-development may require change: self-regulatory abilities, perspective on the self, and deployment of talents and skills. For relationships with others, we can consider both perspective on others and interpersonal behavior.

As noted in chapter two, a focus on affects rather than drives dominates current relational psychoanalytic thinking, and most such treatments concentrate on a patient's affective experience, including defensive avoidance of certain affects, affects within the treatment relationship, and impulsive or excessive expression of affects. The unintegrated and potentially threatening affect states of the dynamic unconscious and the influence of past experiences on present affect states are processed. As attachment security increases in the context of the therapy relationship, a concomitant growth is seen in the patient's ability to explore distressing internal experiences. A therapeutic ambience of empathic responsiveness enables the patient to experience affects within the context of a helpful relationship rather than in isolation, thus promoting the titration and modulation of intense emotional experiences.

Some patients have responded to affective regulatory difficulties with symptomatic adaptations that may be dangerous or distressing, or that may impede their ability to engage in treatment and make productive use of the exploratory processes of psychoanalytic psychotherapy. Certain cognitive behavioral techniques may supplement standard psychoanalytic psychotherapy by offering additional ways to assist patients in regulating affects and self-states. Self-monitoring with the collaboration of the therapist promotes affect articulation and differentiation. Relaxation techniques further patients' ability to deescalate when states of overarousal threaten; potential benefits include the avoidance of fragmented states and their often deleterious consequences as well as the gradual development of greater affect tolerance. Self-management techniques offer patients a means to decrease reliance on addictive or compulsive strategies for responding to affective states while increasing awareness and acceptance of emotions. Overall, these techniques aid patients in viewing their internal processes as more comprehensible and less dangerous. Patients learn that they can have some degree of control over their internal states and expression of them, and have less need to rely on the extreme solutions of overcontrol (avoidance and suppression) or undercontrol (unmodulated experiences of affect and impulsive discharge).

The second aspect of self-functioning relates to the self's view of itself. Patients commonly hold views of the self as globally bad, defective, ugly, unlovable, and so forth, and relate to the self with harshness, judgmental attitudes, and a marked lack of compassion. Gaining insight into the impact of historical occurrences such as traumatic events and insufficient selfobject experiences fosters reevaluation of limited views of the self and more accurate assessments of family interactions and subsequent attributions. Identification with the clinician's perspective enables further revision of extreme views of the self. As powerful as insight and identification with the therapist are, however, it is difficult to transform internal representations of self. "Structures are configurations of a slow rate of change" (Rapaport and Gill, 1959, p. 803). In some treatments this process will be furthered by judicious application of cognitive techniques. Articulation of current cognitions and more adaptive views expands consciousness of organizing principles not previously expressed to oneself. Clarification of such habitual cognitive errors as overly personalized interpretations of situations and dichotomous thinking promotes more moderate and realistic perspectives. Cognitive restructuring helps nascent positively toned views of the self become integrated into daily experience.

The third aspect of self-functioning is the ability to deploy one's talents and skills in the world. This capacity may be affected by such factors as self-inhibition in the service of maintaining needed relationships, which I mentioned as a possible pathway to symptom formation. Other patients, such as Ken, who have suffered traumatic criticism for all efforts, take refuge in grandiose fantasy but have retreated from serious attempts to accomplish anything in the world because doing nothing seems less painful than doing something flawed. Finally, some patients experienced such a lack of mirroring that potential talents and skills have remained largely unknown as part of the invalidated unconscious.

The transformation of self-regulatory abilities and views of the self I have described should have an ameliorative effect on a person's ability to use talents and skills. Increased affect tolerance enables less involvement with symptoms such as addictions that impair functioning, and this tolerance, coupled with broadened views of self and other, promotes less self-suppression and blocking. Even if the inhibitory factors relating to internal conflict are undone in the context of a secure therapeutic relationship, however, the patient may be left with skills deficits in the actualization of abilities in the world because parental modeling was insufficient. Therapeutic provision of self-management skills, such as goal setting, teaches essential strategies for becoming an effective and accomplished person, often in the context of meeting instructional selfobject needs.

Relations with others are intricately connected to the relationship with the self, but in considering therapeutic goals and the effects of various interventions it is useful to examine this area separately. With regard to perspective on others, it is not uncommon for patients to progress from viewing the self as all bad while idealizing others through a state in which blame is reattributed to family members and the patient feels much anger. A final broader perspective (not reached by all patients) involves some capacity to appreciate the psychological and systems factors affecting others' behavior as well as their own, such as recognizing that one's parent was the victim of abuse as well as a perpetrator. Ultimately, achieving insight into one's own organizing principles in the context of a new type of relationship furthers attachment security. This advance, in conjunction with increased affective regulation, facilitates a view of the other as potentially helpful and reliable rather than as inevitably retraumatizing; moreover, the patient's need for the other can be acted on in a balanced fashion rather than being either reprehended or felt with panicky desperation. Although psychanalytic psychotherapy is preeminantly suited to have positive impact on a patient's perspective on others, cognitive techniques may provide a useful adjunct. As was described in the transformation of aspects of self, the use of cognitive techniques may help to identify, clarify, and institute changes in constricted views of others.

The other aspect of relations with others pertains to actual interpersonal behavior. Some elements of needed changes here are tied to complex combinations of exploratory processes within a responsive relationship and symptom-focused interventions. The improved management of self-states entailing intense affect has a beneficial effect on interpersonal relationships, decreasing such phenomena as angry outbursts and clingy anxiety, which are likely to be experienced by others as aversive. Moreover, increased engagement in positive relationships is associated reciprocally with reduced involvement with such symptoms as addictions. For example, in the case of Carol, decreased binge eating promoted greater relationship seeking, and positive experiences in the relational world led to less reliance on the selfobject experiences provided by food. The technique of assertiveness training specifically addresses interpersonal behavior and fosters patients' use of direct communication, which produces more satisfactory experiences in relationships and reduce dependence on passive-aggressive or aggressive means of making oneself heard. Assertive behavior furthers self-esteem and self-respect even if it does not always lead to the desired response from the other. Again, it is clear that relating to self and relating to the other are inextricably linked; the shifts in one or the other generate further alterations in a complex cascade of mutual influence. Similarly, the positive developmental processes described here are stimulated by combinations of interventions informed by relational psychotherapy and those pertaining to active techniques in an ultimately indistinguishable fashion.

CONCLUDING COMMENTS

The overall goals of the psychoanalytic theories that I employ all pertain to living an enriched and enlarged life, with greater self-cohesion, with increased attachment security, and in a subjective world that has been explored and transformed in desired directions. Often psychoanalytic treatment enables an individual to accomplish such goals with no need for active techniques. Some people who are troubled by their symptoms and find such techniques usable may, however, make more rapid progress with the overarching goals of treatment as well as with the specific symptom when an integrative approach is used. The optimal provision of such techniques can supply important selfobject functions, including long-thwarted needs to be instructed in life skills in the context of an important relationship. Use of symptom-focused techniques may facilitate a more secure attachment to the therapist by helping dismissive patients to gain trust and assisting preoccupied and disorganized ones to tolerate limitations on therapist availability. Furthermore, application of such techniques may illuminate some aspects of a patient's internal world, as well as nuances of the intersubjective field, in ways that would not otherwise occur. Use of symptom-focused dynamic psychotherapy involves direct intervention with the symptom that cooccurs with application of psychoanalytic psychotherapy techniques to the person as a whole. Multiple complex processes ensue, with interplay between symptomatic change and overall development such that one facilitates the other. I have argued both that symptoms may require a unique focus and that they must be viewed in the context of the entire intersubjective field. They represent the tip of the iceberg, as it were, and symptom-focused dynamic treatment excludes neither the portion that is visible nor that which is hidden from therapeutic attention.

REFERENCES

Adam, K., Sheldon-Keller, A. & West, S. (1996), Attachment organization and vulnerability to loss, separation, and abuse in disturbed adolescents. In: *Attachment Theory: Social, Developmental, and Clinical Perspectives,* ed. S. Goldberg, R. Muir & J. Kerr. Hillsdale, NJ: The Analytic Press, pp. 309–341.

Adams, E. & Sutker, P., eds. (2001), *Comprehensive Handbook of Psychopathology,* 3rd ed. New York: Kluwer Academic/Plenum.

Ainsworth, M. (1989), Attachments beyond infancy. *Amer. Psychol.,* 44:709–716.

———— Blehar, M., Waters, E. & Wall, S. (1978), *Patterns of Attachment.* Hillsdale, NJ: Lawrence Erlbaum Associates.

Alexander, F. (1950), Analysis of the therapeutic factors in psychoanalytic treatment. In: *The Scope of Psychoanalysis: Selected Papers of Franz Alexander.* New York: Basic Books, 1961, pp. 261–275.

———— & French, T. (1946), *Psychoanalytic Therapy: Principles and Application.* New York: Ronald Press.

American Psychiatric Association (1994), *Diagnostic and Statistical Manual of Mental Disorders,* 4th ed. Washington, DC: American Psychiatric Association.

Atwood, G. & Stolorow, R. (1984), *Structures of Subjectivity: Explorations in Psychoanalytic Phenomenology.* Hillsdale, NJ: The Analytic Press.

Bacal, H. (1985), Optimal responsiveness and the therapeutic process. In: *Progress in Self Psychology, Vol. 1,* ed. A. Goldberg. Hillsdale, NJ: The Analytic Press, pp. 202–226.

———— (1990), The elements of a corrective selfobject experience. *Psychoanal. Inq.,* 10:197–220.

———— (1994), The selfobject relationship in psychoanalytic treatment. In: *A Decade of Progress: Progress in Self Psychology, Vol. 10,* ed. A. Goldberg. Hillsdale, NJ: The Analytic Press, pp. 21–30.

———— ed. (1998), *Optimal Responsiveness: How Therapists Heal Their Patients.* Northvale, NJ: Aronson.

———— & Herzog, B. (2003), Specificity theory and optimal responsiveness: An outline. *Psychoanal. Psychol.,* 20:635–649.

———— & Newman, K. (1990), *Theories of Object Relations: Bridges to Self Psychology.* New York: Columbia University Press.

Bader, M. (1994), The tendency to neglect therapeutic aims in psychoanalysis. *Psychoanal. Quart.,* 63:246–270.

Balint, E. (1993), *Before I Was I.* New York: Guilford Press.

Bandura, A. (1977), Self-efficacy: Toward a unifying theory of behavioral change. *Psychol. Rev.,* 84:191–215.

Barlow, D. (1988), *Anxiety and Its Disorders.* New York: Guilford Press.

Bartholomew, K. (1990), Avoidance of intimacy: An attachment perspective. *J. Soc. Pers. Rel.,* 7:147–178.

Basch, M. (1988), *Understanding Psychotherapy.* New York: Basic Books.

———— (1995), Kohut's contribution. *Psychoanal. Dial.,* 5:367–373.

Beck, A. (1976), *Cognitive Therapy and the Emotional Disorders.* New York: International Universities Press.

———— & Emery, G. (1985), *Anxiety Disorders and Phobias: A Cognitive Perspective.* New York: Basic Books.

———— Rush, A., Shaw, B. & Emery, G. (1979), *Cognitive Therapy of Depression.* New York: Guilford Press.

———— Wright, F., Newman, C. & Liese, B. (1993), *Cognitive Therapy of Substance Abuse.* New York: Guilford Press.

Beebe, B. (2004), Faces in relation: A case study. *Psychoanal. Dial.,* 14:1–51.

———— Knoblauch, S., Rustin, J. & Sorter, D. (2003a), Introduction: A systems view. *Psychoanal. Dial.,* 13:743–775.

———— & Lachmann, F. (1992), The contribution of mother–infant mutual influence to the origins of self- and object representations. In: *Relational Perspectives in Psychoanalysis,* ed. N. Skolnick & S. Warshaw. Hillsdale, NJ: The Analytic Press, pp. 83–117.

———— & ———— (2002), *Infant Research and Adult Treatment: Co-constructing Interactions.* Hillsdale, NJ: The Analytic Press.

———— Rustin, J., Sorter, D. & Knoblauch, S. (2003b), An expanded view of intersubjectivity in infancy and its application to psychoanalysis. *Psychoanal. Dial.,* 13:805–841.

Belsky, J. (1999), Interactional and contextual determinants of attachment security. In: *Handbook of Attachment: Theory, Research, and Clinical Applications,* ed. J. Cassidy & P. Shaver. New York: Guilford Press, pp. 249–264.

Benjamin, J. (1988), *The Bonds of Love*. New York: Pantheon.

Benson, H. (1975), *The Relaxation Response*. New York: Morrow.

Blagys, M. & Hilsenroth, M. (2000), Distinctive features of short-term psychodynamic-interpersonal psychotherapy: A review of the comparative psychotherapy process literature. *Clin. Psychol.: Sci. Prac.*, 7:167–188.

Blizard, R. (2001), Masochistic and sadistic ego states: Dissociative solutions to the dilemma of attachment to an abusive caretaker. *J. Trauma Dissoc.*, 2:37–58.

Blumenthal, J., Babyak, M., Moore, K., Craighead, W., Herman, S., Khatri, P., Waugh, R., Napolitano, M., Forman, L., Appelbaum, P., Doranswamy, P. & Krishnan, K. (1999), Effects of exercise training in older patients with major depression. *Arch. Internat. Med.*, 159:2349–2356.

Bollas, C. (1987), *The Shadow of the Object*. New York: Columbia University Press.

Borkovec, T. (2002), Life in the future versus life in the present. *Clin. Psychol.: Sci. Prac.*, 9:76–80.

Bowlby, J. (1969), *Attachment and Loss, Vol. 1: Attachment*. New York: Basic Books.

———— (1973), *Attachment and Loss, Vol. 2: Separation*. New York: Basic Books.

———— (1988), *A Secure Base: Clinical Applications of Attachment Theory*. London: Routledge.

Brandchaft, B. (1988), A case of intractable depression. In: *Learning from Kohut: Progress in Self Psychology, Vol. 4*, ed. A. Goldberg. Hillsdale, NJ: The Analytic Press, pp. 133–154.

———— (1994), Structures of pathologic accommodation and change in psychoanalysis. Presented at the Association for Psychoanalytic Self Psychology, March, New York.

Brennan, K. & Shaver, P. (1995), Dimensions of adult attachment, affect regulation, and romantic functioning. *Personal. Social Psychol. Bull.*, 21:267–283.

Bretherton, I. & Munholland, K. (1999), Internal working models in attachment relationships: A construct revisited. In: *Handbook of Attachment: Theory, Research, and Clinical Applications*, ed. J. Cassidy & P. Shaver. New York: Guilford Press, pp. 89–111.

Briere, J. (1992), *Child Abuse Trauma: Theory and Treatment of the Lasting Effects*. Newbury Park, CA: Sage.

Bromberg, P. (2001), Treating patients with symptoms—and symptoms with patience: Reflections on shame, dissociation, and eating disorders. *Psychoanal. Dial.*, 11:891–912.

Bucci, W. (1997), *Psychoanalysis and Cognitive Science: A Multiple Code Theory*. New York: Guilford Press.

Bulik, C., Sullivan, P. & Kendler, K. (1998), Heritability of binge eating and broadly defined bulimia nervosa. *Biol. Psychiat.*, 44:1210–1218.

Burke, W. (1992), Countertransference disclosure and the asymmetry/mutuality dilemma. *Psychoanal. Dial.*, 2:241–271.

Carlson, E. (1998), A prospective longitudinal study of disorganized/disoriented attachment. *Child Devel.*, 69:1970–1979.

Cassidy, J. (1988), Child-mother attachment and the self in six-year-olds. *Child Devel.*, 59:121–134.

────── & Kobak, R. (1988), Avoidance and its relation to other defensive processes. In: *Clinical Implications of Attachment*, ed. J. Belsky & T. Nezwerski. Hillsdale, NJ: Lawrence Erlbaum Associates, pp. 300–323.

Center for Disease Control and Prevention (1994), HIV/AIDS Surveillance Report. Atlanta, GA.

Cloitre, M., Chase Stovall-McClough, K., Miranda, R. & Chemtob, C. (1994), Therapeutic alliance, negative mood regulation, and treatment outcome in child abuse-related post traumatic stress disorder. *J. Consult. Clin. Psychol.*, 72:411–416.

Connors, M. (1992), Bulimia: A multidimensional team approach. In: *The Addictions*, ed E. Freeman. White Plains, NY: Longman Publishing, pp. 192–203.

────── (1994), Symptom formation: An integrative self-psychological perspective. *Psychoanal. Psychol.*, 11:509–523.

────── (1996), Developmental vulnerabilities for eating disorders. In: *The Developmental Psychopathology of Eating Disorders*, ed. L. Smolak, M. Levine & R. Striegel-Moore. Mahwah, NJ: Lawrence Erlbaum Associates, pp. 285–310.

────── (1997a), The renunciation of love: Dismissive attachment and its treatment. *Psychoanal. Psychol.*, 14:475–493.

────── (1997b), Need and responsiveness in the treatment of a severely traumatized patient: A relational perspective. *Amer. J. Psychother.*, 51:86–101.

────── (2000), Dimensions of experience in relationship seeking. In: *How Responsive Should We Be? Progress in Self Psychology, Vol. 16*, ed. A. Goldberg. Hillsdale, NJ: The Analytic Press, pp.199–216.

────── (2001a), Integrative treatment of symptomatic disorders. *Psychoanal. Psychol.*, 18:74–91.

────── (2001b), Relationship of sexual abuse to body image and eating problems. In: *Body Image, Eating Disorders, and Obesity in Youth*, ed. J. K. Thompson & L. Smolak. Washington, DC: American Psychological Association, pp. 149–167.

────── & Morse, W. (1993), Sexual abuse and eating disorders: A review. *Internat. J. Eating Disorders*, 13:1–11.

Cortois, C. (1988), *Healing the Incest Wound: Adult Survivors in Therapy*. New York: Norton.

Craighead, W., Sheets., E., Bjornsson, A. & Arnarson, E. (2005), Specificity and nonspecificity in psychotherapy. *Clin. Psychol.: Sci. Prac.,* 12:189–193.

Crittenden, P. (1995), Attachment and psychopathology. In: *Attachment Theory: Social, Developmental, and Clinical Perspectives,* ed. S. Goldberg, R. Muir & J. Kerr. Hillsdale, NJ: The Analytic Press, pp. 367–406.

Curtis, R., Field, C., Knaan-Kostman, I. & Mannix, K. (2004), What 75 psychoanalysts found helpful and hurtful in their own analyses. *Psychoanal. Psychol.,* 21:183–202.

Cushman, P. (1990), Why the self is empty. *Amer. Psychol.,* 45:599–611.

Director, L. (2002), The value of relational psychoanalysis in the treatment of chronic drug and alcohol use. *Psychoanal. Dial.,* 12:551–579.

Doctors, S. (1996), Notes on the contribution of the analyst's self-awareness to optimal responsiveness. In: *Basic Ideas Reconsidered: Progress in Self Psychology, Vol. 12,* ed. A. Goldberg. Hillsdale, NJ: The Analytic Press, pp. 55–63.

Donegan, D., Rodin, J., O'Brien, C. & Solomon, R. (1983), A learning theory approach to commonalities. In: *Commonalities in Substance Abuse and Habitual Behavior,* ed. D. Gerstein & D. Maloff. Lexington, MA: Lexington Books, pp. 111–156.

Donnelley, C. (1980), Active development of the positive introject in severely disturbed patients. *Brit. J. Med. Psychiat.,* 53:307–312.

Dozier, M. (1990), Attachment organization and treatment use for adults with serious psychopathological disorders. *Devel. & Psychopathol.,* 2:47–60.

Ehrenberg, D. (1992), *The Intimate Edge.* New York: Norton.

Eissler, K. (1953), The effect of the structure of the ego on psychoanalytic technique. *J. Amer. Psychoanal. Assn.,* 1:104–143.

Elson, M. (1989), Teacher as learner, learner as teacher. In: *Learning and Education: Psychoanalytic Perspectives,* ed. K. Field, B. Cohler & G. Wool. Madison, CT: International Universities Press, pp. 789–808.

Epstein, S. (1994), Integration of the cognitive and the psychodynamic unconscious. *Amer. Psychol.,* 49:709–724.

Feeney, J. & Noller, P. (1990), Attachment style as a predictor of adult romantic relationships. *J. Pers. Soc. Psychol.,* 58:281–291.

Ferenczi, S. (1927), The elasticity of psychoanalytic technique. In: *Final Contributions to the Problems and Methods of Psycho-Analysis,* ed. M. Balint (trans. E. Mosbacher). New York: Basic Books, 1955, pp. 87–101.

——— (1931), Child analysis in the analysis of adults. In: *Final Contributions to the Problems and Methods of Psycho-Analysis,* ed. M.

Balint (trans. E. Mosbacher). New York: Basic Books, 1955, pp. 126–142.

Fonagy, P. (2001), *Attachment Theory and Psychoanalysis*. New York: Other Press.

—— Leigh, T., Steele, M., Steele, H., Kennedy, G., Mattoon, M., Target, M. & Gerber, A. (1996), The relation of attachment status, psychiatric classification, and response to psychotherapy. *J. Consult. Clin. Psychol.*, 64:22–31.

—— Steele, M., Steele, H., Leigh, T., Kennedy, R., Mattoon, G. & Target, M. (1995), Attachment, the reflective self, and borderline states: The predictive specificity of the Adult Attachment Interview and pathological emotional development. In: *Attachment Theory: Social, Developmental, and Clinical Perspectives*, ed. S. Goldberg, R. Muir & J. Kerr. Hillsdale, NJ: The Analytic Press, pp. 233–278.

—— & Target, M. (1997), Attachment and reflective function: Their role in self-organization. *Devel. & Psychopathol.*, 9:679–700.

Fosshage, J. (1992), Self psychology: The self and its vicissitudes within a relational matrix. In: *Relational Perspectives in Psychoanalysis*, ed. N. Skolnick & S. Warshaw. Hillsdale, NJ: The Analytic Press, pp. 21–42.

—— (1995), Interaction in psychoanalysis: A broadening horizon. *Psychoanal. Dial.*, 5:459–478.

—— (1997), Listening/experiencing perspectives and the quest for a facilitating responsiveness. In: *Conversations in Self Psychology: Progress in Self Psychology, Vol. 13*, ed. A. Goldberg. Hillsdale, NJ: The Analytic Press, pp. 33–55.

Frank, K. (1990), Action techniques in psychoanalysis. *Contemp. Psychoanal.*, 26:732–756.

—— (1992), Combining action techniques with psychoanalytic therapy. *Internat. Rev. Psycho-Anal.*, 19:57–79.

—— (1993), Action, insight, and working through: Outlines of an integrative approach. *Psychoanal. Dial.*, 3:535–577.

—— (1999), *Psychoanalytic Participation: Action, Interaction, and Integration*. Hillsdale, NJ: The Analytic Press.

Freud, S. (1896), The aetiology of hysteria. *Standard Edition*, 3:191–221. London: Hogarth Press, 1962.

—— (1905), Three essays on the theory of sexuality. *Standard Edition*, 7:125–248. London: Hogarth Press, 1953.

—— (1917a), The paths to the formation of symptoms. *Standard Edition*, 16:358–377. London: Hogarth Press, 1963.

—— (1917b), Introductory lectures on psycho-analysis: Part III. General theory of the neuroses. *Standard Edition*, 16:412–430. London: Hogarth Press, 1963.

———— (1917c), Analytic therapy. *Standard Edition*, 16:448–463. London: Hogarth Press, 1963.

———— (1919), Lines of advance in psycho-analytic therapy. *Standard Edition*, 17:157–168. London: Hogarth Press, 1955.

———— (1937), Analysis terminable and interminable. *Standard Edition*, 23:209–253. London: Hogarth Press, 1964.

———— (1940), An outline of psycho-analysis. *Standard Edition*, 23:144–207. London: Hogarth Press, 1964.

Gabbard, G. (2002), Addiction as mind-body bridge: Commentary on paper by Lisa Director. *Psychoanal. Dial.*, 12:581–584.

Gedo, J. (1979), *Beyond Interpretation*. New York: International Universities Press.

———— (1988), *The Mind in Disorder*. Hillsdale, NJ: The Analytic Press.

———— (1991), *The Biology of Clinical Encounters: Psychoanalysis as a Science of Mind*. Hillsdale, NJ: The Analytic Press.

———— (1999), *The Evolution of Psychoanalysis: Contemporary Theory and Practice*. New York: Other Press.

———— & Goldberg, A. (1973), *Models of the Mind*. Chicago: University of Chicago Press.

George, C., Kaplan, N. & Main, M. (1996), Adult Attachment Interview (3rd ed). Unpublished manuscript, University of California at Berkeley.

Ghent, E. (2002), Wish, need, drive: Motive in the light of dynamic systems theory and Edelman's selectionist theory. *Psychoanal. Dial.*, 12:763–808.

Gill, M. (1982), *The Analysis of Transference, Vol. 1*. New York: International Universities Press.

———— (1984), Psychoanalytic, psychodynamic, cognitive behavior, and behavior therapies compared. In: *Psychoanalytic Therapy and Behavior Therapy: Is Integration Possible?* ed. H. Arkowitz & S. B. Messer. New York: Plenum Press, pp. 179–187.

———— (1988), Converting psychotherapy into psychoanalysis. *Contemp. Psychoanal.*, 24:262–274.

———— (1994), *Psychoanalysis in Transition: A Personal View*. Hillsdale, NJ: The Analytic Press.

Gold, J. & Stricker, G. (2001), Relational psychoanalysis as a foundation of assimilative integration. *J. Psychother. Integration*, 11:43–58.

Goldberg, A. (1978), *The Psychology of the Self: A Casebook*. New York: International Universities Press.

———— (1999), *Being of Two Minds: The Vertical Split in Psychoanalysis and Psychotherapy*. Hillsdale, NJ: The Analytic Press.

Goldfried, M. & Davison, G. (1994), *Clinical Behavior Therapy* (expanded ed.). New York: Wiley.

Goodwin, D. (1984), Studies of familial alcoholism: A review. *J. Clin. Psychiat.*, 45:14–17.

Gottman, J. (1994), *Why Marriages Succeed or Fail.* New York: Fireside.

Grabe, H., Spitzer, C. & Freyberger, H. (2004), Alexithymia and personality in relation to dimensions of psychopathology. *Amer. J. Psychiat.*, 161:1299–1301.

Greenberg, J. & Mitchell, S. (1983), *Object Relations in Psychoanalytic Theory.* Cambridge, MA: Harvard University Press.

Grossmann, K. E. & Grossmann, K. (1991), Attachment quality as an organizer of emotional and behavioral responses in a longitudinal perspective. In: *Attachment across the Life Cycle,* ed. C. M. Parkes, J. Stevenson-Hinde & P. Marris. London: Tavistock/Routledge, pp. 93–114.

Haft, W. & Slade, A. (1989), Affect attunement and maternal attachment: A pilot study. *Infant Ment. Health J.*, 10:157–172.

Havens, L. (2004), The American impact on psychoanalysis. *Psychoanal. Dial.*, 14:255–264.

Hayes, S., Strosahl, K. & Wilson, K. (1999), *Acceptance and Commitment Therapy: An Experiential Approach to Behavior Change.* New York: Guilford Press.

Hazan, C. & Shaver, P. (1987), Romantic love conceptualized as an attachment process. *J. Pers. Soc. Psychol.*, 52:511–524.

——— (1990), Love and work: An attachment-theoretical perspective. *J. Pers. Soc. Psychol.*, 59:270–280.

Herman, J. (1992), *Trauma and Recovery.* New York: Basic Books.

Hesse, E. (1999), The Adult Attachment Interview: Historical and current perspectives. In: *Handbook of Attachment,* ed. J. Cassidy & P. Shaver. New York: Guilford Press, pp. 395–433.

Hoffer, P. (2005), The wise baby meets the enfant terrible: The evolution of Ferenczi's views on development. *Psychoanal. Psychol.*, 20:18–29.

Hoffman, I. (1998), *Ritual and Spontaneity in the Psychoanalytic Process.* Hillsdale, NJ: The Analytic Press.

Hollander, M. & Ford, C. (1990), *Dynamic Psychotherapy: An Introductory Approach.* Northvale, NJ: Aronson.

Horowitz, M. (1986), *Stress Response Syndromes,* 2nd ed. Northvale, NJ: Aronson.

Jack, D. (1991), *Silencing the Self: Women and Depression.* New York: Harper Perennial.

Jaycox, L., Zoellner, L. & Foa, E. (2002), Cognitive-behavior therapy for PTSD in rape survivors. *J. Clin. Psychol.*, 58:891–906.

Jenike, M., Baer, L. & Minichiello, W. (1998), *Obsessive Compulsive Disorders: Practical Management.* St. Louis, MO: Mosby.

Johnson, C. & Connors, M. (1987), *The Etiology and Treatment of*

Bulimia Nervosa: A Biopsychosocial Perspective. New York: Basic Books.

———— Connors, M. & Tobin, D. (1987), Symptom management of bulimia. *J. Consult. Clin. Psychol.*, 55:668–676.

Kabat-Zinn, J. (1990), *Full Catastrophe Living.* New York: Dell.

Kagan, J. (1989), *Unstable Ideas: Temperament, Cognition, and the Self.* Cambridge, MA: Harvard University Press.

Kazdin, A. (1973), Covert modeling and the reduction of avoidance behavior. *J. Abnorm. Psychol.*, 81:87–95.

Kernberg, O. (2004), Rewards, dangers, findings, and attitudes in psychoanalytic research. *Can. J. Psychoanal.*, 12:178–194.

Kobak, R. (1999), The emotional dynamics of disruptions in attachment relationships: Implications for theory, research, and clinical intervention. In: *Handbook of Attachment,* ed. J. Cassidy & P. Shaver. New York: Guilford Press, pp. 21–43.

Kohut, H. (1968), The psychoanalytic treatment of narcissistic personality disorders: Outline of a systematic approach. In: *The Search for the Self,* ed. P. Ornstein. New York: International Universities Press, pp. 477–509.

———— (1971), *The Analysis of the Self.* New York: International Universities Press.

———— (1977), *The Restoration of the Self.* New York: International Universities Press.

———— (1984), *How Does Analysis Cure?* ed. A. Goldberg & P. Stepansky. Chicago: University of Chicago Press.

———— & Wolf, E. (1978), The disorders of the self and their treatment: An outline. *Internat. J. Psychoanal.*, 59:413–425.

Krystal, H. (1988), *Integration and Self-Healing: Affect, Trauma, Alexithymia.* Hillsdale, NJ: The Analytic Press.

Lasch, C. (1978), *The Culture of Narcissism: American Life in an Age of Diminishing Expectations.* New York: Norton.

Layton, L. (2004), Dreams of America/American dreams. *Psychoanal. Dial.*, 14:233–254.

Lichtenberg, J. (1989), *Psychoanalysis and Motivation.* Hillsdale, NJ: The Analytic Press.

———— (1990), Rethinking the scope of the patient's transference and the therapist's counterresponsiveness. In: *The Realities of Transference: Progress in Self Psychology, Vol. 6,* ed. A. Goldberg. Hillsdale, NJ: The Analytic Press, pp. 23–33.

Lindon, J. (1994), Gratification and provision in psychoanalysis: Should we get rid of "the rule of abstinence"? *Psychoanal. Dial.*, 4:459–582.

Linehan, M. (1993), *Cognitive-Behavioral Treatment of Borderline Personality Disorder.* New York: Guilford Press.

Locke, E. & Latham, G. (2002), Building a practically useful theory of goal setting and task motivation: A 35-year odyssey. *Amer. Psychol.*, 57:705–717.

London, P. (1986). *The Modes and Morals of Psychotherapy*, 2nd ed. New York: Hemisphere.

Lyons-Ruth, K. (1991), Rapprochement or approchement: Mahler's theory reconsidered from the vantage point of recent research on early attachment relationships. *Psychoanal. Psychol.*, 6:1–23.

Main, M. (1995), Recent studies in attachment: Overview, with selected implications for clinical work. In: *Attachment Theory: Social, Developmental, and Clinical Perspectives*, ed. S. Goldberg, R. Muir & J. Kerr. Hillsdale, NJ: The Analytic Press, pp. 407–474.

———— & Hesse, E. (1990), Parents' unresolved traumatic experiences are related to infant disorganized attachment status: Is frightened and/or frightening parental behavior the linking mechanism? In: *Attachment in the Preschool Years: Theory, Research, and Intervention*, ed. M. T. Greenberg, D. Cicchetti & E. M. Cummings. Chicago: University of Chicago Press, pp. 161–182.

———— & Solomon (1986), Discovery of an insecure-disorganized/disoriented attachment pattern. In: *Affective Development in Infancy*, ed. T. B. Brazelton & M. Yogman. Norwood, NJ: Ablex, pp. 95–124.

Markson, E. (1992), Transference and structure formation. In: *New Therapeutic Visions: Progress in Self Psychology, Vol. 8*, ed. A. Goldberg. Hillsdale, NJ: The Analytic Press, pp. 20–26.

Marlatt, G. A. (1998), *Harm Reduction*. New York: Guilford Press.

———— & Gordon, J. (1980), Determinants of relapse: Implications for the maintenance of behavior change. In: *Behavioral Medicine: Changing Health Lifestyles*, ed. P. Davidson & S. Davidson. New York: Brunner/Mazel, pp. 410–452.

———— & ———— eds. (1985), *Relapse Prevention: Maintenance Strategies in the Treatment of Addictive Behavior*. New York: Guilford Press.

———— & Parks, G. (1982), Self-management of addictive behaviors. In: *Self Management and Behavior Change: From Theory to Practice*, ed. P. Karoly & F. H. Kanfer. New York: Pergamon, pp. 443–488.

Masling, J. (2003), Stephen A. Mitchell, relational psychoanalysis, and empirical data. *Psychoanal. Psychol.*, 20:587–608.

McCullough, L. & Andrews, S. (2001), Assimilative integration: Short-term dynamic psychotherapy for treating affect phobias. *Clin. Psychol.: Sci. Pract.*, 8:82–97.

McGinnis, J. & Foege, W. (1993), Actual causes of death in the United States. *J. Amer. Med. Assn.*, 270:2207–2212.

McWilliams, N. (2003), The educative aspects of psychoanalysis. *Psychoanal. Psychol.*, 20:245–260.

———— (2004), *Psychoanalytic Psychotherapy: A Practitioner's Guide.* New York: Guilford Press.

Messer, S. & Warren, C. (1995), *Models of Brief Psychodynamic Therapy: A Comparative Approach.* New York: Guilford Press.

Miller, W. & Rollnick, S. (1991), *Motivational Interviewing.* New York: Guilford Press.

Mikulincer, M. (1995), Attachment style and the mental representation of self. *J. Pers. Soc. Psychol.,* 69:1203–1215.

———— Florian, V. & Weller, A. (1993), Attachment styles, coping strategies, and posttraumatic psychological distress: The impact of the Gulf War in Israel. *J. Pers. Soc. Psychol.,* 64:817–826.

———— & Nachshon, O. (1991), Attachment style and patterns of self-disclosure. *J. Pers. Soc. Psychol.,* 61:321–331.

———— & Orbach, I. (1995), Attachment styles and repressive defensiveness: The accessibility and architecture of affective memories. *J. Pers. Soc. Psychol.,* 68:917–925.

Mitchell, S. (1988), *Relational Concepts in Psychoanalysis.* Cambridge, MA: Harvard University Press.

———— (1993), *Hope and Dread in Psychoanalysis.* New York: Basic Books.

———— (1997), *Influence and Autonomy in Psychoanalysis.* Hillsdale, NJ: The Analytic Press.

———— (2000), *Relationality: From Attachment to Intersubjectivity.* Hillsdale, NJ: The Analytic Press.

———— & Black, M. (1995), *Freud and Beyond: A History of Modern Psychoanalytic Thought.* New York: Basic Books.

———— & Harris, A. (2004), What's American about American psychoanalysis? *Psychoanal. Dial.,* 14:165–191.

Nanamoli, B. & Bodhi, B., trans. (1995), *The Middle Length Discourses of the Buddha.* Boston: Wisdom Publications.

Neumann, D., Houskamp, B., Pollock, V. & Briere, J. (1996), The long-term sequelae of childhood sexual abuse in women: A meta-analytic review. *Child Maltreatment,* 1:6–16.

Newman, K. (1998), Optimal responsiveness from abstinence to usability. In: *Optimal Responsiveness: How Therapists Heal Their Patients,* ed. H. Bacal. Northvale, NJ: Aronson, pp. 97–115.

Nijenhuis, E. & Van der Hart, O. (1999), Somatoform dissociative phenomena: A Janetian perspective. In: *Splintered Reflections: Images of the Body in Trauma,* ed. J. Goodwin & R. Attias. New York: Basic Books, pp. 89–127.

Orange, D. (2003), Antidotes and alternatives: Perspectival realism and the new reductionisms. *Psychoanal. Psychol.,* 20:472–486.

Ornstein, P. (1991), Why self psychology is not an object relations theory:

Clinical and theoretical considerations. In: *The Evolution of Self Psychology: Progress in Self Psychology, Vol. 7*, ed. A. Goldberg. Hillsdale, NJ: The Analytic Press, pp. 17–29.

——— & Ornstein, A. (1995), Some distinguishing features of Heinz Kohut's self psychology. *Psychoanal. Dial.*, 5:385–391.

Pariser, M. (2005), Splitting and reductive identification: Comment on Orange (2003). *Psychoanal. Psychol.*, 22:120–130.

Peebles-Kleiger, M.J. (2002), *Beginnings: The Art and Science of Planning Psychotherapy*. Hillsdale, NJ: The Analytic Press.

Peele, S., ed. (1985), *The Meaning of Addiction: A Compulsive Experience and Its Interpretation*. Lexington, MA: Lexington Books.

Piers, C. (2005), The mind's multiplicity and continuity. *Psychoanal. Dial.*, 15:229–254.

Pizer, B. (2003), When the crunch is a (k)not: A crimp in relational dialogue. *Psychoanal. Dial.*, 13:171–192.

Poppen, R. (1988), *Behavioral Relaxation Training and Assessment*. New York: Pergamon.

Premack, D. (1959), Toward empirical behavior laws. I: Positive reinforcement. *Psychol. Rev.*, 66:219–233.

Prochaska, J., DiClemente, C. & Norcross, J. (1992), In search of how people change: Applications to addictive behaviors. *Amer. Psychol.*, 47:1102–1114.

——— Norcross, J. & DiClemente, C. (1994), *Changing for Good*. New York: William Morrow.

Rapaport, D. & Gill, M. (1959), The points of view and assumptions of metapsychology. In: *The Collected Papers of David Rapaport*, ed. M. Gill. New York: Basic Books, 1967, pp. 795–811.

Reis, B. (2005), The self is alive and well and living in relational psychoanalysis. *Psychoanal. Psychol.*, 22:86–95.

Renik, O. (1993), Analytic interactions: Conceptualizing technique in light of the analyst's irreducible subjectivity. *Psychoanal. Quart.*, 62:553–571.

——— (1995), The ideal of the anonymous analyst and the problem of self-disclosure. *Psychoanal. Quart.*, 64:466–495.

Rimm, D. & Masters, J. (1974), *Behavior Therapy: Techniques and Empirical Findings*. New York: Academic Press.

Ringstrom, P. (2001), Cultivating the improvisational in psychoanalytic treatment. *Psychoanal. Dial.*, 11:727–754.

Rosner, R., Lyddon, W. & Freeman, A., eds. (2004), *Cognitive Therapy and Dreams*. New York: Springer Publishing Co.

Rowe, C. (1994), Reformulations of the concept of selfobject: A misalliance of self psychology with object relations theory. In: *A Decade of Progress: Progress in Self Psychology, Vol. 10*, ed. A. Goldberg. Hillsdale, NJ: The Analytic Press, pp. 9–20.

Rozee, P. & Van Boemel, G. (1989), The psychological effects of war trauma and abuse on older Cambodian refugee women. *Women & Therapy*, 8:23–50.

Safran, J. (2001), When worlds collide: Psychoanalysis and the empirically supported treatment movement. *Psychoanal. Dial.*, 11:659–691.

——— & Aron, L. (2001), Introduction to symposium on implications of the empirically supported treatment controversy for psychoanalysis. *Psychoanal. Dial.*, 11:571–582.

——— & Siegel, Z. (1990), *Interpersonal Process in Cognitive Therapy.* New York: Guilford Press.

Sampson, H. (1994), Repeating pathological relationships to disconfirm pathogenic beliefs. *Psychoanal. Dial.*, 4:357–361.

Schore, A.N. (1994), *Affect Regulation and the Origin of the Self: The Neurobiology of Emotional Development.* Hillsdale, NJ: Lawrence Erlbaum Associates.

Schuckit, M. (1989), Biological and genetic markers of alcoholism. In: *Alcoholism: Biomedical and Genetic Aspects*, eds. H. Goedde & D. Agarwal. Elmsford, NY: Pergamon, pp. 290–302.

Seligman, S. (2005), Dynamic systems theories as a metaframework for psychoanalysis. *Psychoanal. Dial.*, 15:285–319.

Shakespeare, W. (1600–1601), *The Tragedy of Hamlet, Prince of Denmark.* New York: New American Library, 1963.

Shane, M. & Shane, E. (1996), Self psychology in search of the optimal: A consideration of optimal responsiveness, optimal provision, optimal gratification, and optimal restraint in the clinical situation. In: *Basic Ideas Reconsidered: Progress in Self Psychology, Vol. 12*, ed. A. Goldberg. Hillsdale, NJ: The Analytic Press, pp. 37–54.

——— Shane, E. & Gales, M. (1997), *Intimate Attachments: Toward a New Self Psychology.* New York: Guilford Press.

Shapiro, F. & Maxfield, L. (2002), Eye movement desensitization and reprocessing (EMDR): Information processing in the treatment of trauma. *J. Clin. Psychol.*, 58:933–946.

Shaver, P. & Mikulincer, M. (2002), Attachment-related psychodynamics. *Attach. Human. Devel.*, 4:133–161.

Shear, N., Cooper, A., Klerman, G., Busch, F. & Shapiro, T. (1993), A psychodynamic model of panic disorder. *Amer. J. Psychiat.*, 150:859–866.

Shitou Xiqian (2004), *The Harmony of Difference and Sameness*, trans. T. Leighton. Chicago, IL: Ancient Dragon Zen Gate Chant Book.

Sibley, D. & Blinder, B. (1988), Anorexia nervosa. In: *The Eating Disorders*, ed. B. Blinder, B. Chaitin & R. Goldstein. New York: PMA, pp. 247–258.

Siegel, D. (1999), *The Developing Mind: Toward a Neurobiology of Interpersonal Experience.* New York: Guilford Press.

Sobell, M. & Sobell, L. (2000), Stepped care as a heuristic approach to the treatment of alcohol problems. *J. Consult. Clin. Psychol.*, 68:573–579.

Solomon, I. (1992), *The Encyclopedia of Evolving Techniques in Psychodynamic Therapy*. Northvale, NJ: Aronson.

Solomon, J. & George, C. (1999), The place of disorganization in attachment theory: Linking classic observations with contemporary findings. In: *Attachment Disorganization*, ed J. Solomon & C. George. New York: Guilford Press, pp. 3–32.

Solomon, R. (1964), Punishment. *Amer. Psychol.*, 19:239–253.

Spezzano, C. (1993), *Affect in Psychoanalysis*. Hillsdale, NJ: The Analytic Press.

——— (1995), "Classical" versus "contemporary" theory: The differences that matter clinically. *Contemp. Psychoanal.*, 31:20–46.

——— (2004), American psychoanalysis: A comparative attempt. *Psychoanal. Dial.*, 14:193–206.

Spiegler, M. & Guevremont, D. (1993), *Contemporary Behavior Therapy*, 2nd ed. Pacific Grove, CA: Brooks/Cole.

Sroufe, L. A. (1996). *Emotional Development: The Organization of Emotional Life in the Early Years*. New York: Cambridge University Press.

——— & Waters, E. (1977), Attachment as an organizational construct. *Child Devel.*, 48:1184–1199.

Stern, S. (2002a), The self as a relational structure: A dialogue with multiple self theory. *Psychoanal. Dial.*, 12:693–714.

——— (2002b), Identification, repetition, and psychological growth: An expansion of relational theory. *Psychoanal. Psychol.*, 19:722–738.

Stolorow, R. (1988), Integrating self psychology and classical psychoanalysis: An experience-near approach. In: *Learning from Kohut: Progress in Self Psychology, Vol. 4*, ed. A. Goldberg. Hillsdale, NJ: The Analytic Press, pp. 63–70.

——— (1992), Subjectivity and self psychology: A personal odyssey. In: *New Therapeutic Visions: Progress in Self Psychology, Vol. 8*, ed. A. Goldberg. Hillsdale, NJ: The Analytic Press, pp. 241–250.

——— (1995), Loyalism and expansionism in self psychology. *Psychoanal. Dial.*, 5:427–430.

——— & Atwood, G. (1979), *Faces in a Cloud*. Northvale, NJ: Aronson.

——— & ——— (1992), *Contexts of Being*. Hillsdale, NJ: The Analytic Press.

——— Brandchaft, B. & Atwood, G. (1987), *Psychoanalytic Treatment: An Intersubjective Approach*. Hillsdale, NJ: The Analytic Press.

Sullivan, H. (1953), *The Interpersonal Theory of Psychiatry*. New York: Norton.

Summers, F. (1994), *Object Relations Theories and Psychopathology: A Comprehensive Text*. Hillsdale, NJ: The Analytic Press.

——— (1999), *Transcending the Self*. Hillsdale, NJ: The Analytic Press.

Terman, D. (1988), Optimum frustration: Structuralization and the therapeutic process. In: *Learning from Kohut: Progress in Self Psychology, Vol. 4*, ed. A. Goldberg. Hillsdale, NJ: The Analytic Press, pp. 113–125.

Thelan, E. (2005), Dynamic systems theory and the complexity of change. *Psychoanal. Dial.*, 15:255–283.

Thompson, M. (2004), Happiness and chance: A reappraisal of the psychoanalytic conception of suffering. *Psychoanal. Psychol.*, 21:134–153.

Thomson, R. & Connors, M. (2001), The instructional selfobject. Presented at Chicago Association for Psychoanalytic Psychology, April.

Tolpin, M. (1983), Corrective emotional experience: A self psychological reevaluation. In: *The Future of Psychoanalysis*, ed. A. Goldberg. New York: International Universities Press, pp. 363–380.

——— (2000), The role of empathy and interpretation. Presented at 23rd Annual International Conference on the Psychology of the Self, November, Chicago, IL.

Torgersen, S. (1983), Genetic factors in anxiety disorders. *Arch. Gen. Psychiat.*, 40:1085–1089.

von Broembsen, F. (1999), *The Sovereign Self: Toward a Phenomenology of Self-Experience*. Northvale, NJ: Aronson.

Wachtel, P. (1977), *Psychoanalysis and Behavior Therapy: Toward an Integration*. New York: Basic Books.

——— (1987), *Action and Insight*. New York: Guilford Press.

——— (1994), Behavior and experience: Allies, not adversaries. *J. Psychother. Integra.* 4:121–131.

——— (1997), *Psychoanalysis, Behavior Therapy, and the Relational World*. Washington, DC: American Psychological Association.

Wegner, D. (1994), Ironic processes of mental control. *Psychol. Rev.*, 101:34–52.

Weiss, J. (1993), *How Psychotherapy Works: Process and Technique*. New York: Guilford Press.

——— Sampson, H. & the Mt. Zion Psychotherapy Research Group (1986), Unconscious pathogenic beliefs. In: *The Psychoanalytic Process: Theory, Clinical Observations, and Empirical Research*. New York: Guilford Press.

West, R., Edwards, M. & Hajek, P. (1998), A randomized controlled trial of a 'buddy' system to improve success at giving up smoking in general practice. *Addiction*, 93:1007–1011.

Westen, D. (1990), Psychoanalytic approaches to personality. In: *Handbook of Personality: Theory and Research*, ed. L. Pervin. New York: Guilford Press, pp. 21–65.

———— (2002), The language of psychoanalytic discourse. *Psychoanal. Dial.*, 12:857–898.

———— Novotny, C. & Thompson-Brenner, H. (2004), The empirical status of empirically supported therapies: Assumptions, methods, and findings. *Psychol. Bull.*, 130:631–663.

Whiston, S. & Sexton, T. (1993), An overview of psychotherapy outcome research: Implications for practice. *Prof. Psychol.: Res. Prac.*, 24:43–51.

White, R. (1959), Motivation reconsidered: The concept of competence. *Psychol. Rev.*, 66:279–333.

Winnicott, D. (1960), The theory of the parent-infant relationship. In: *The Maturational Processes and the Facilitating Environment.* New York: International Universities Press, 1965, pp. 37–55.

Wolf, E. (1983), Aspects of neutrality. *Psychoanal. Inq.*, 3:675–689.

———— (1988), *Treating the Self.* New York: Guilford Press.

———— (1989), The psychoanalytic self psychologist looks at learning. In: *Learning and Education: Psychoanalytic Perspectives*, ed. K. Field, B. Cohler & G. Wool. Madison, CT: International Universities Press, pp. 377–394.

———— (1998), Optimal responsiveness and disruptions-restorations. In: *Optimal Responsiveness: How Therapists Heal Their Patients*, ed. H. Bacal. Northvale, NJ: Aronson, pp. 237–248.

Wolpe, J. (1958), *Psychotherapy by Reciprocal Inhibition.* Stanford, CA: Stanford University Press.

Index